AF479339

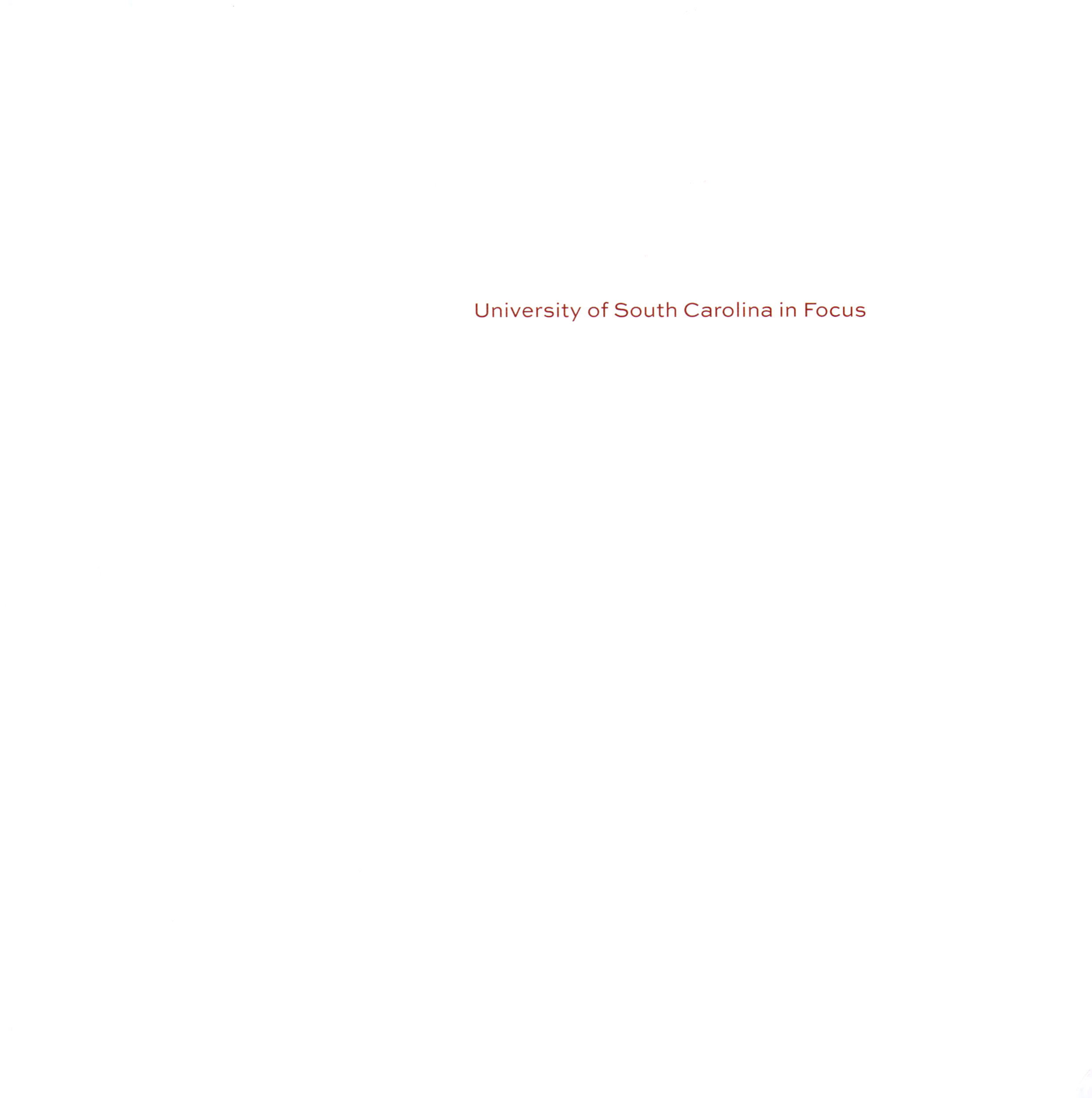

University of South Carolina in Focus

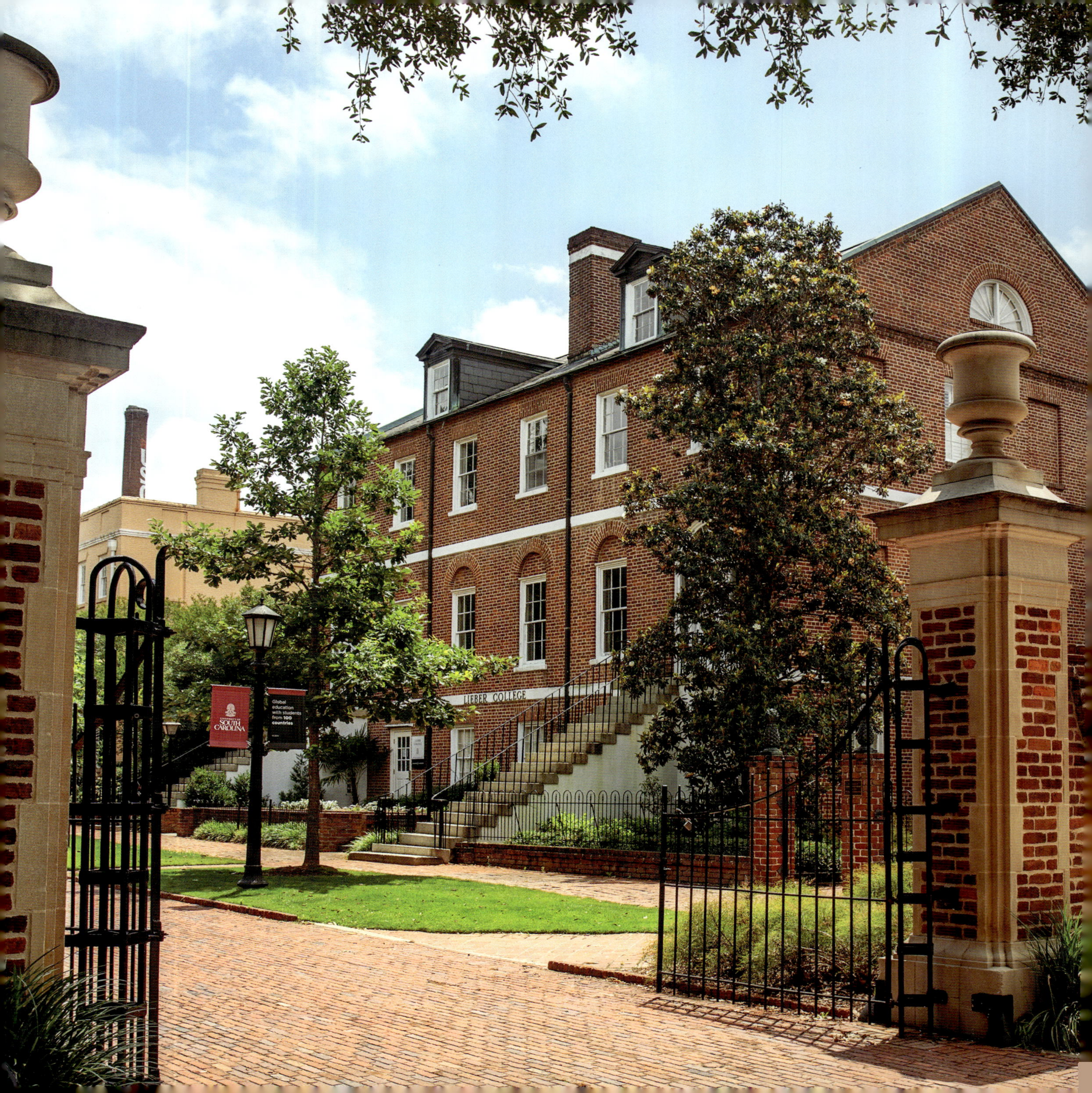

UNIVERSITY OF SOUTH CAROLINA
Global education with students from 100 countries
LIEBER COLLEGE

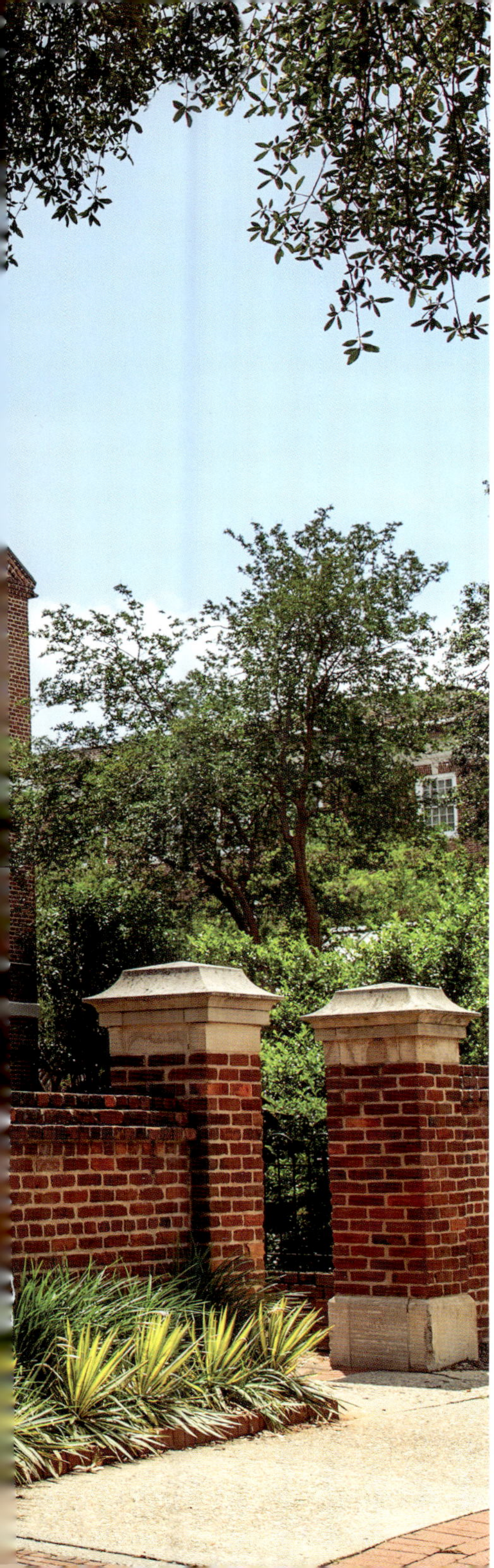

UNIVERSITY of SOUTH CAROLINA in FOCUS

CHRIS HORN

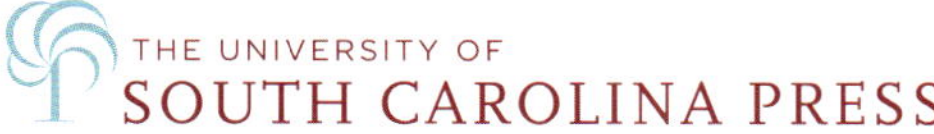

Published by the
University of South Carolina Press
Columbia, South Carolina 29208

www.uscpress.com

Manufactured in Korea

31 30 29 28 27 26 25 24 23 22
10 9 8 7 6 5 4 3 2 1

Library of Congress
Cataloging-in-Publication Data
can be found at http://catalog.loc.gov/.

ISBN: 978-1-64336-312-7 (hardcover)

Frontispiece: Iconic gates mark the entryways to the U-shaped brick driveway that gives the historic district of campus its name—the Horseshoe.

The reflecting pool in front of the Thomas Cooper Library.

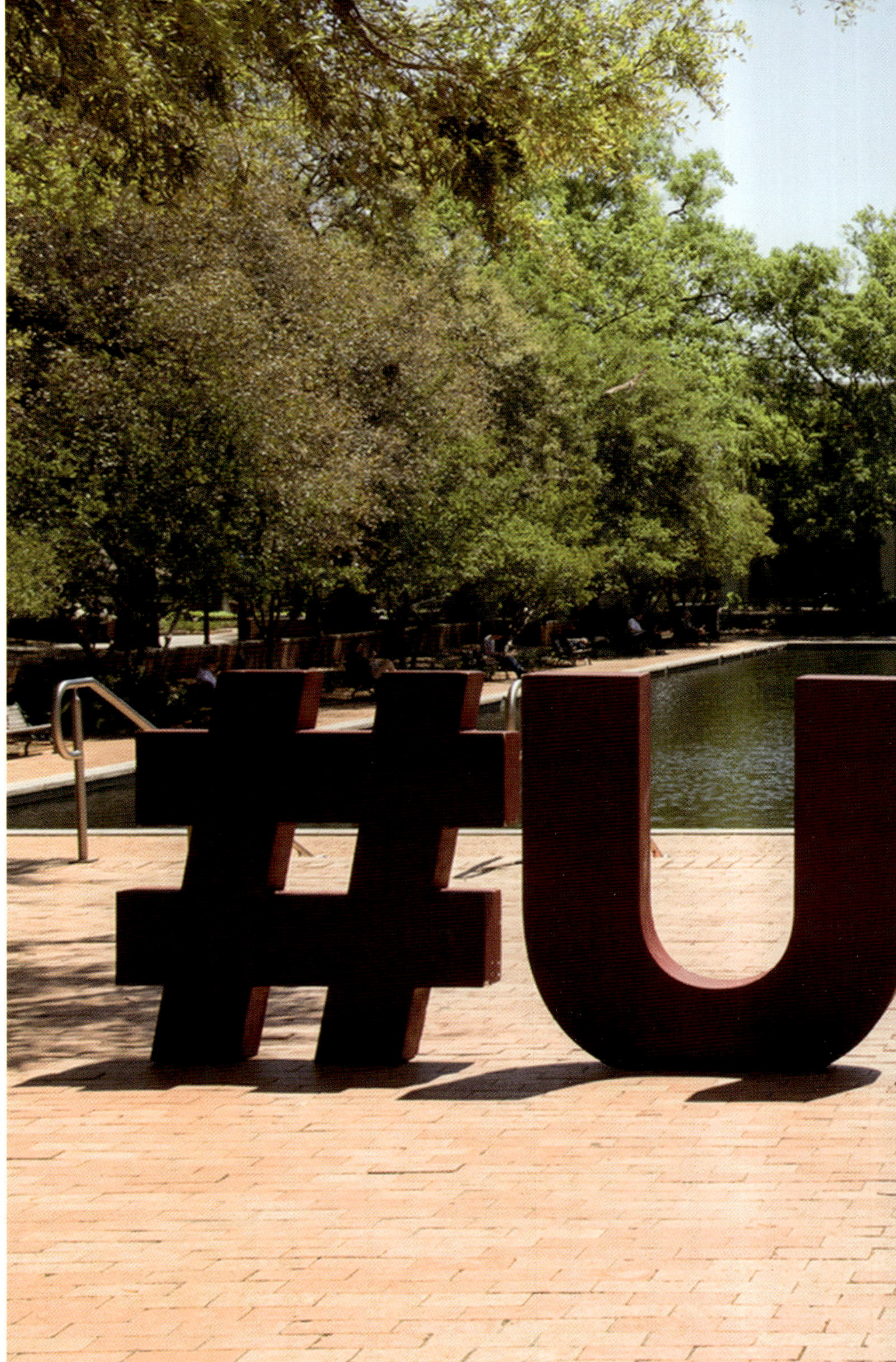

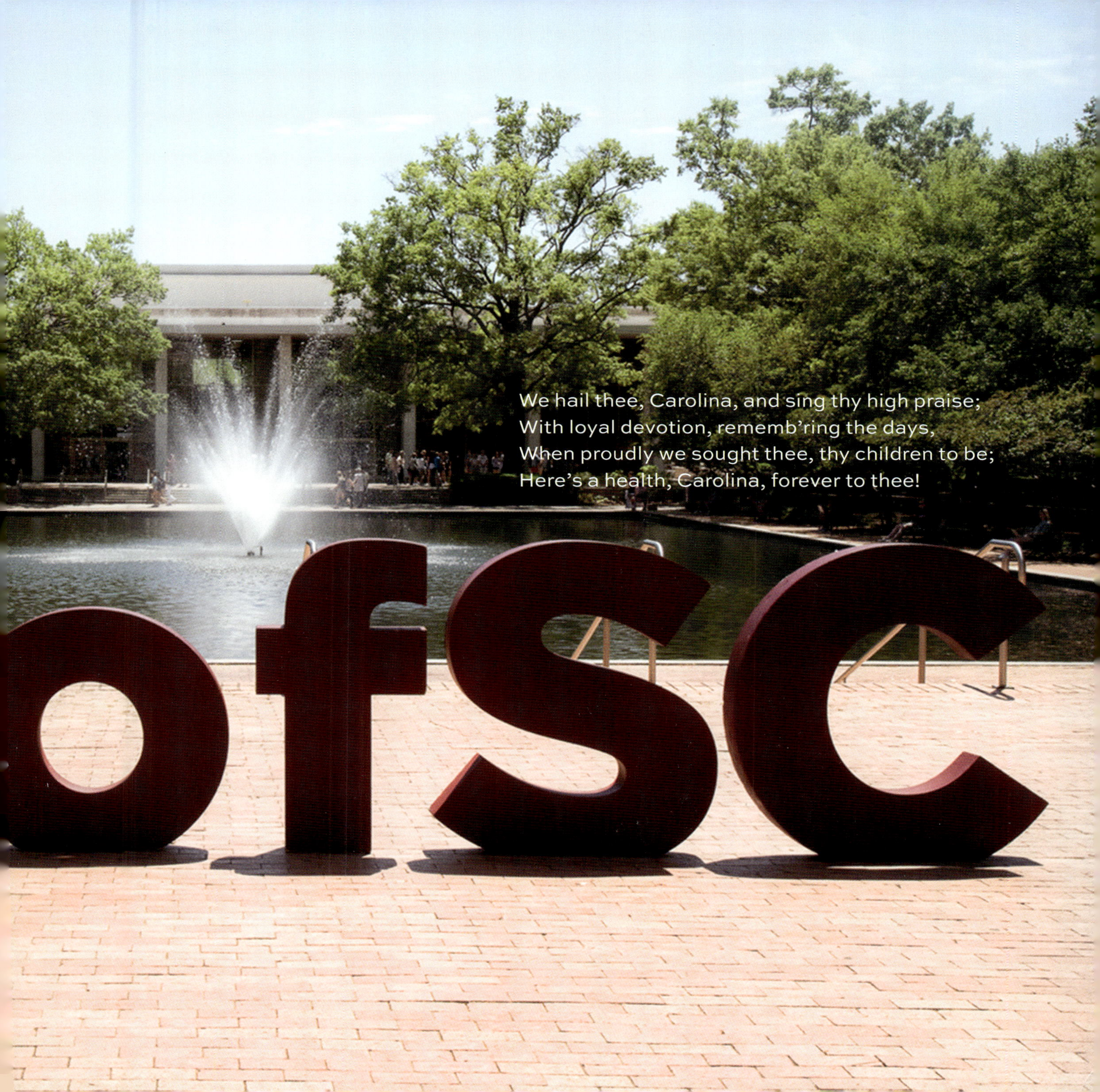

We hail thee, Carolina, and sing thy high praise;
With loyal devotion, rememb'ring the days,
When proudly we sought thee, thy children to be;
Here's a health, Carolina, forever to thee!

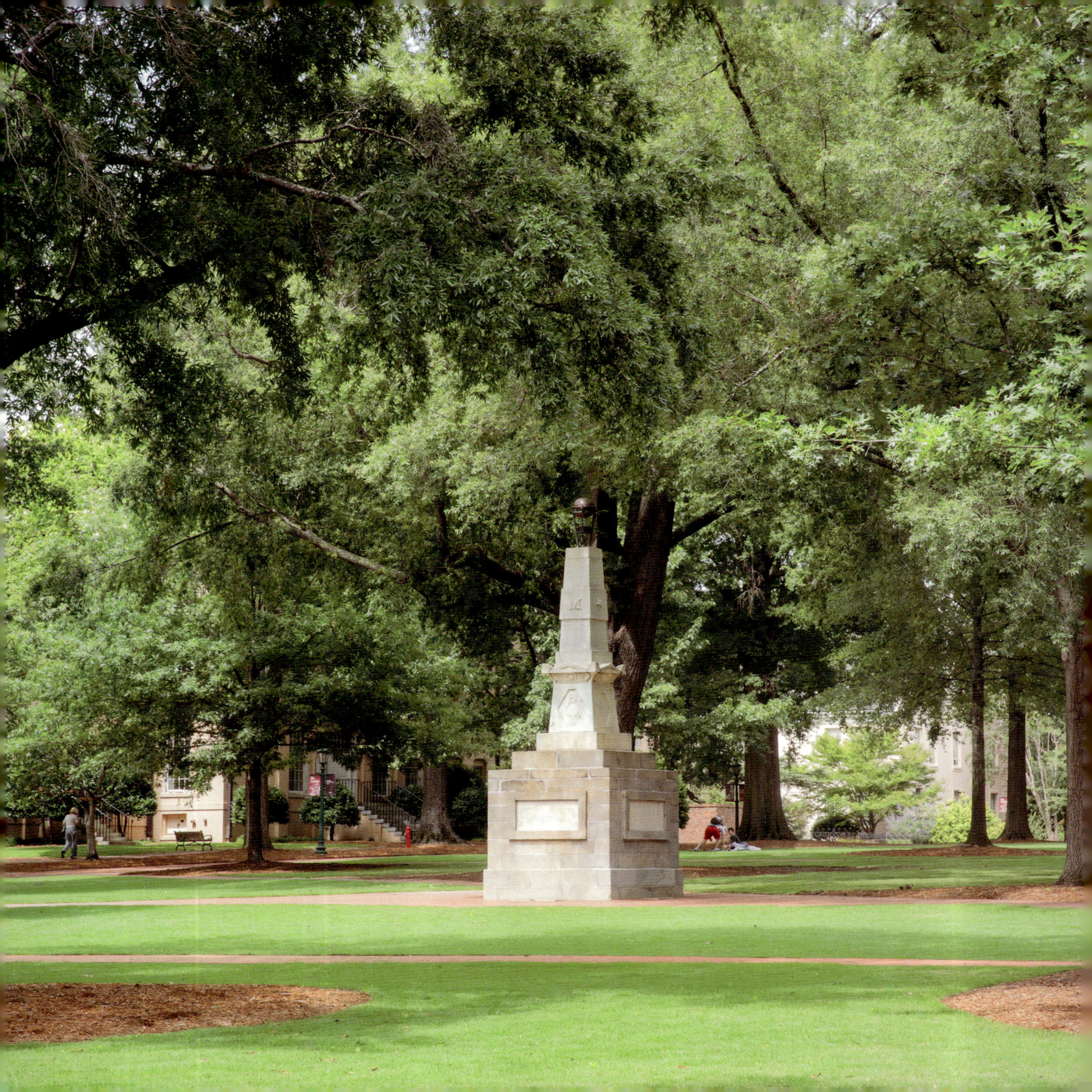

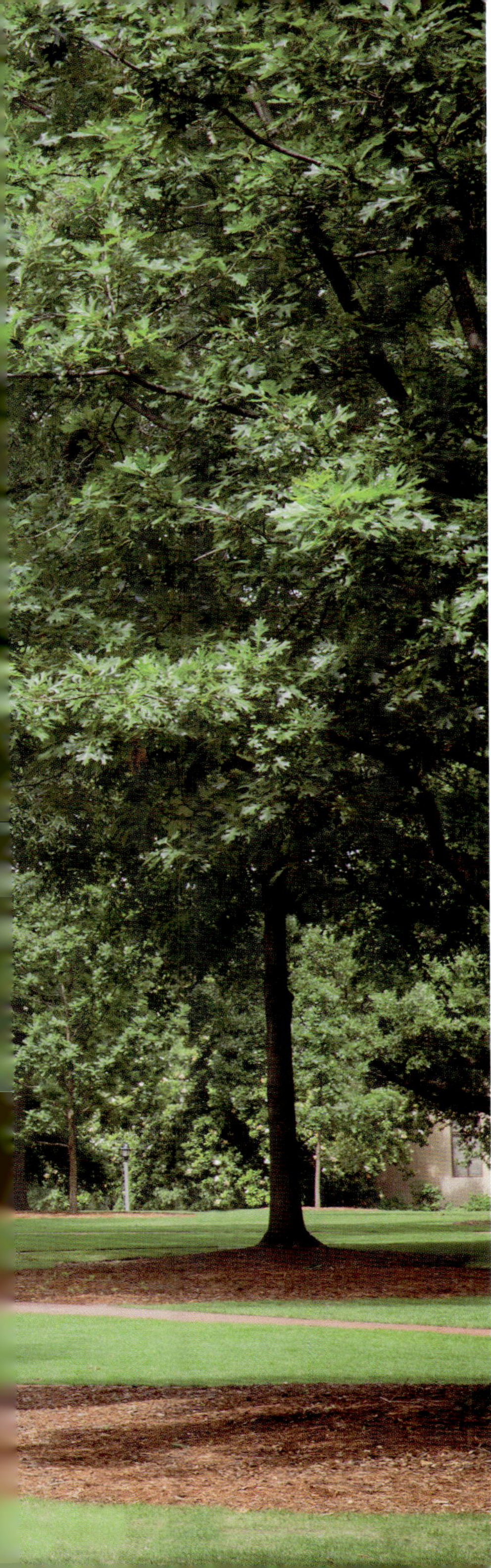

Introduction

Walk across the University of South Carolina campus and you'll find yourself immersed in a beautiful urban forest of 7,000 trees that shade the nearly 360 acres of rolling landscape. A campus stroll will also expose you to a timeline of architectural history, from the early nineteenth-century classical lines on historic Horseshoe buildings to the neoclassical features of Longstreet Theatre to the mid-century modern style of the main library and student union building.

Beyond the visual delight of the campus's natural and built environments is a palpable spirit of wonder and discovery. It dates back to the late eighteenth century when South Carolina's leaders began discussing the formation of South Carolina College—the precursor of the University of South Carolina—chartered in 1801. For its first several decades, the college enjoyed a reputation as one of the nation's premier institutions of classical learning and was the first in the country to build a freestanding library for its students.

In the aftermath of the Civil War, the college was rechartered as the University of South Carolina, and for several years during the Reconstruction era it was the only previously segregated institution of higher learning in the South to admit and graduate Black men, whose later accomplishments were impressive. Women were admitted in the 1890s, and in 1963 the university admitted its first African American students since Reconstruction.

In its more than two centuries of service, the university has weathered two world wars and the Great Depression, while keeping step with the steady advance of modernity. Today it is known as one of the nation's top research universities with more than 310 degree programs of which 60 are nationally ranked, more than any other university in the state. Some 35,000 students pursue undergraduate and advanced degrees on the Columbia campus, and it is their energy—guided and shaped by a diverse and capable faculty—that gives this place its own special identity.

This brief chronology of the University of South Carolina offers a small taste of the institution's more than 220 years of history. Now immerse yourself in the pages that follow, each one a portrait of the charm and spirit of a campus considered to be one of America's most beautiful.

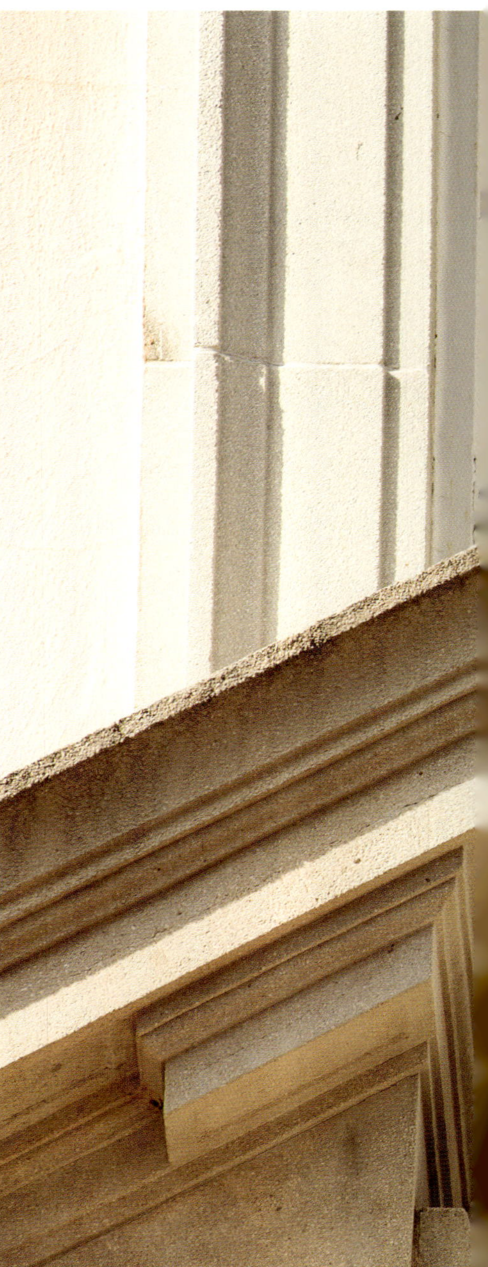

Previous: Designed by Washington Monument architect Robert Mills, the Maxcy Monument honors President Jonathan Maxcy, South Carolina College's first president who served from 1804 until his death in 1820.

The university's seal, perched above the entrance of the Osborne Administration Building, includes the Latin inscription *Emollit Mores Nec Sinit Esse Feros:* "Learning humanizes character and does not permit it to be cruel."

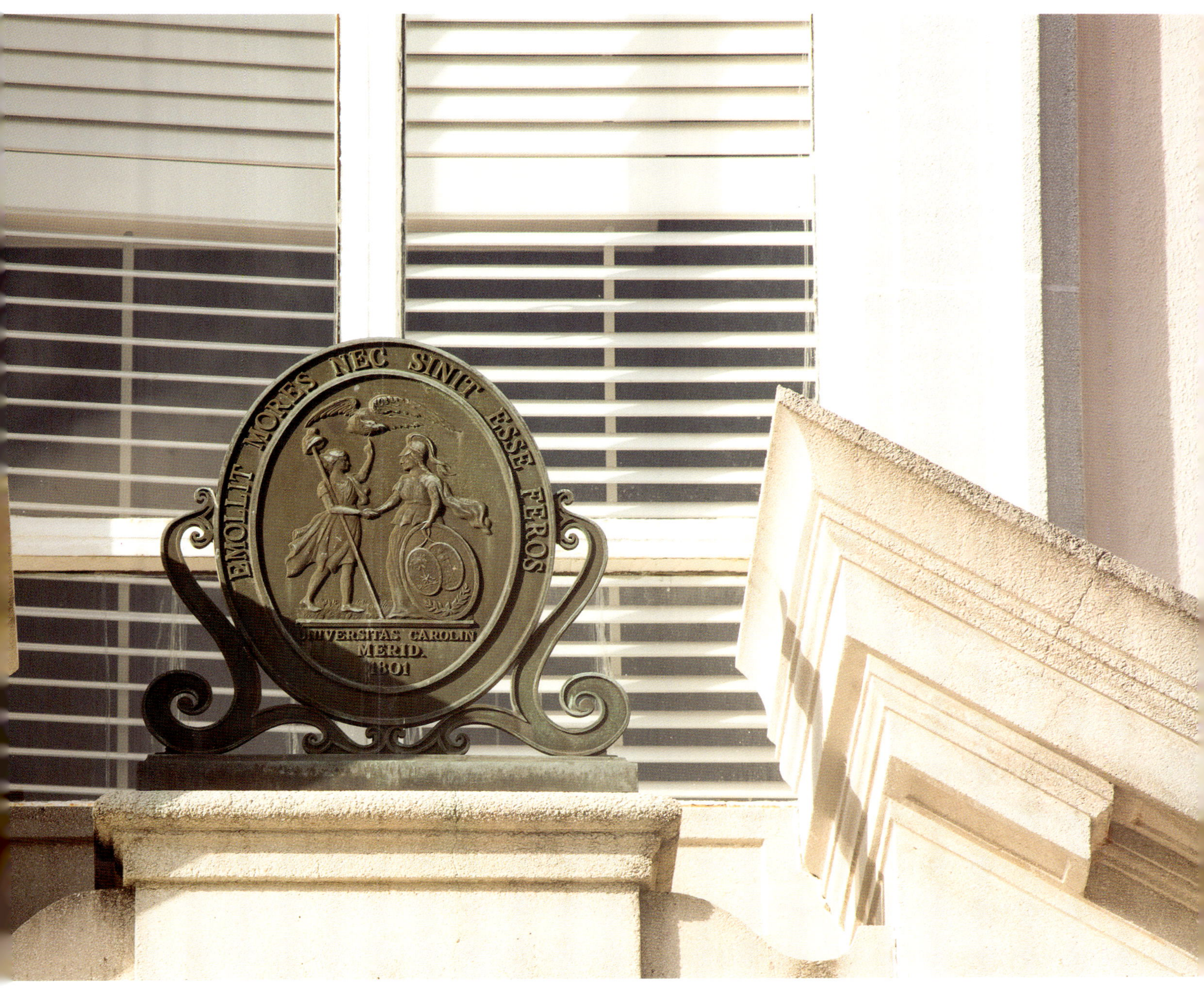

EMOLLIT MORES NEC SINIT ESSE FEROS
UNIVERSITAS CAROLIN
MERID.
1801

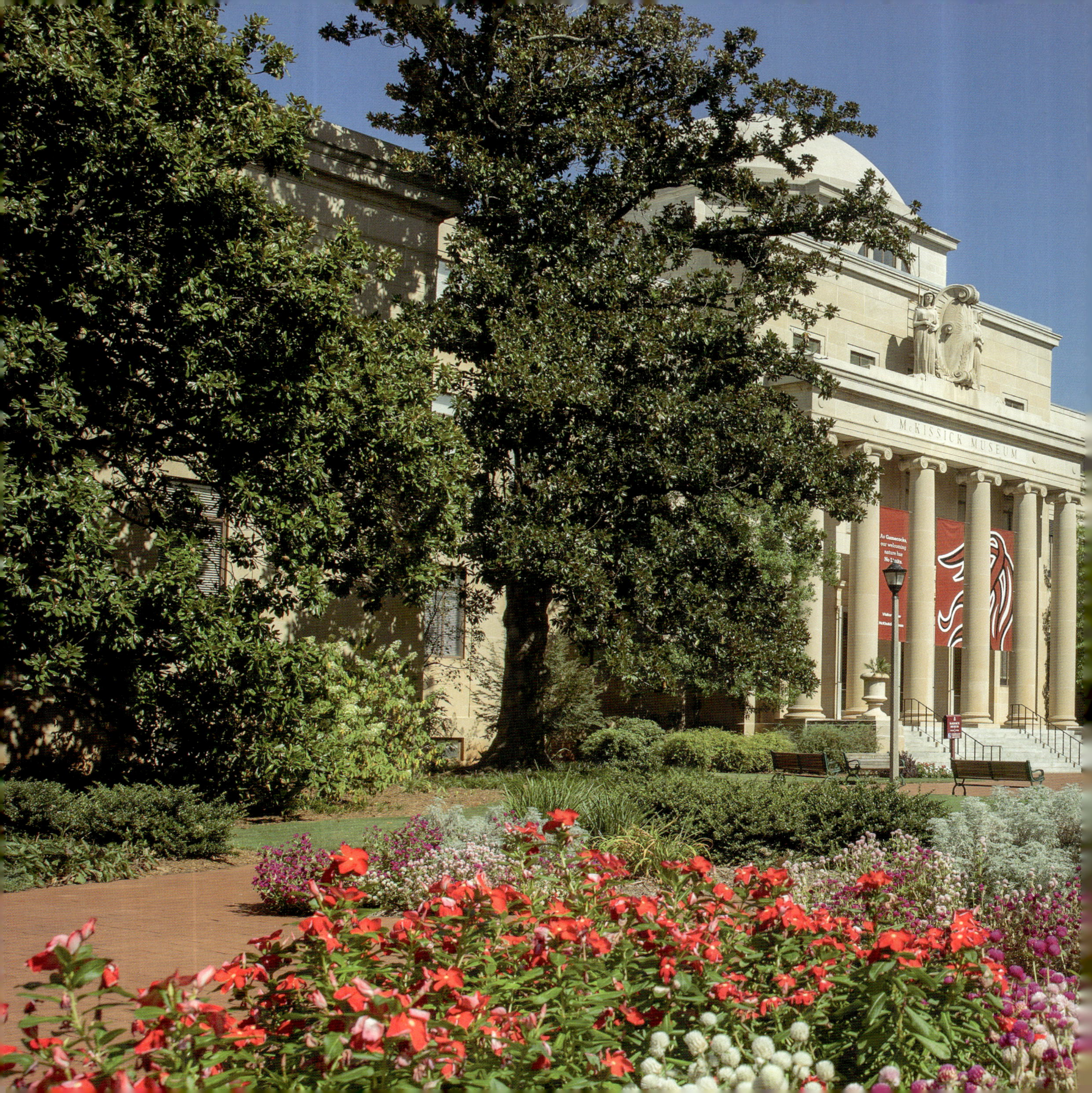

McKISSICK MUSEUM
As Gamecocks, our welcoming nature has No Limits.

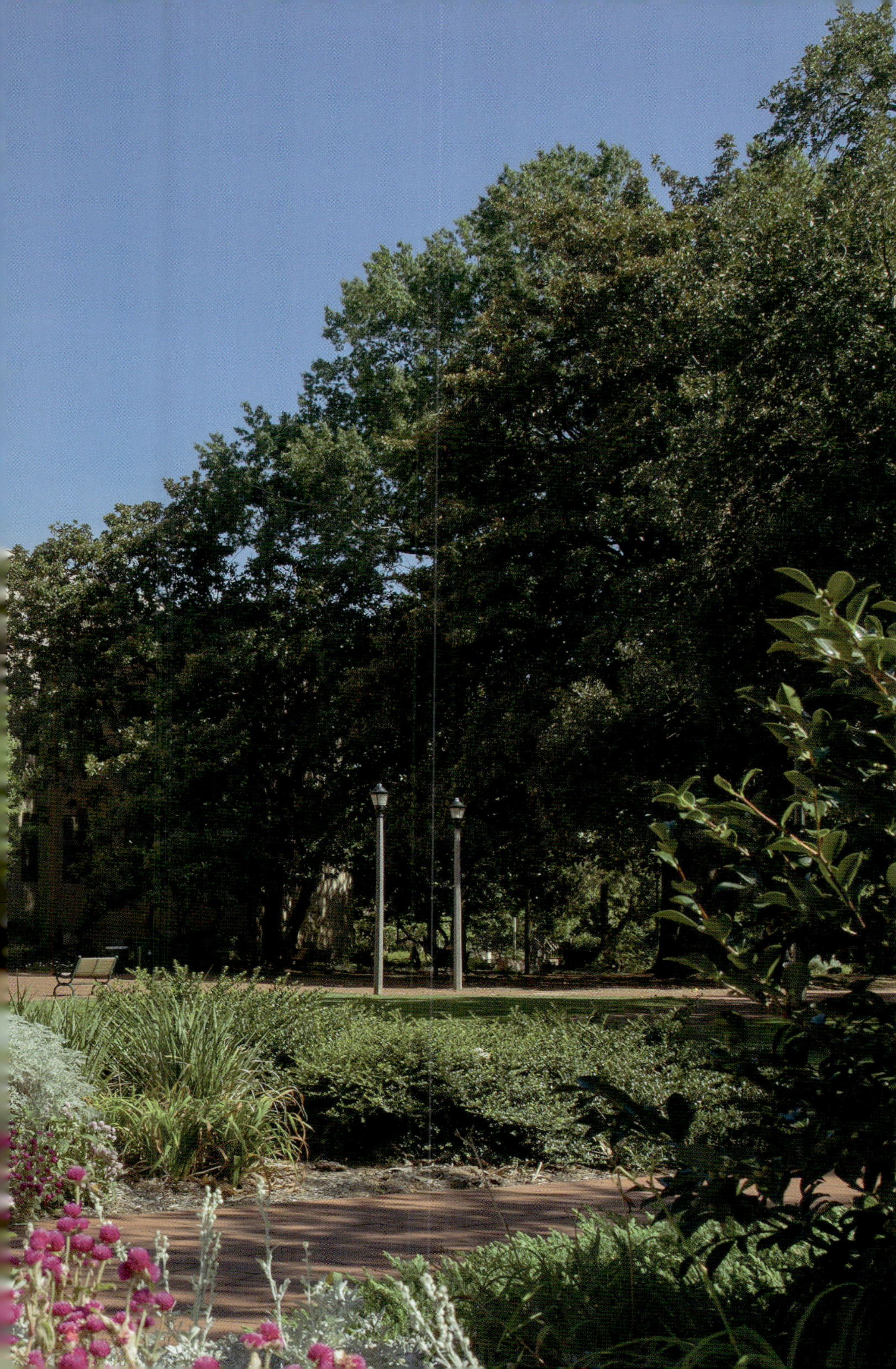

McKissick was constructed in 1940 as the university's second freestanding library and was named in memory of university President J. Rion McKissick. The building now houses McKissick Museum, the Visitor Center, and university admissions offices.

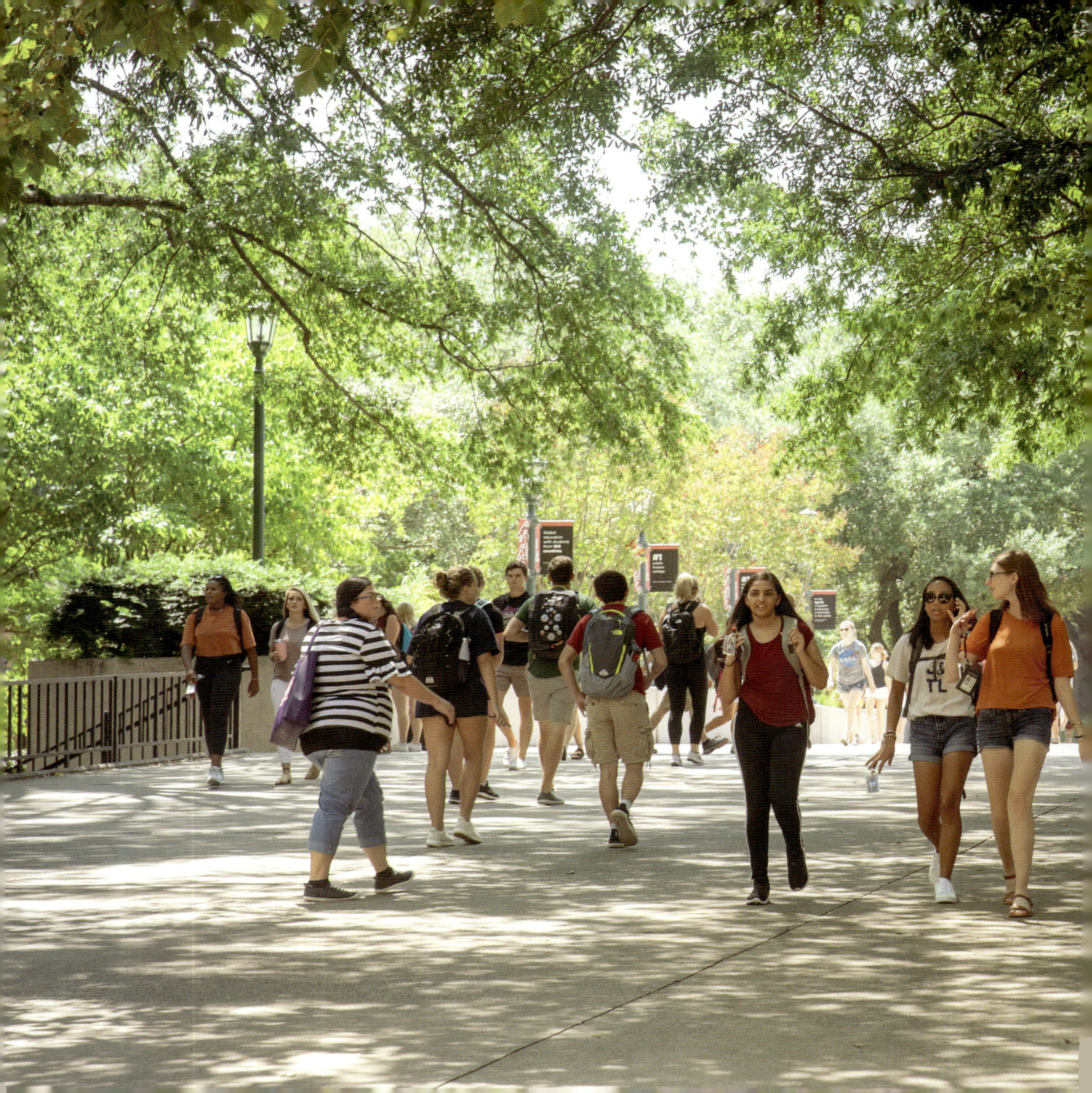

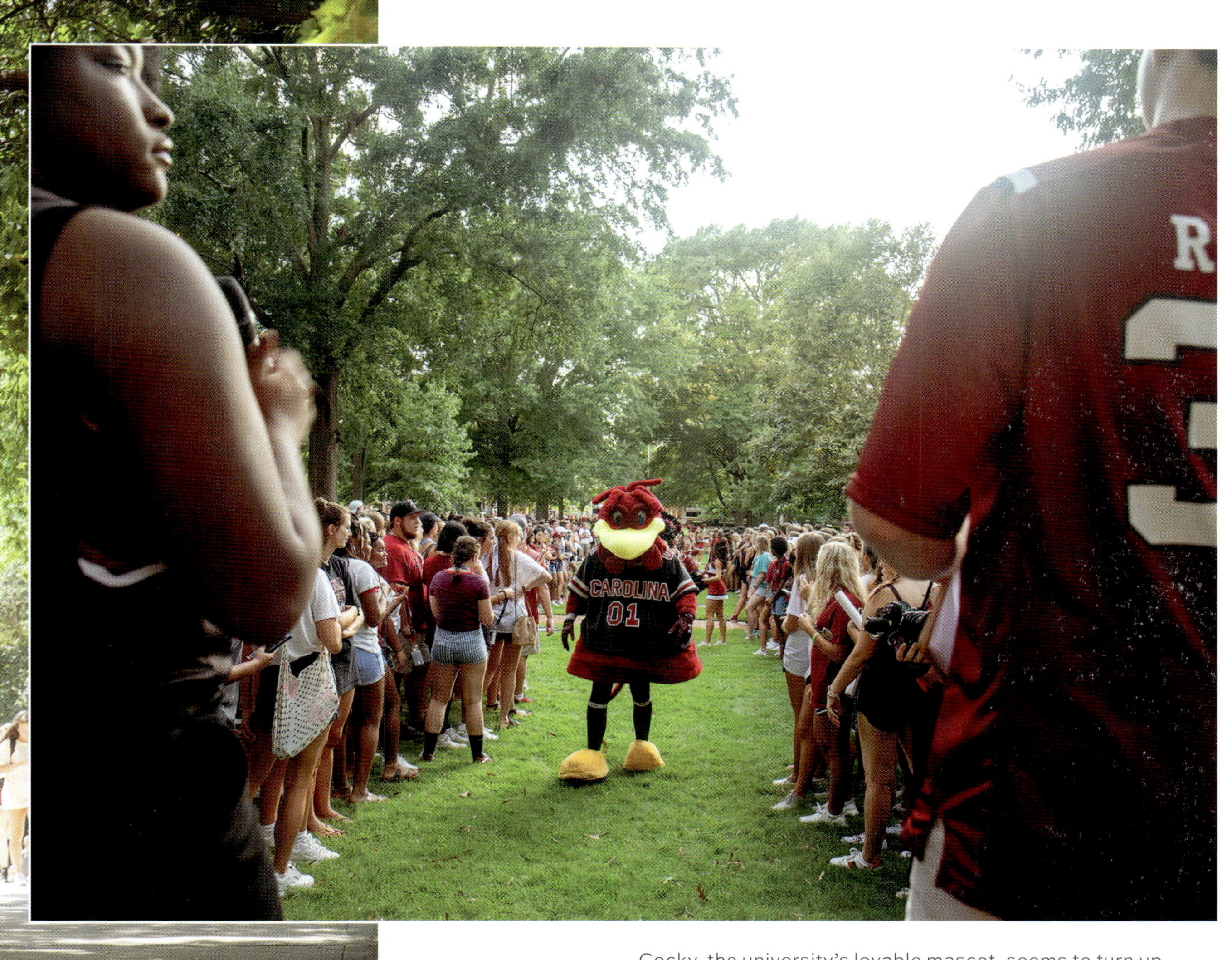

Cocky, the university's lovable mascot, seems to turn up everywhere on campus, bringing his inimitable antics and good humor to the scene.

Students bustle across the Pickens Street pedestrian bridge, the broad corridor that connects east campus with Gibbes Green and beyond.

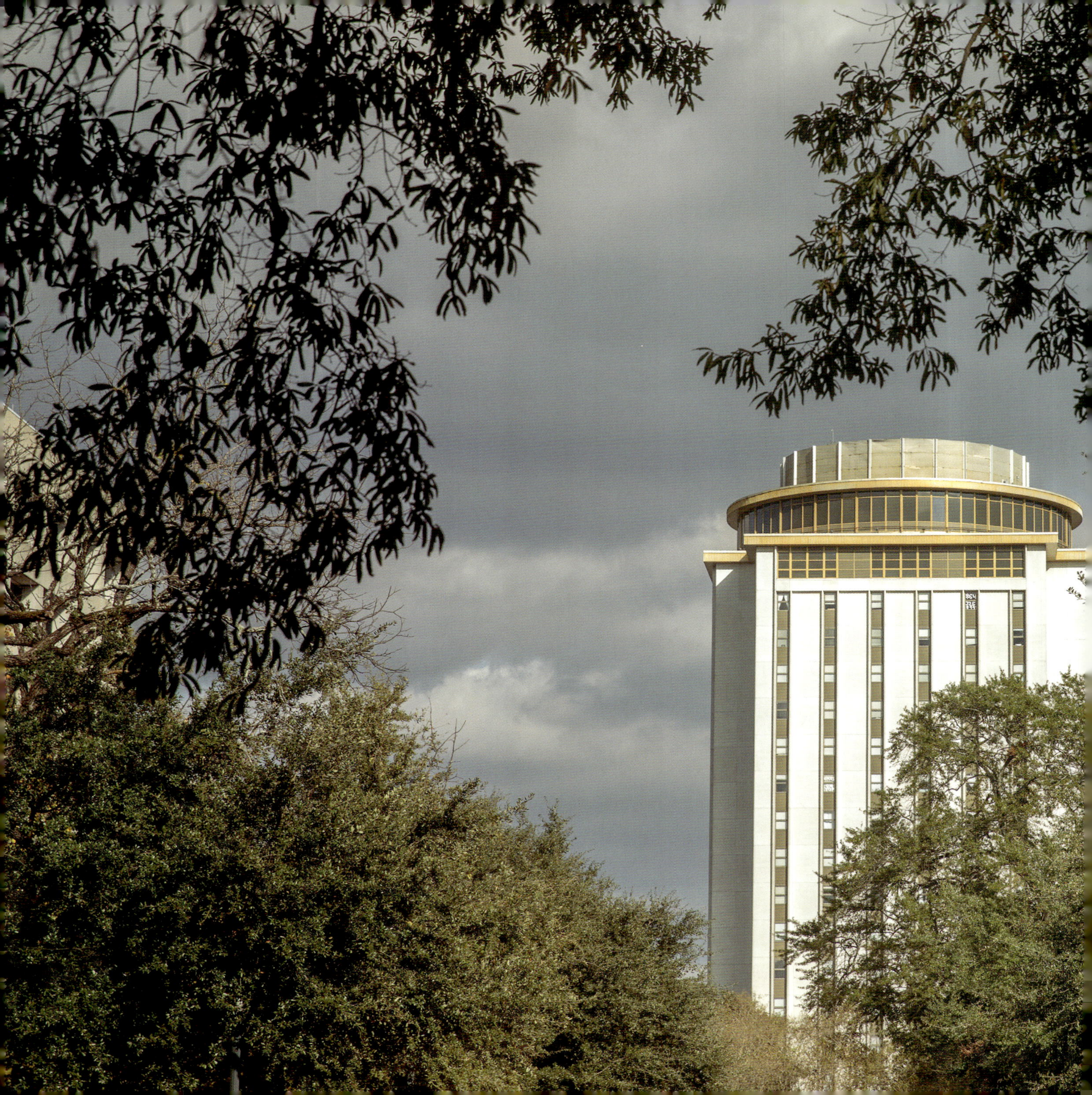

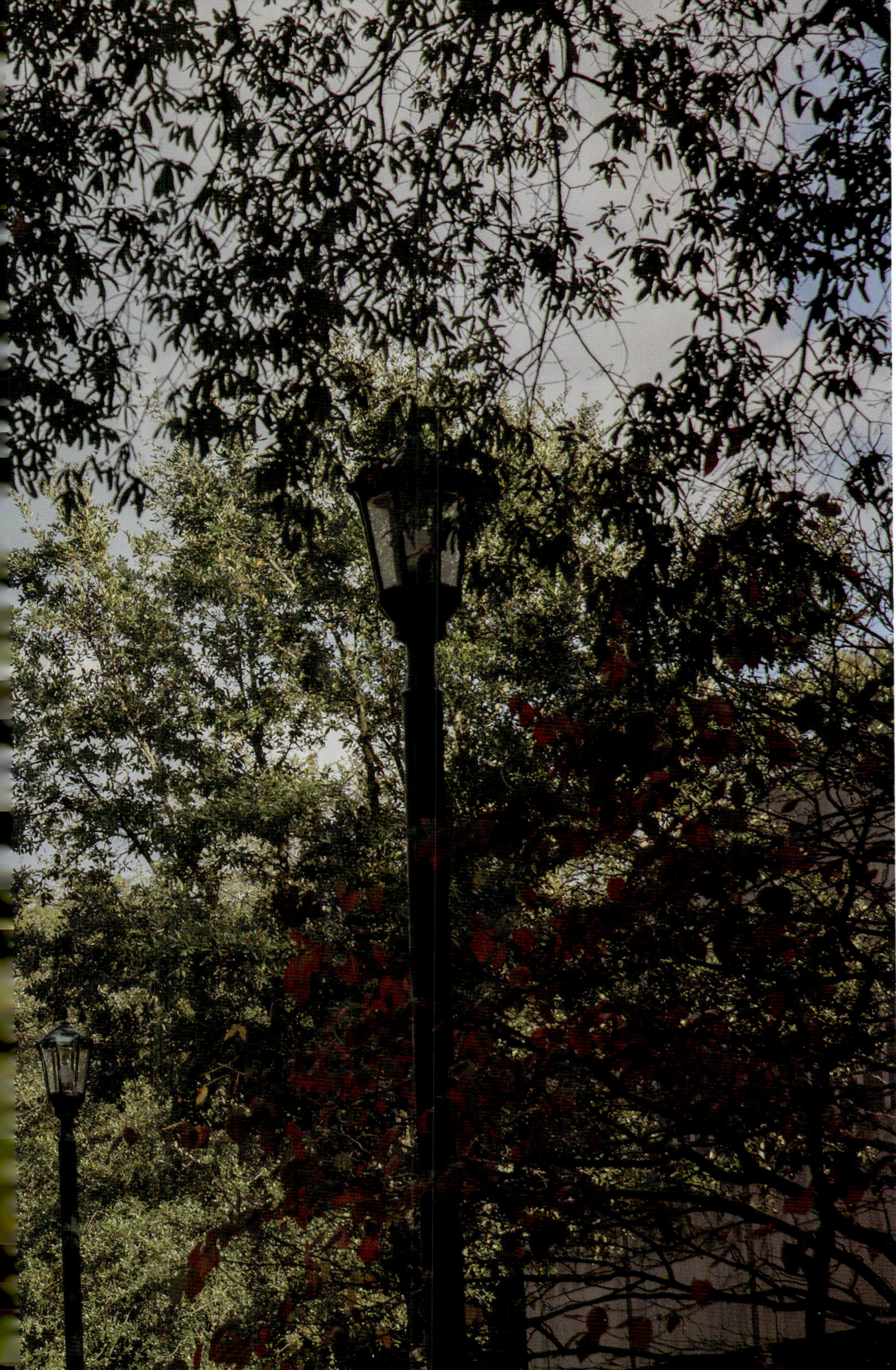

The eighteen-story Capstone House's distinctive revolving top is an unmistakable landmark on the Columbia skyline. The residence hall for Capstone Scholars also houses the Top of Carolina restaurant, which offers patrons a panoramic view of the city.

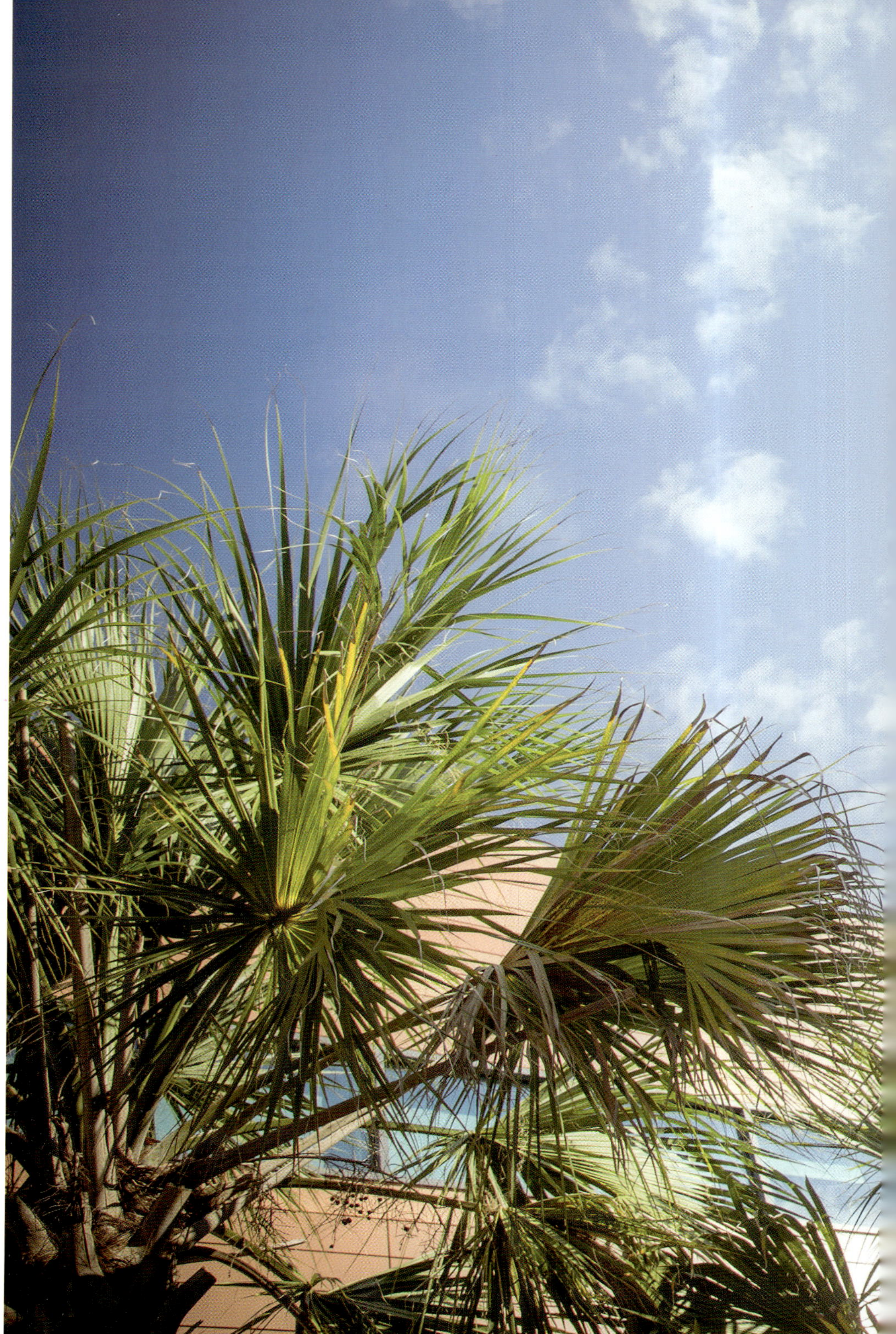

A small grove of palmettos, South Carolina's state tree, provides a distinctly southern charm to the courtyard at the Darla Moore School of Business.

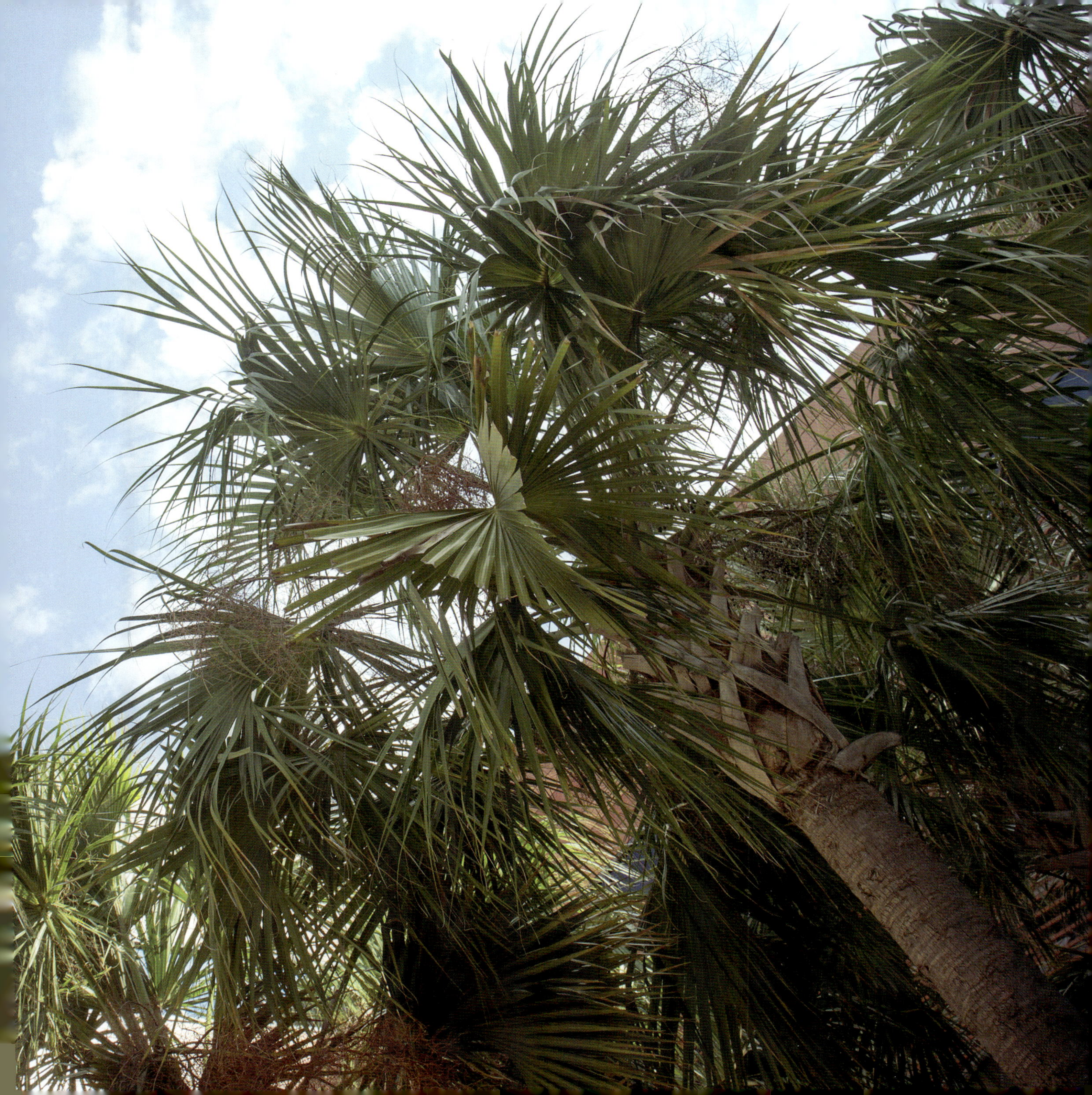

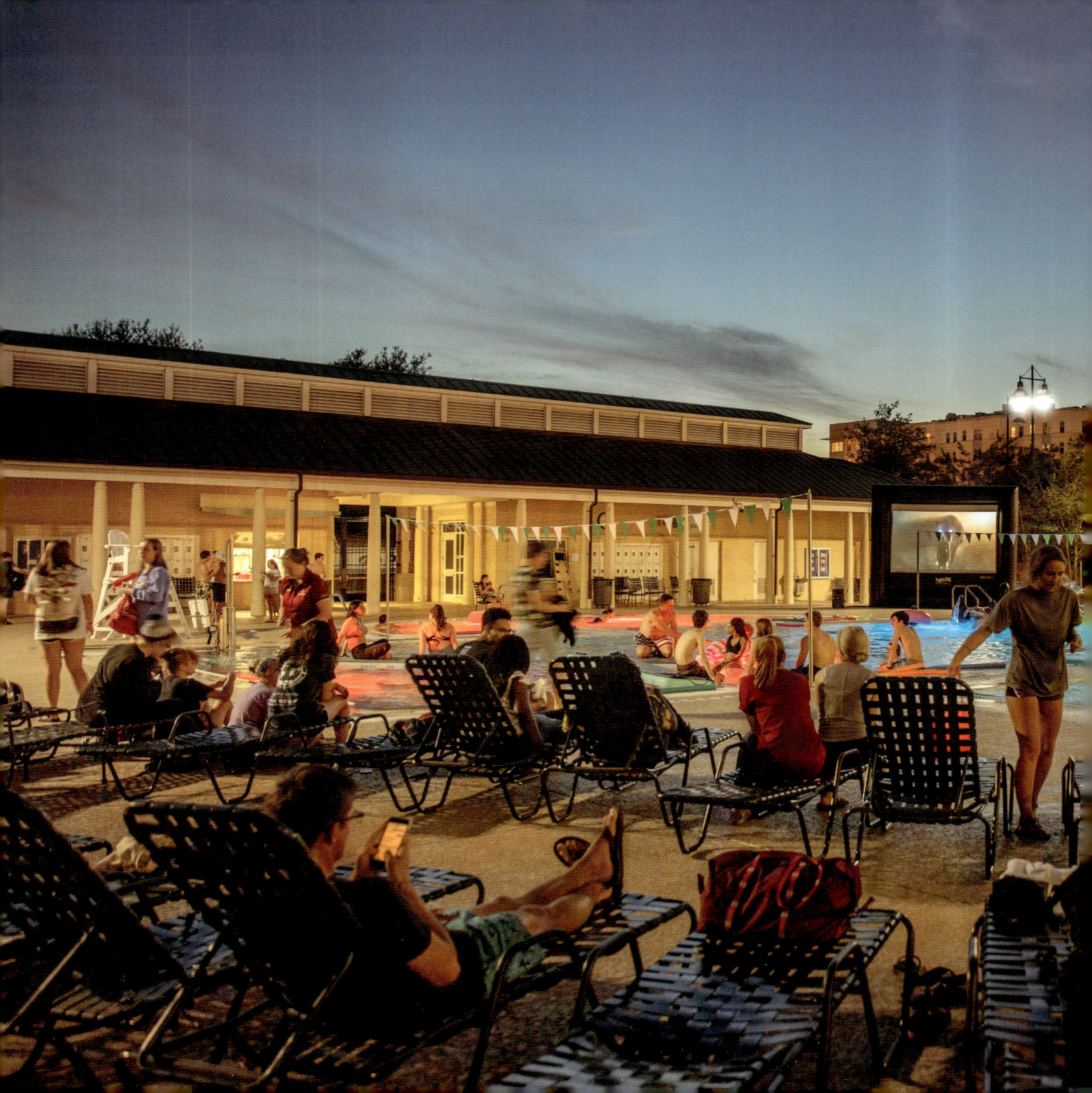

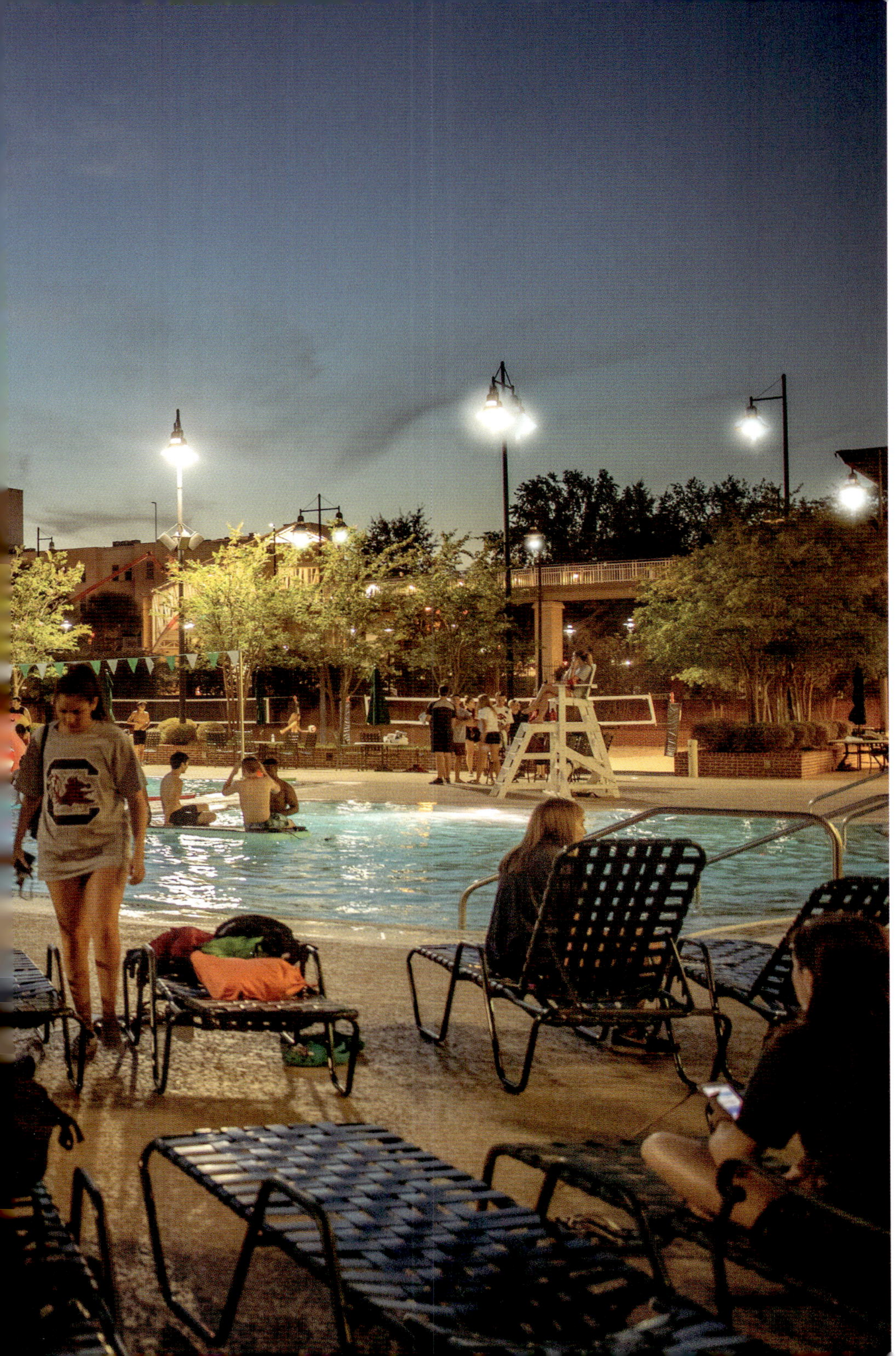

Combine an outdoor pool and an outdoor movie screen and what do you get? A dive-in movie, of course—one of many amenities at the Strom Thurmond Wellness and Fitness Center.

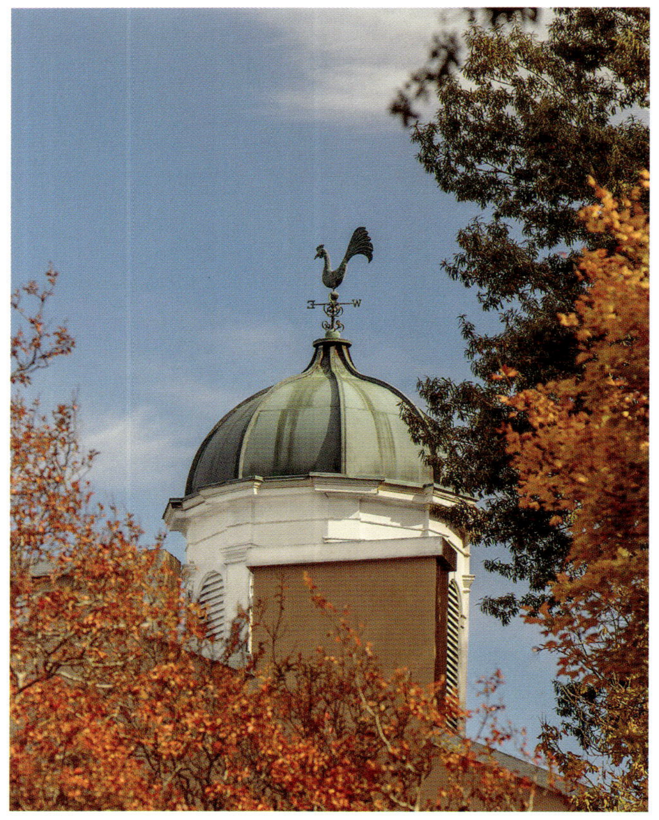

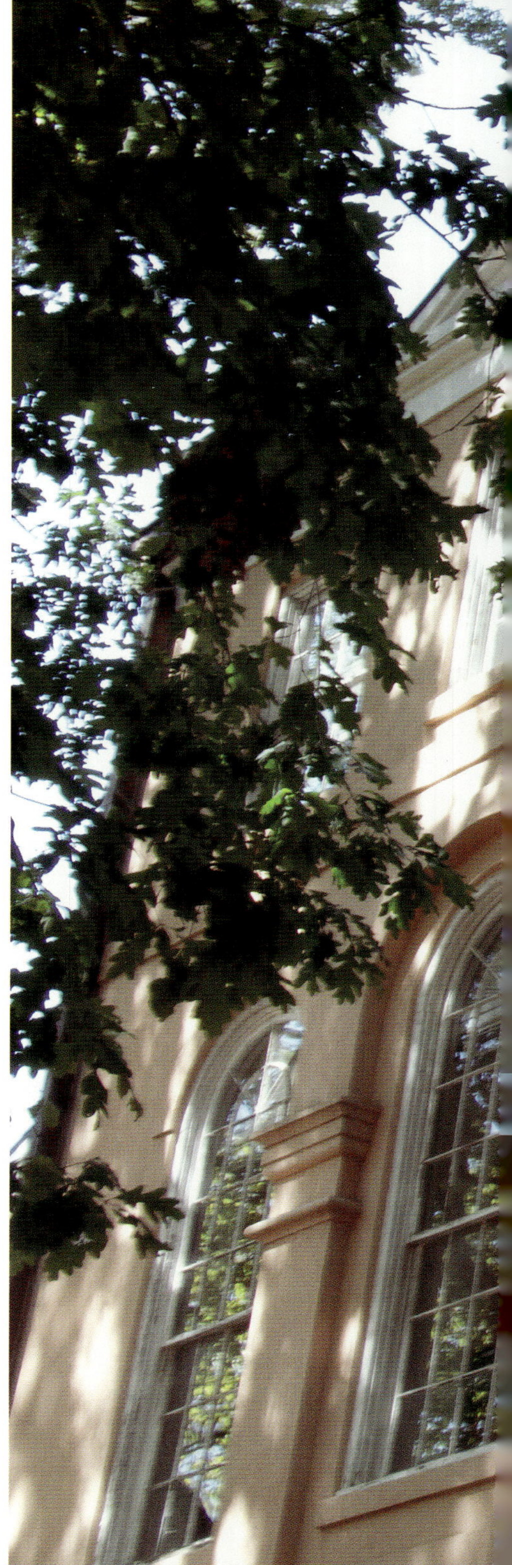

DeSaussure is the university's second oldest building, constructed in 1809 and named for Henry William DeSaussure,
a Revolutionary War veteran who helped establish South
Carolina College. The central portion of the building houses
the university's highly ranked South Carolina Honors College.

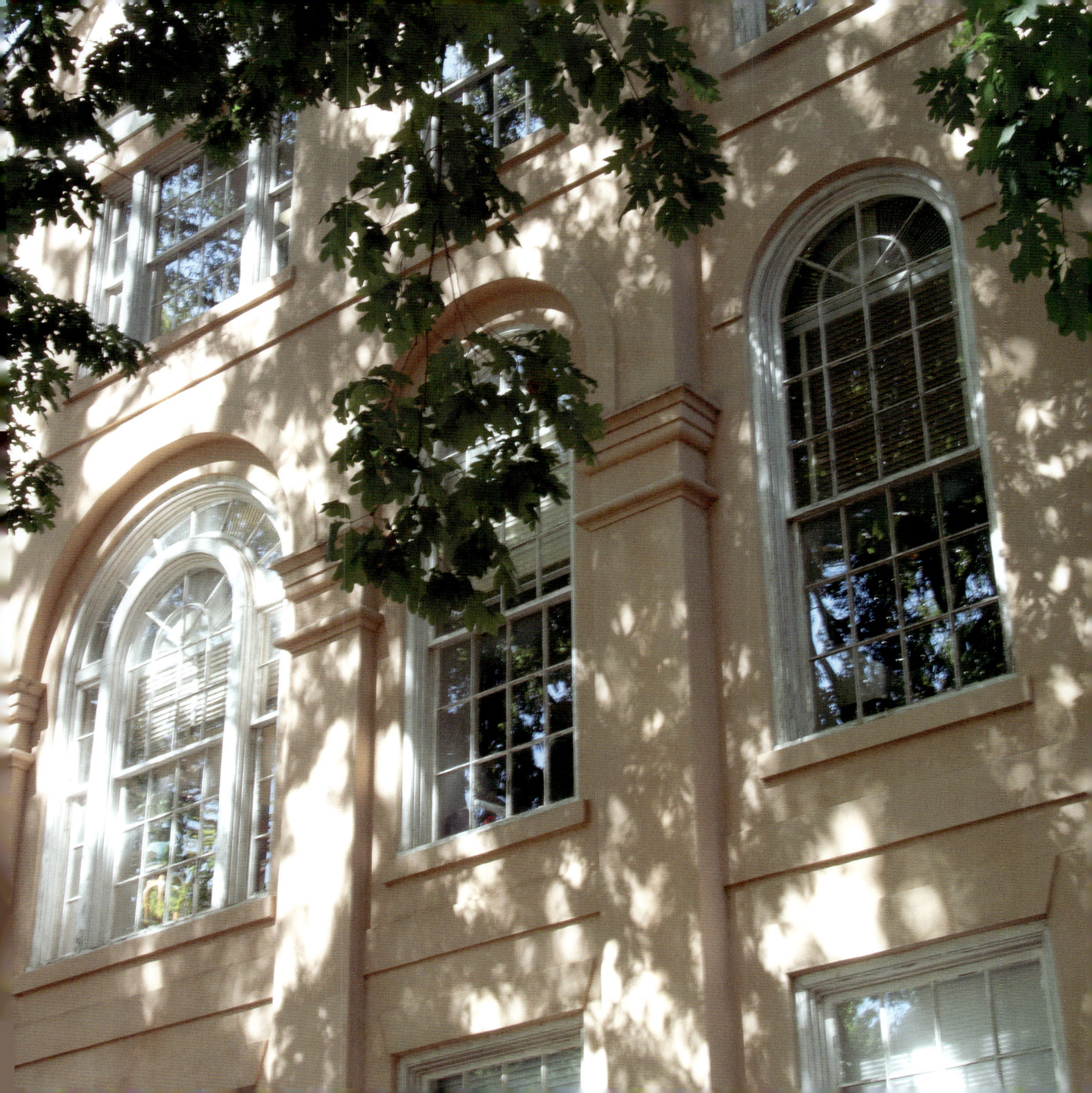

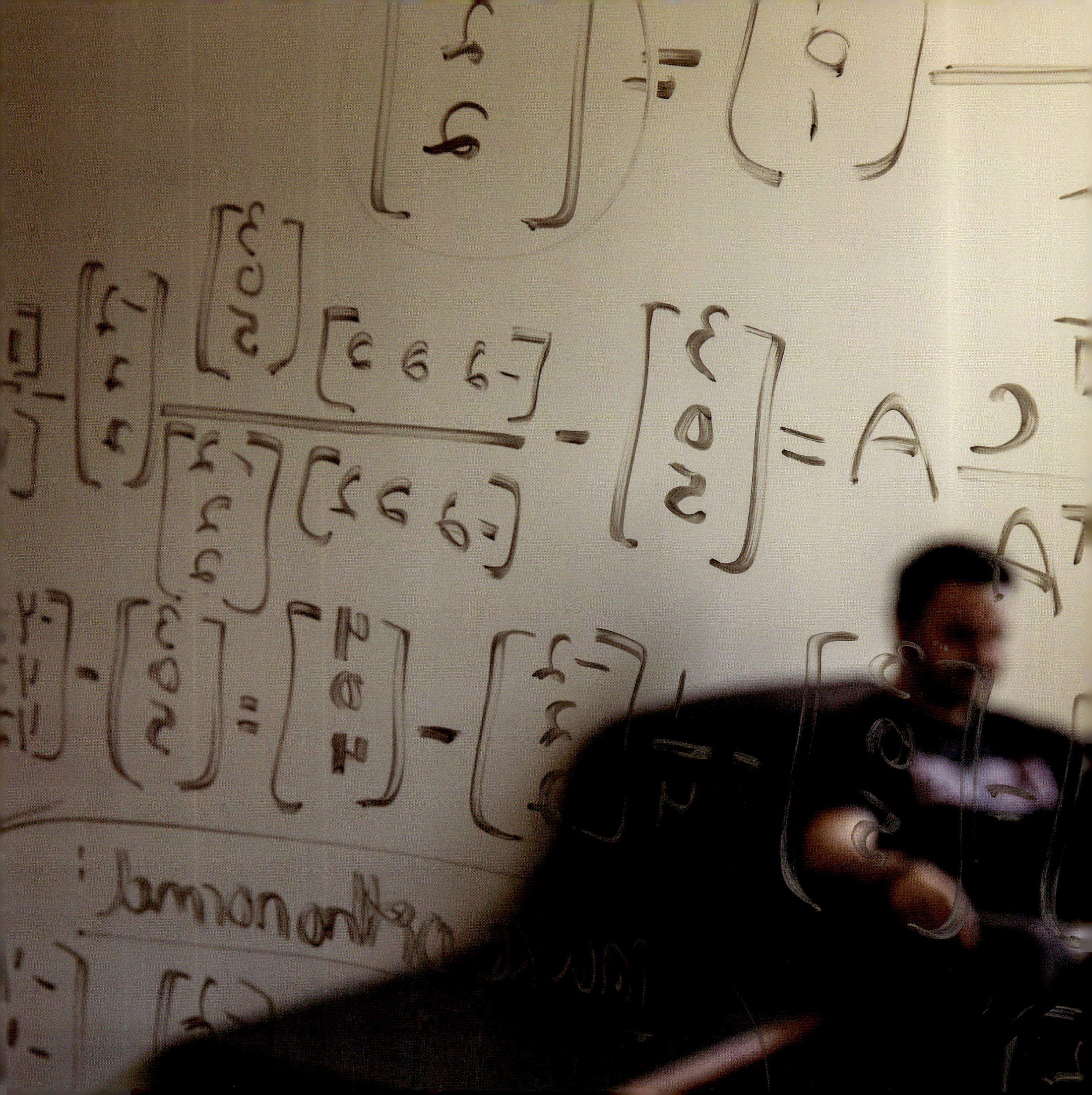

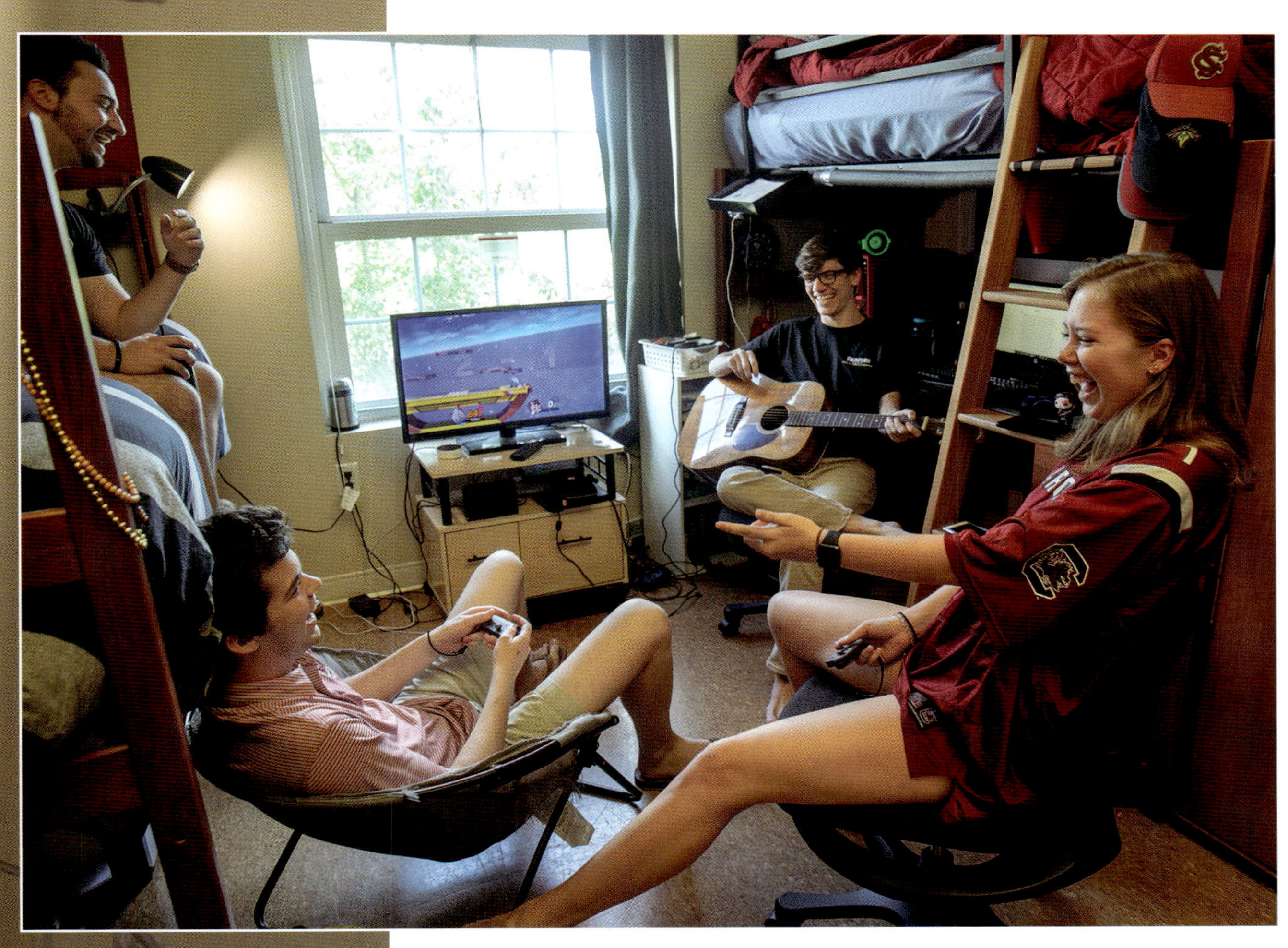

Dorm life: a moment of levity, an afternoon of camaraderie, a lifetime of memories.

Scientific equations scrawled on a transparent marker board chart the daily quest for knowledge that is the lifeblood of a research university.

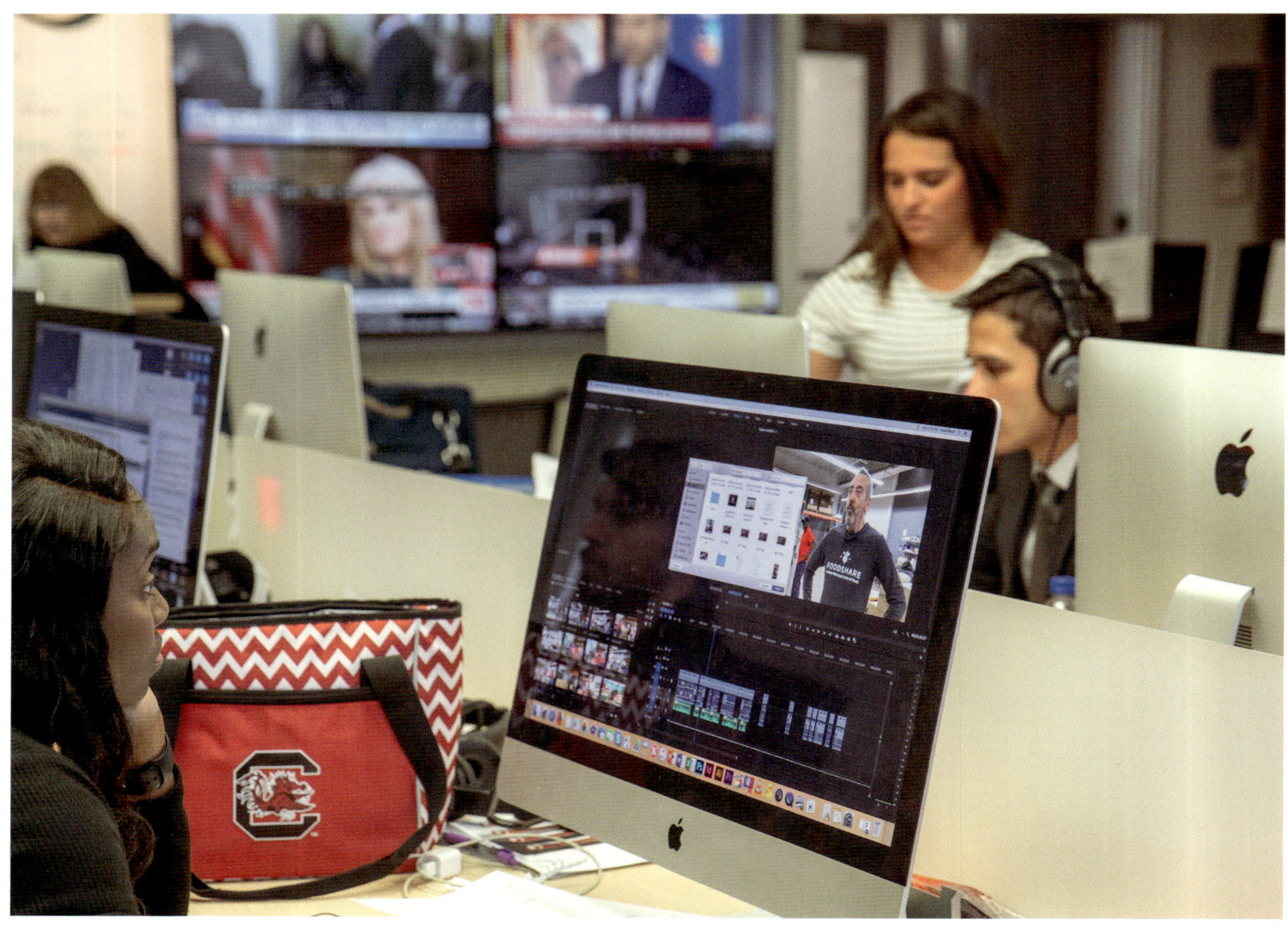

Whether learning side by side or on digital platforms, Carolina students get leading-edge instruction from top faculty members recruited from around the world.

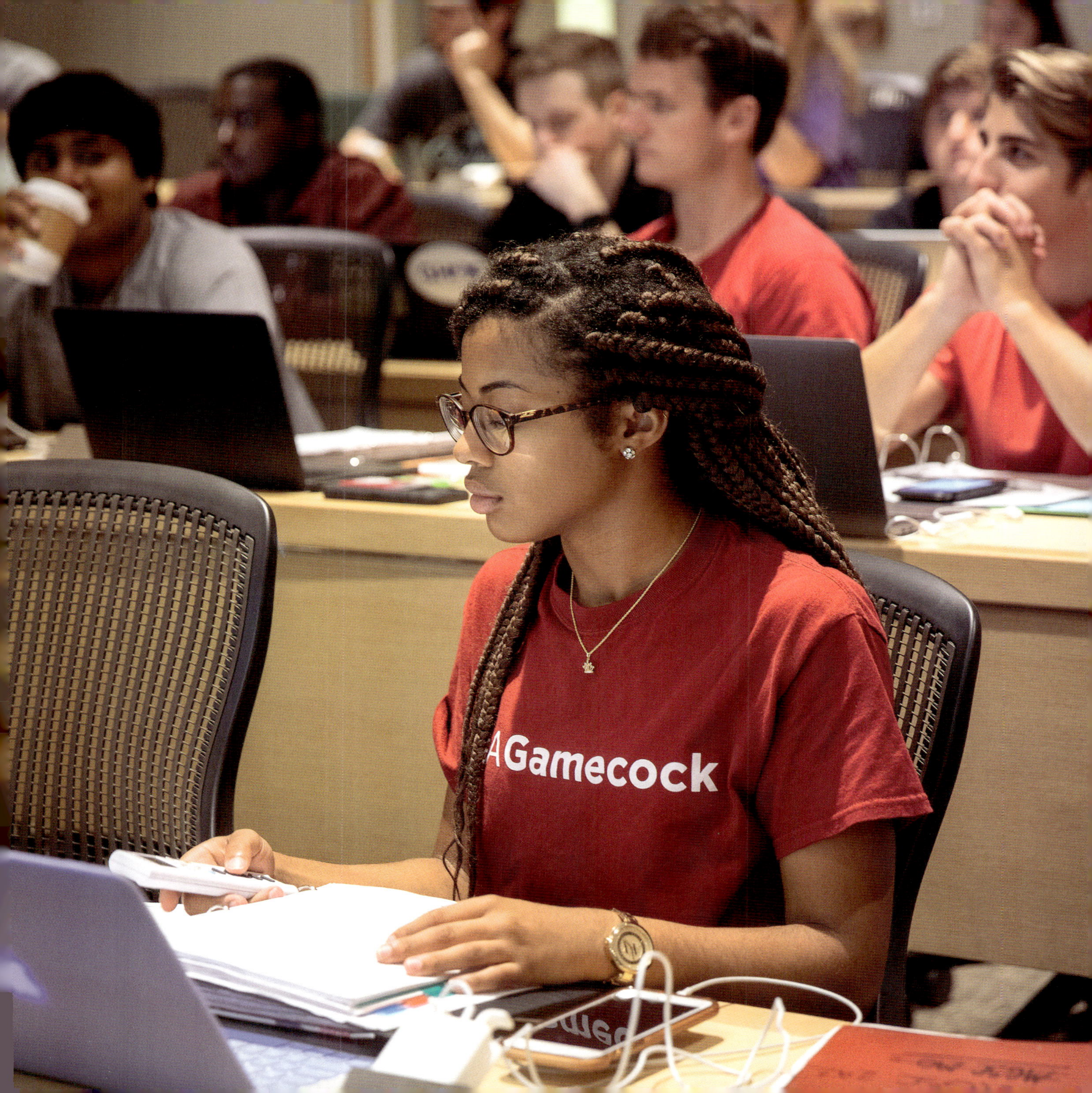

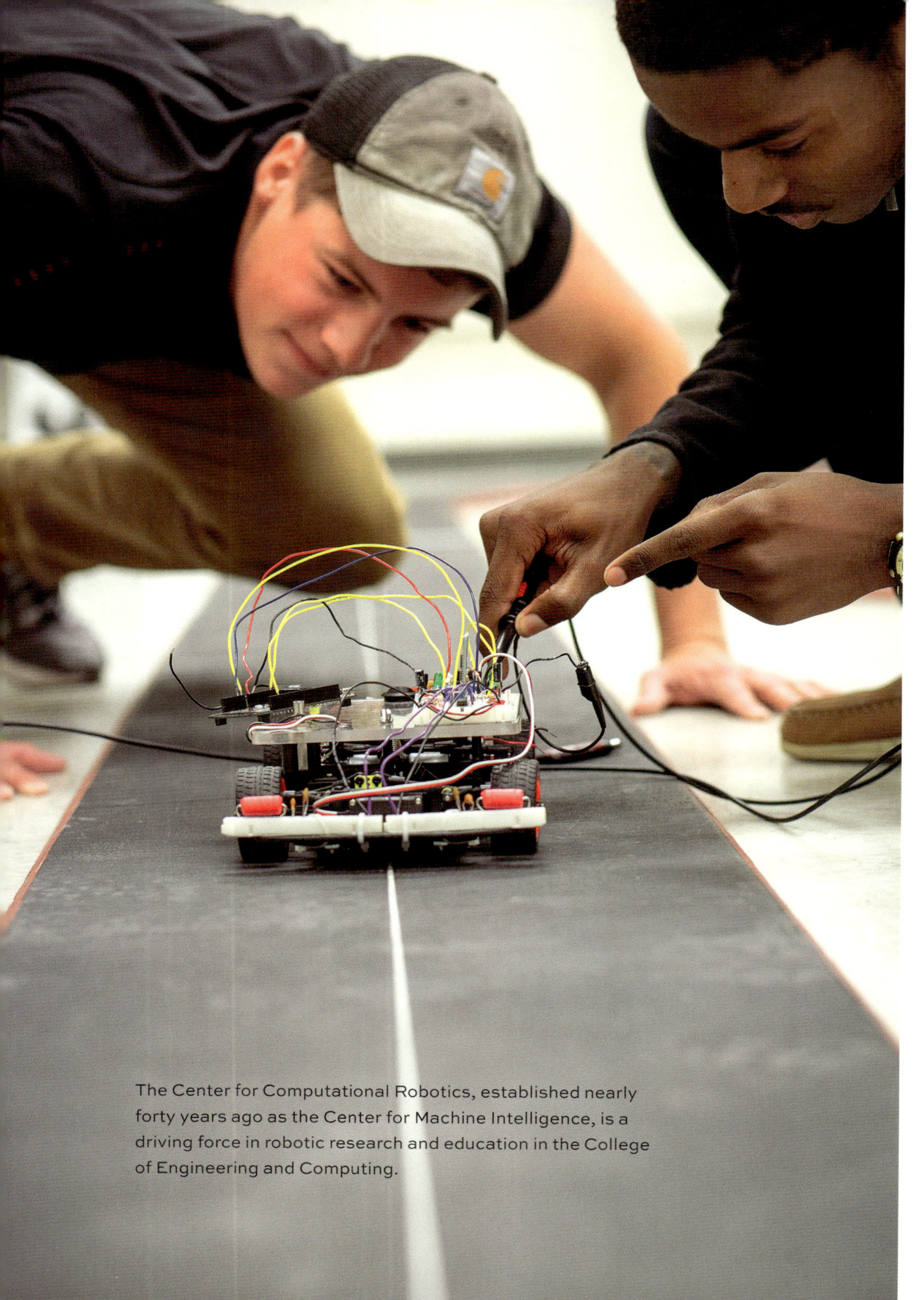

The Center for Computational Robotics, established nearly forty years ago as the Center for Machine Intelligence, is a driving force in robotic research and education in the College of Engineering and Computing.

Scientists in the clean room of the Photonics and Microelectronics Lab use novel materials to develop LEDs, lasers, microwave transistors, and photodetectors.

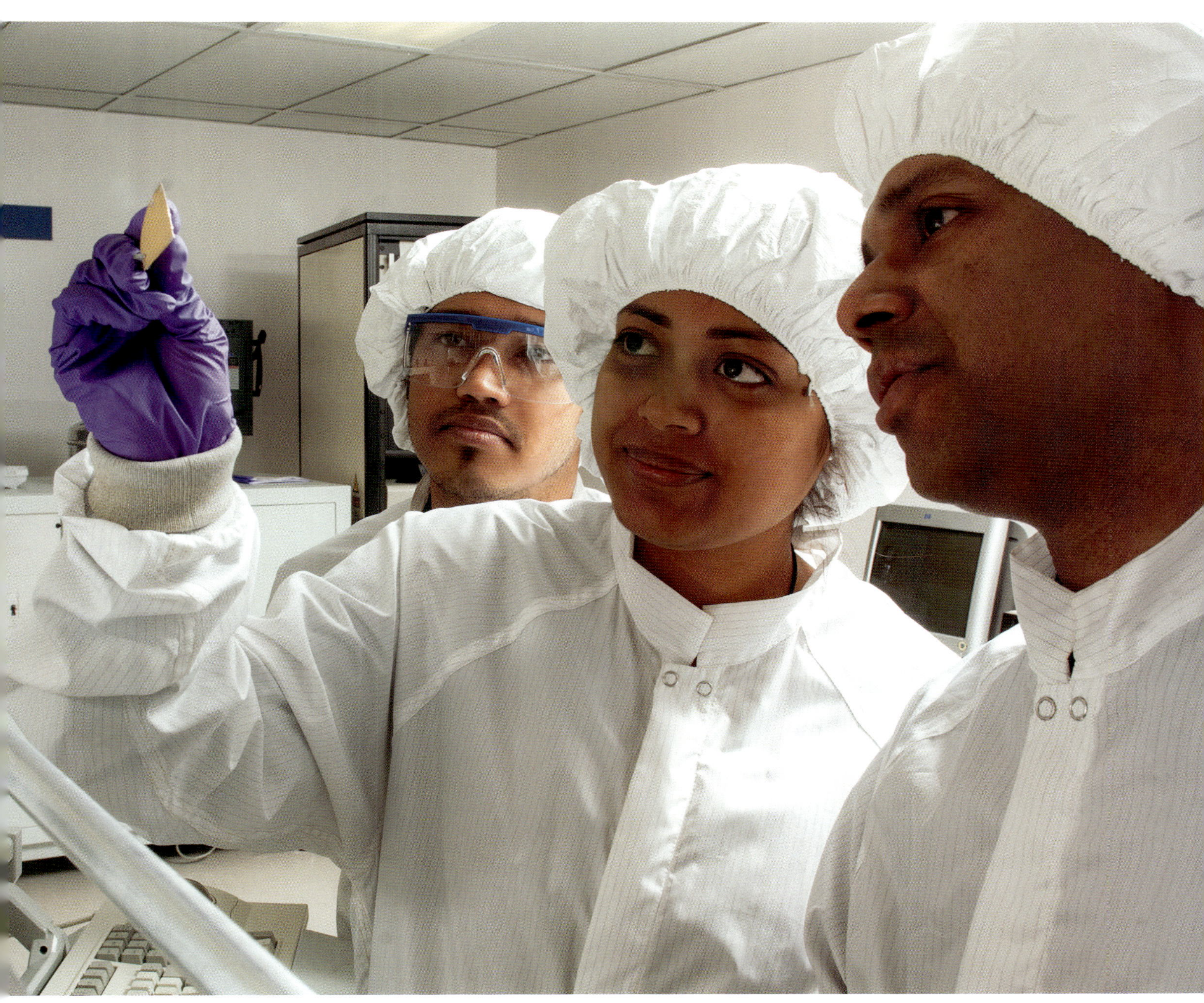

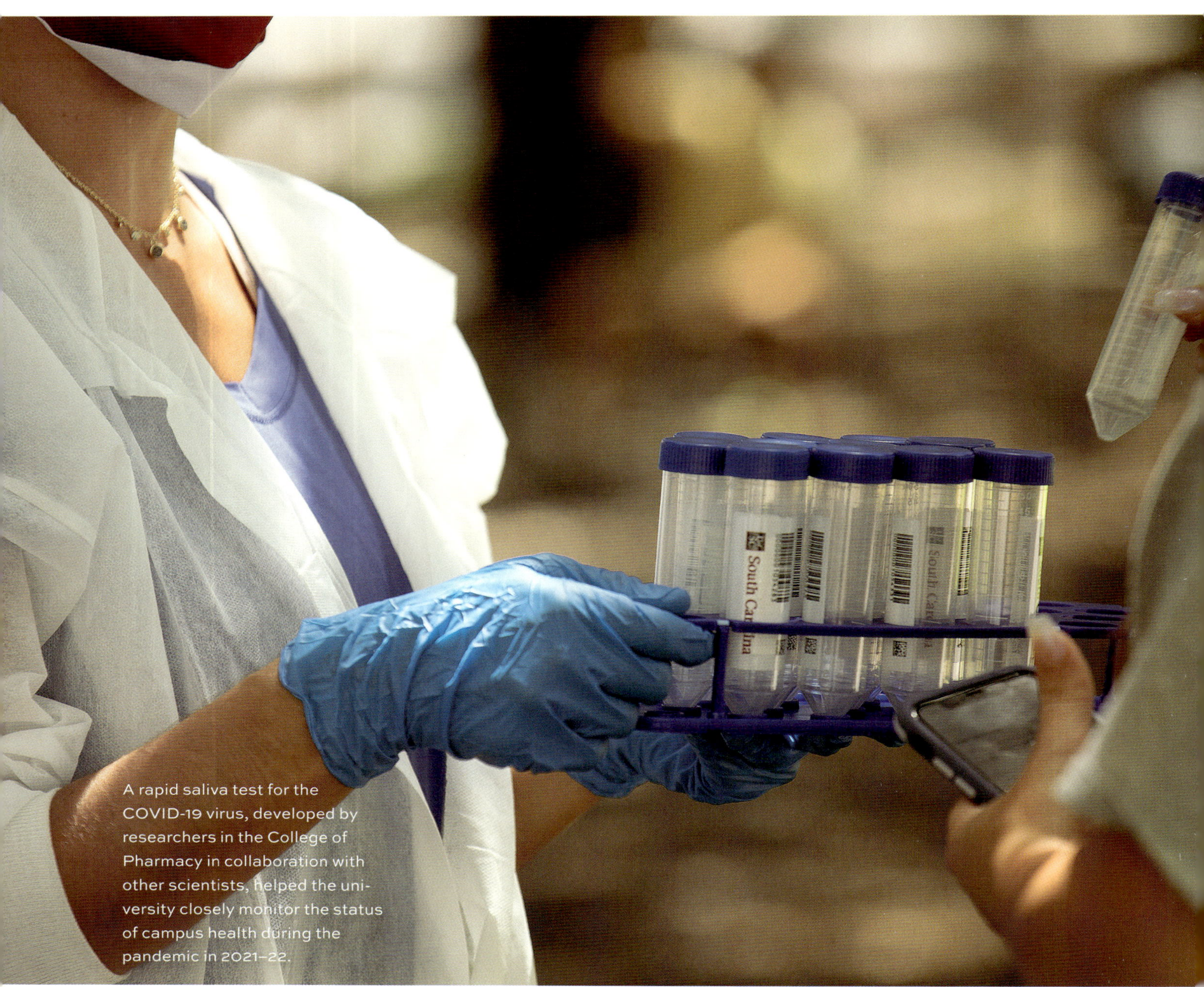

A rapid saliva test for the COVID-19 virus, developed by researchers in the College of Pharmacy in collaboration with other scientists, helped the university closely monitor the status of campus health during the pandemic in 2021–22.

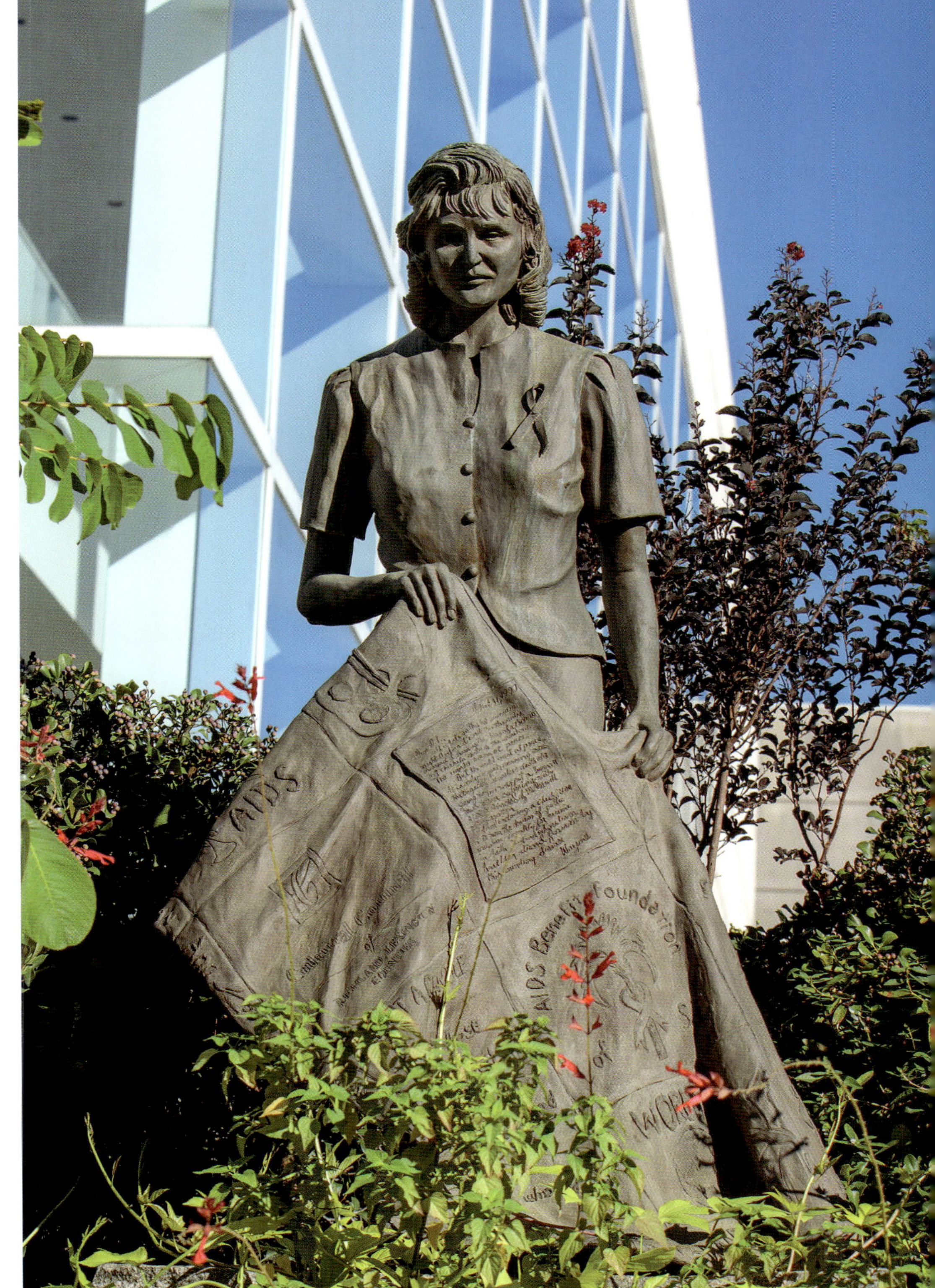

The AIDS Awareness Sculpture, created by Lexington artist Estelle Frierson, was installed beside the Koger Center for the Arts in 2003 as a tribute to the university's commitment to AIDS research and education. Many of those efforts involve scientists at the Arnold School of Public Health, who continue to be on the front lines of AIDS-related research.

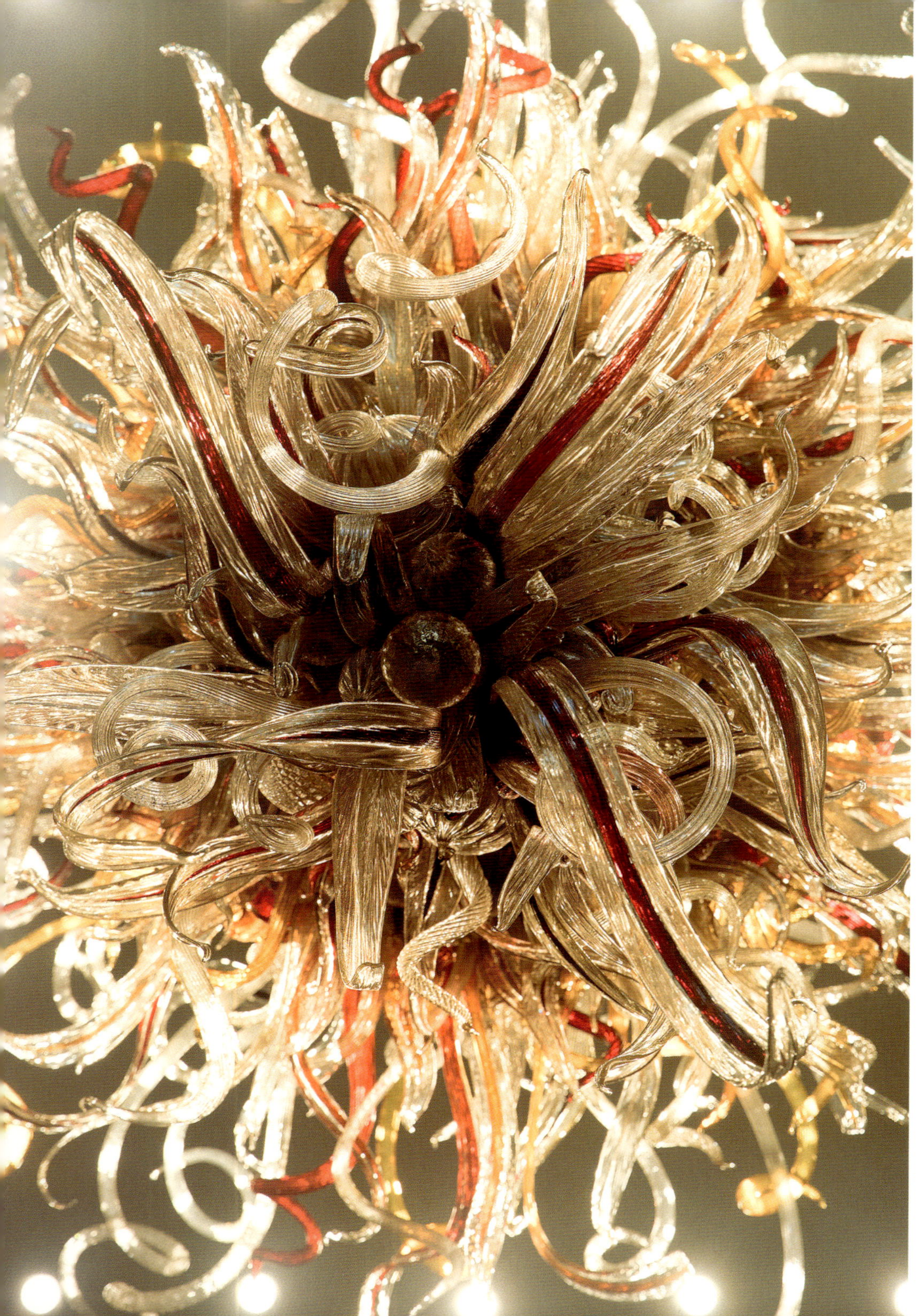

Designed by the studio of renowned artist Dale Chihuly, the Burnished Bronze and Garnet Chandelier hangs in the Perrin Family Lobby at the University of South Carolina School of Law. Given by an anonymous donor, it is an elegantly contemporary accent in the law school building, which incorporates historic architectural elements from former judicial and correctional facilities in Columbia.

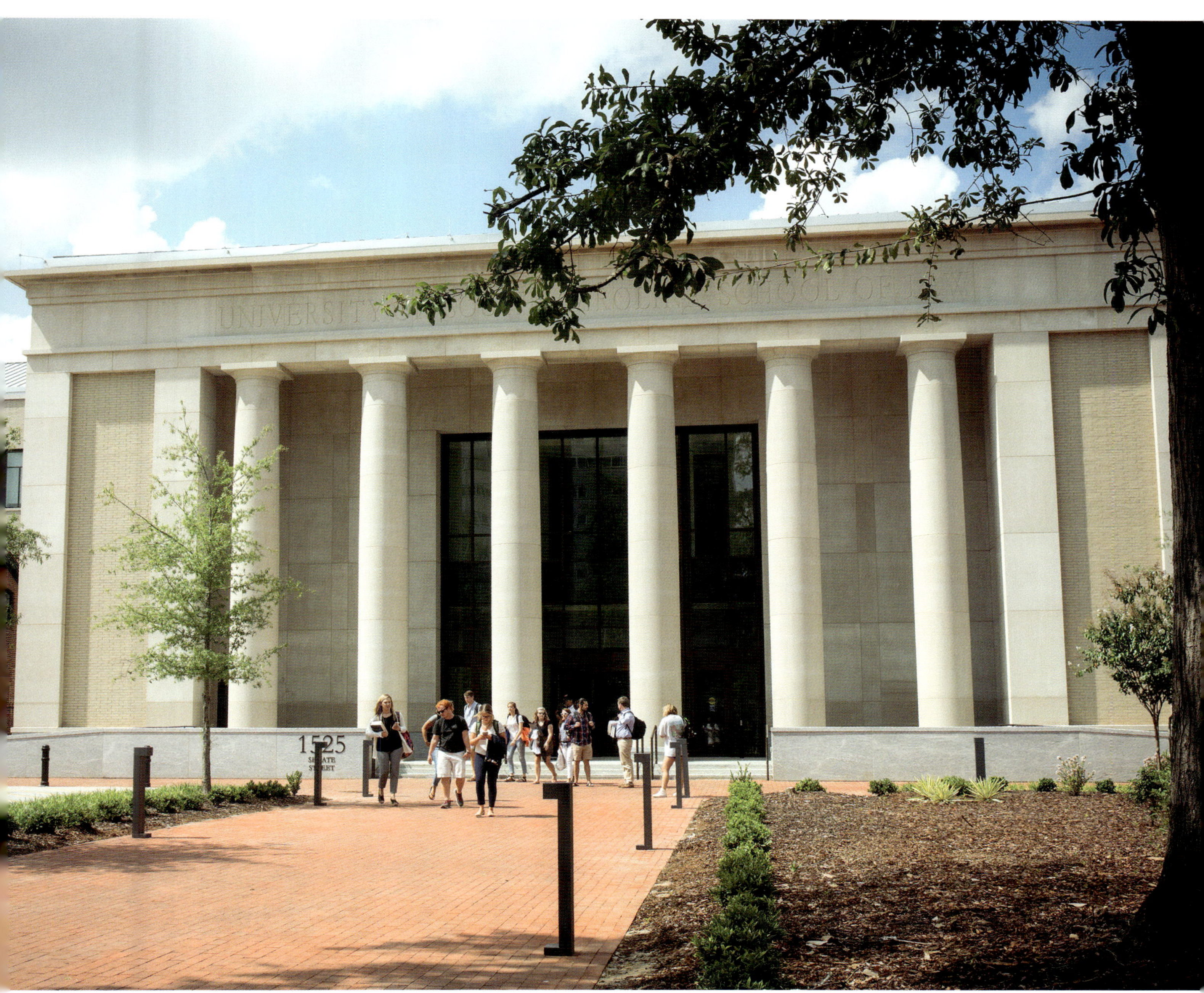

UNIVERSITY OF SOUTH CAROLINA SCHOOL OF LAW
1525
SENATE
STREET

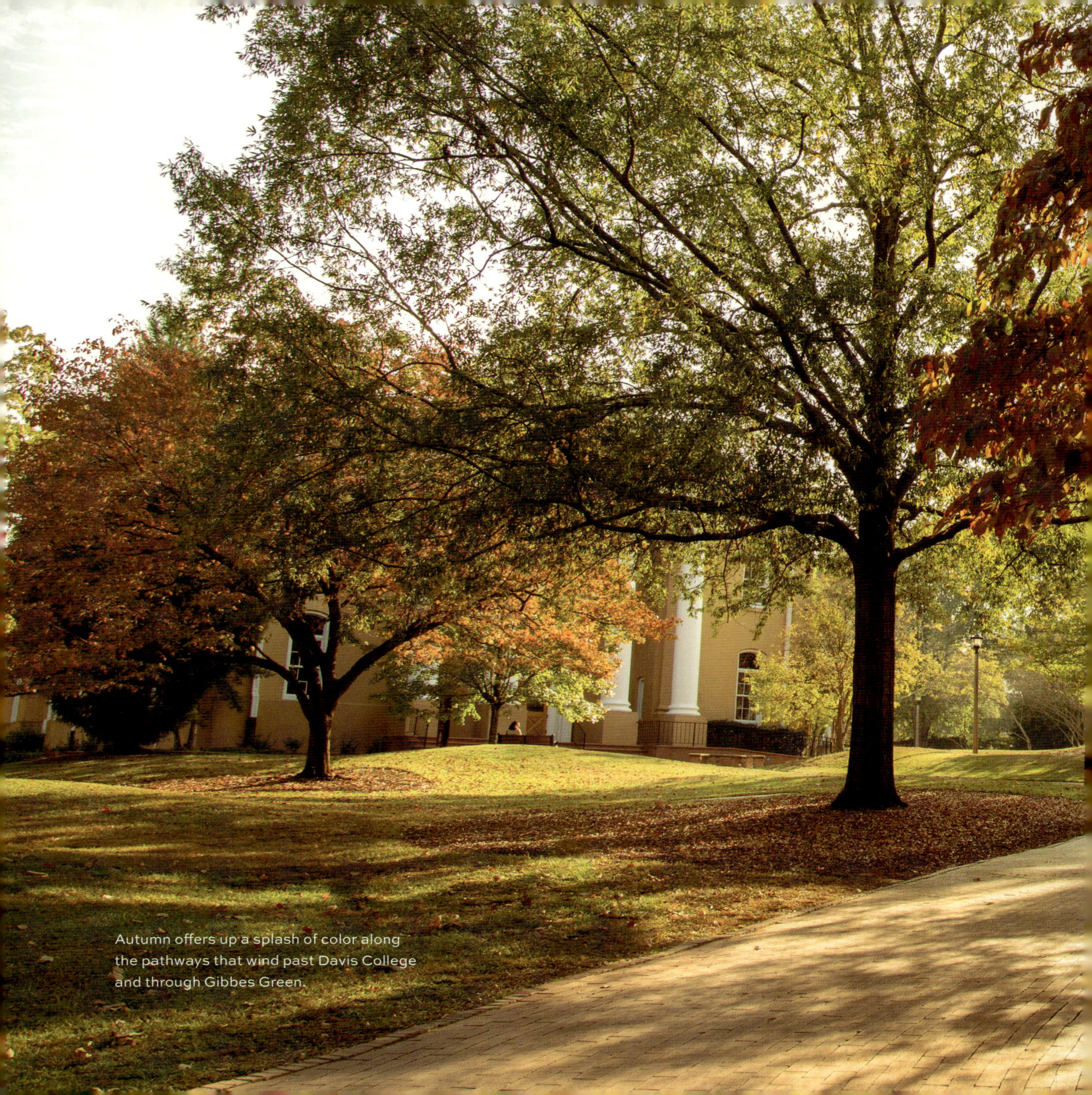

Autumn offers up a splash of color along the pathways that wind past Davis College and through Gibbes Green.

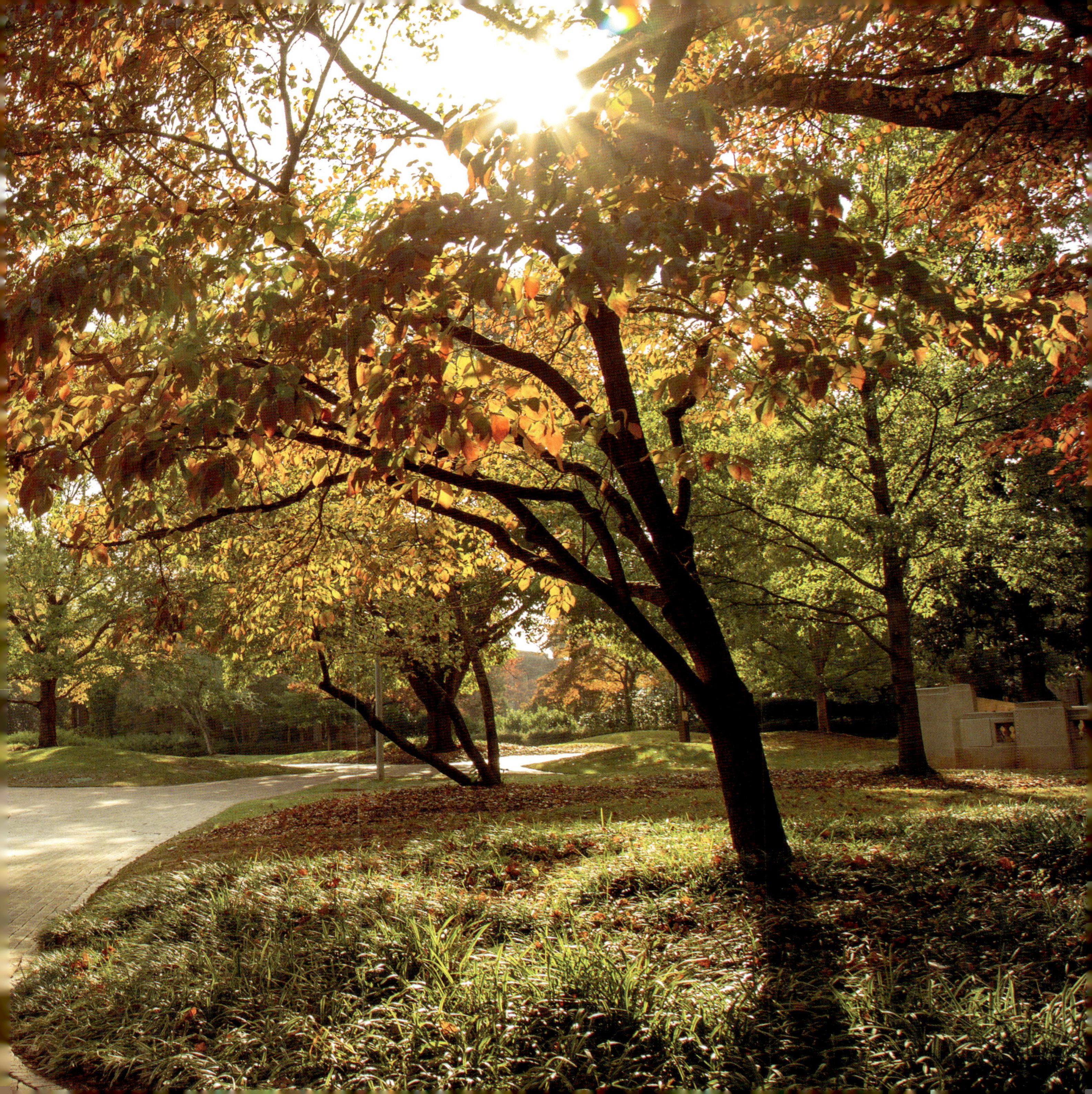

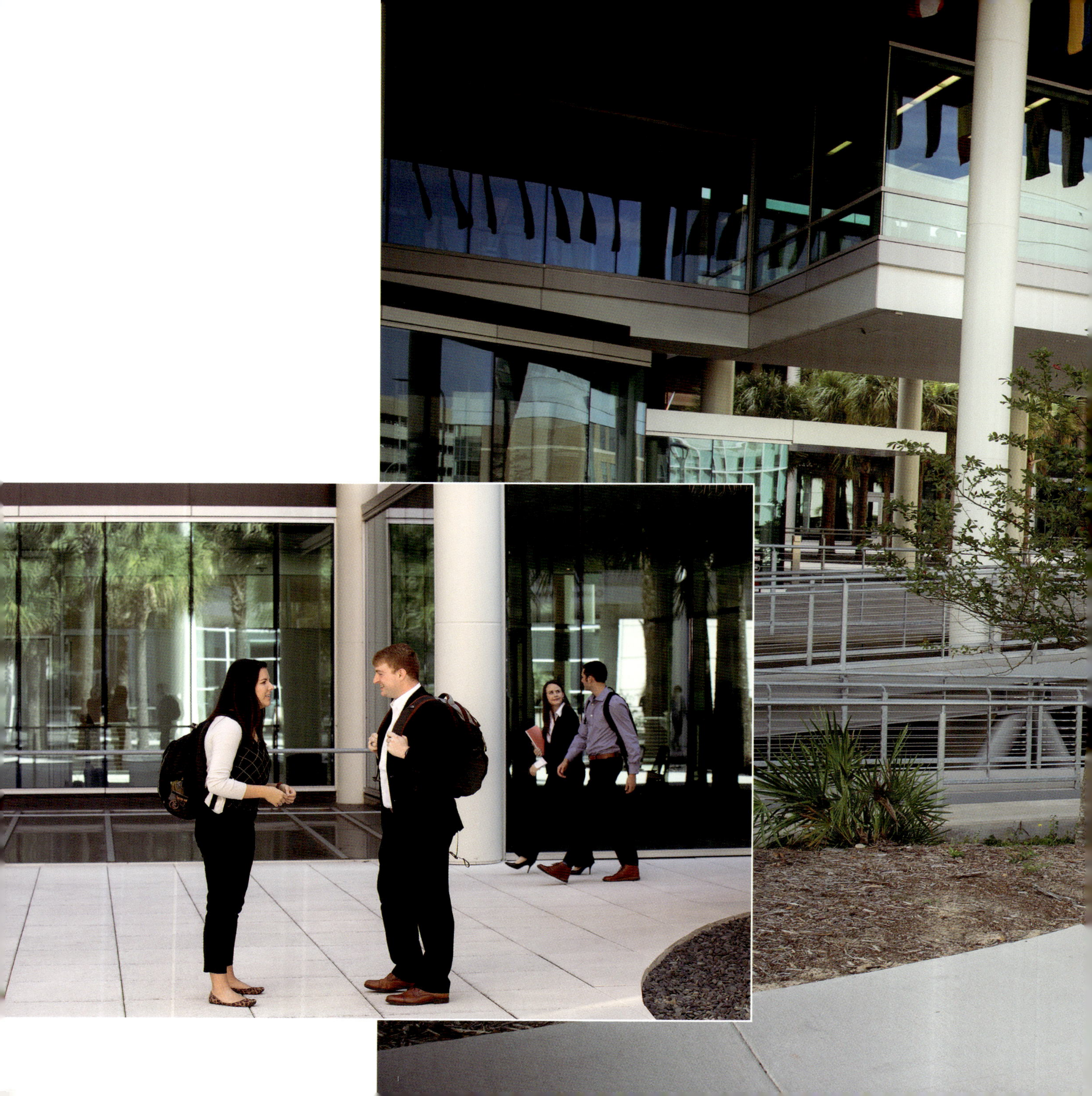

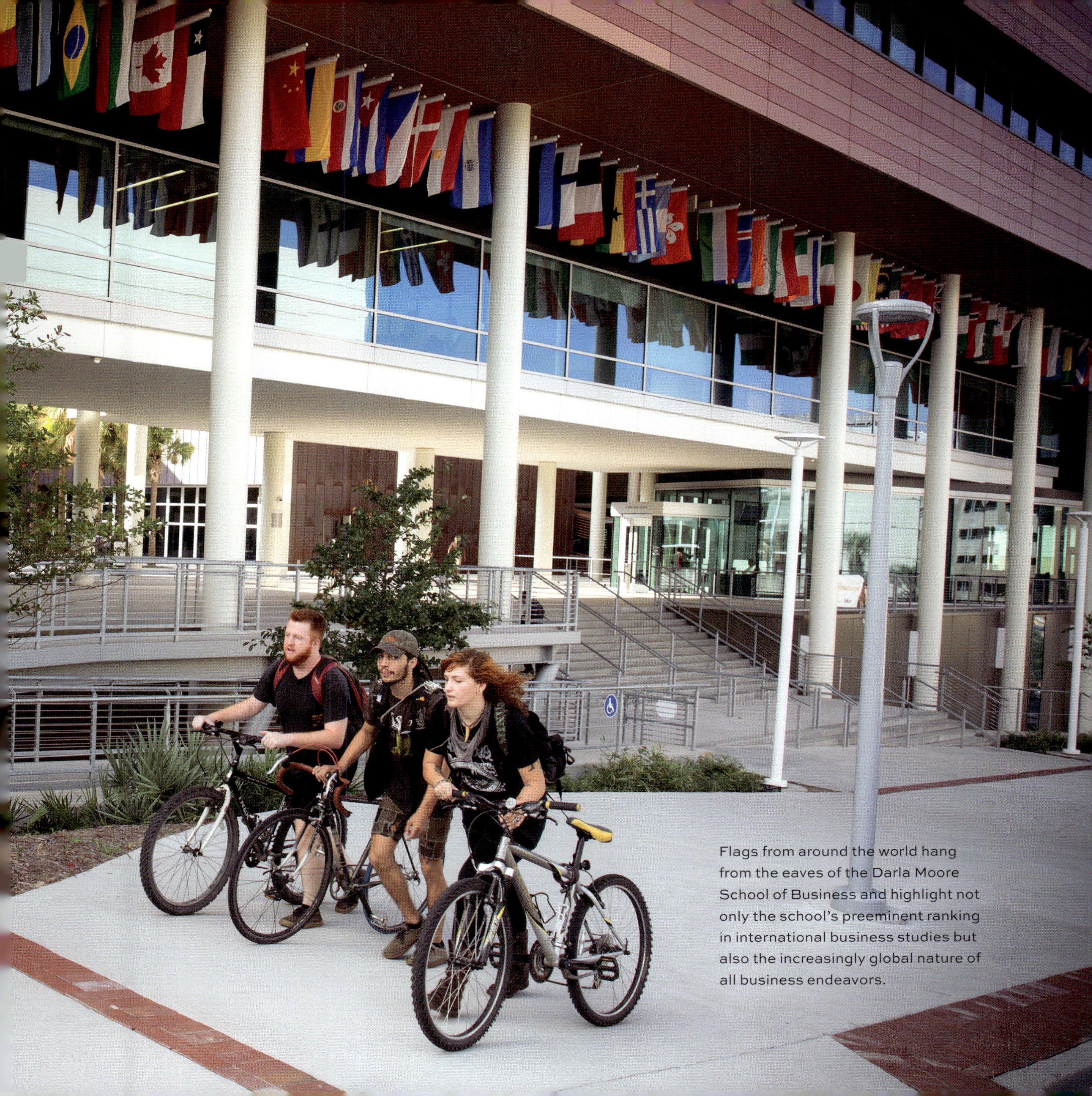

Flags from around the world hang from the eaves of the Darla Moore School of Business and highlight not only the school's preeminent ranking in international business studies but also the increasingly global nature of all business endeavors.

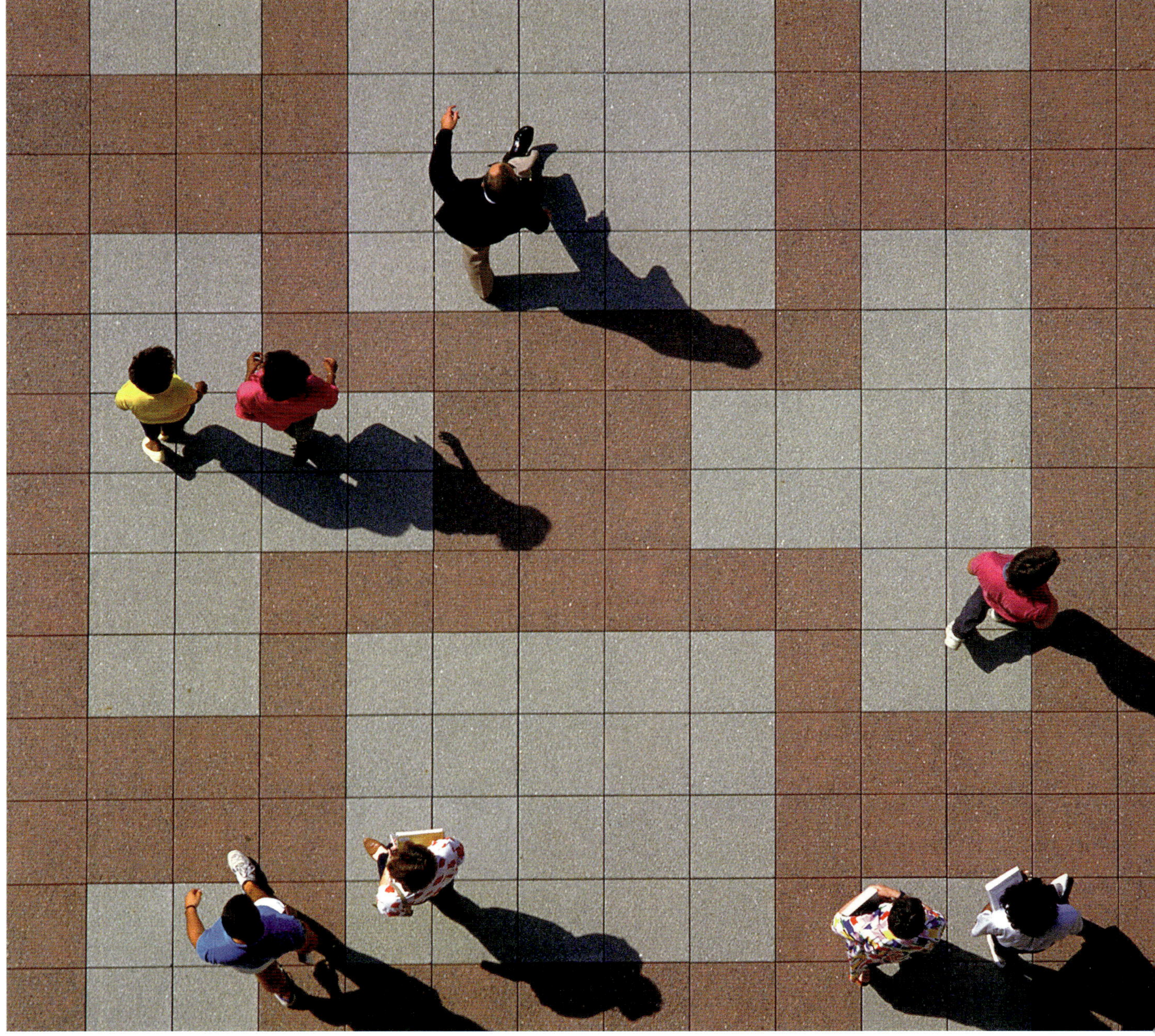

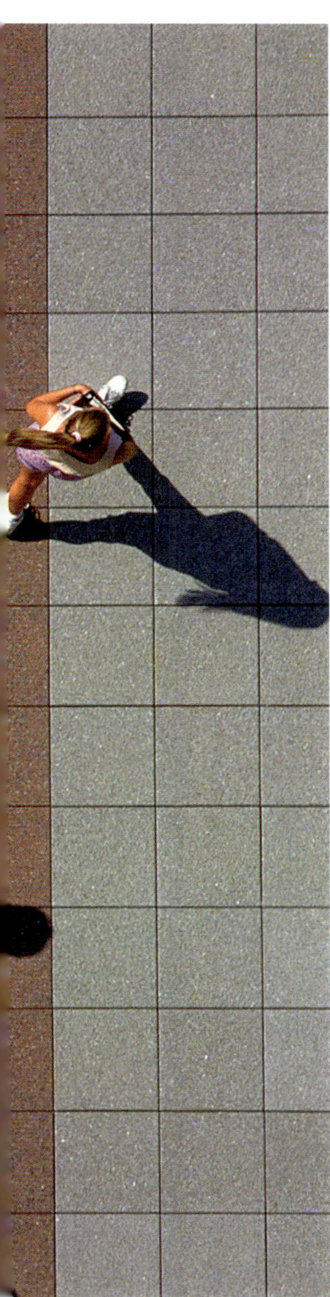

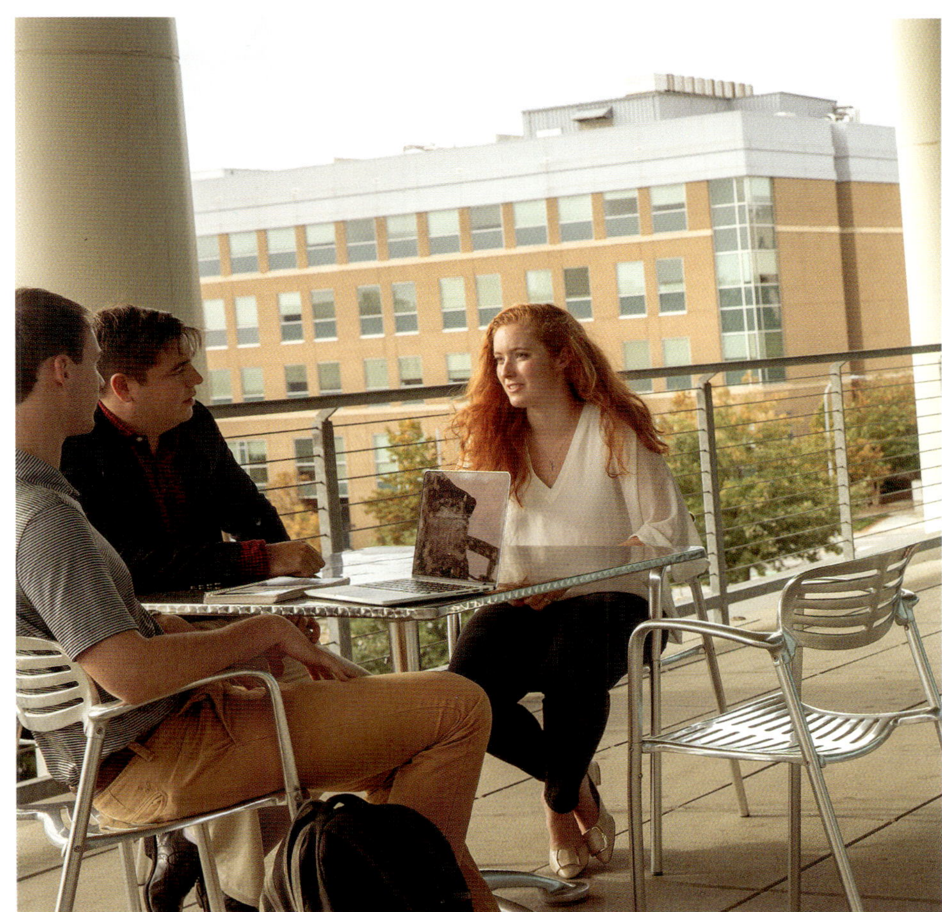

A covered patio at the Darla Moore School of Business is the perfect place to catch up with classmates.

Pedestrians' shadows dance across the plaza in front of the Close-Hipp Building, home of the College of Hospitality, Retail and Sport Management.

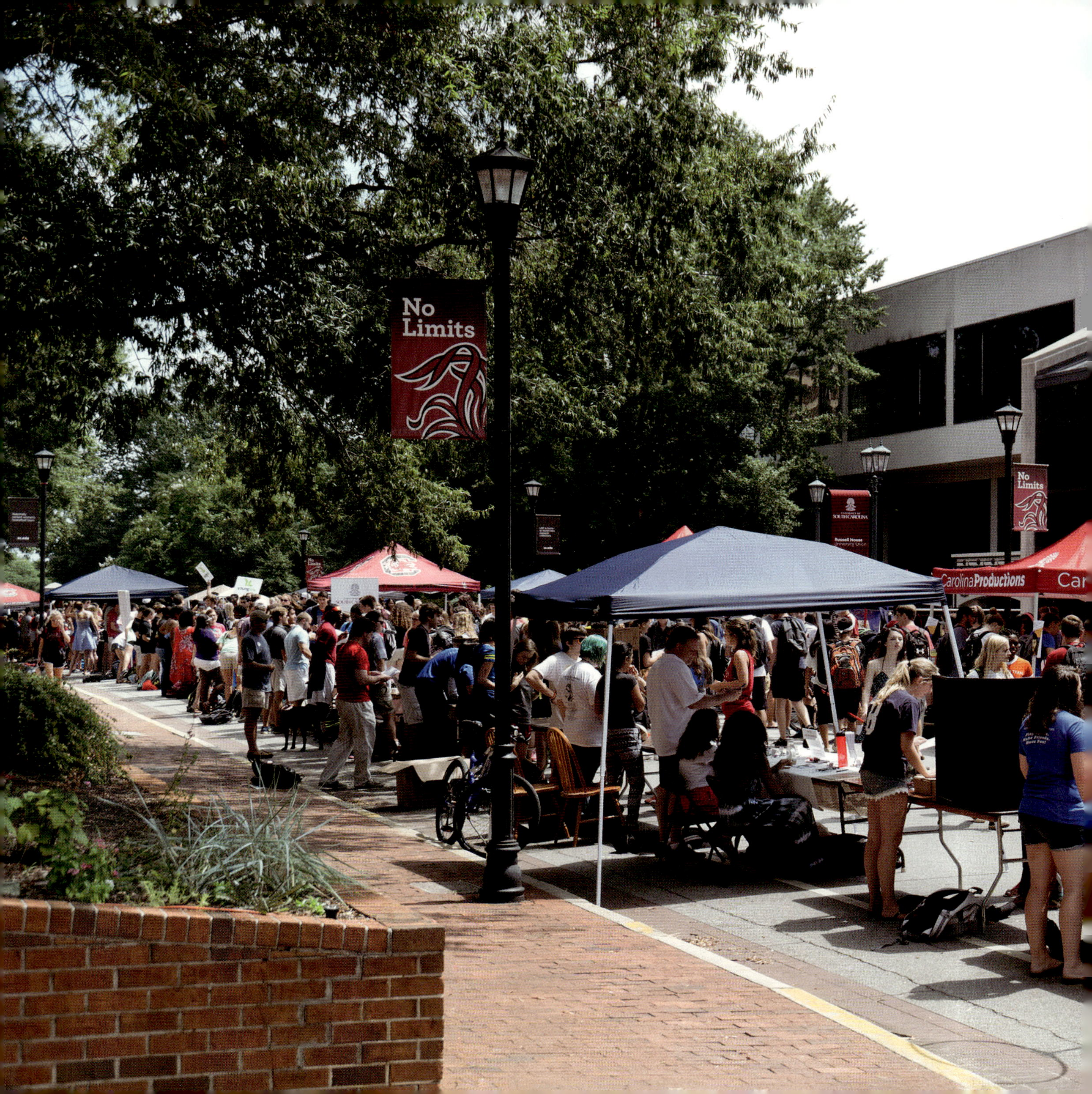

No Limits
No Limits
Carolina Productions
Russell House
University Union

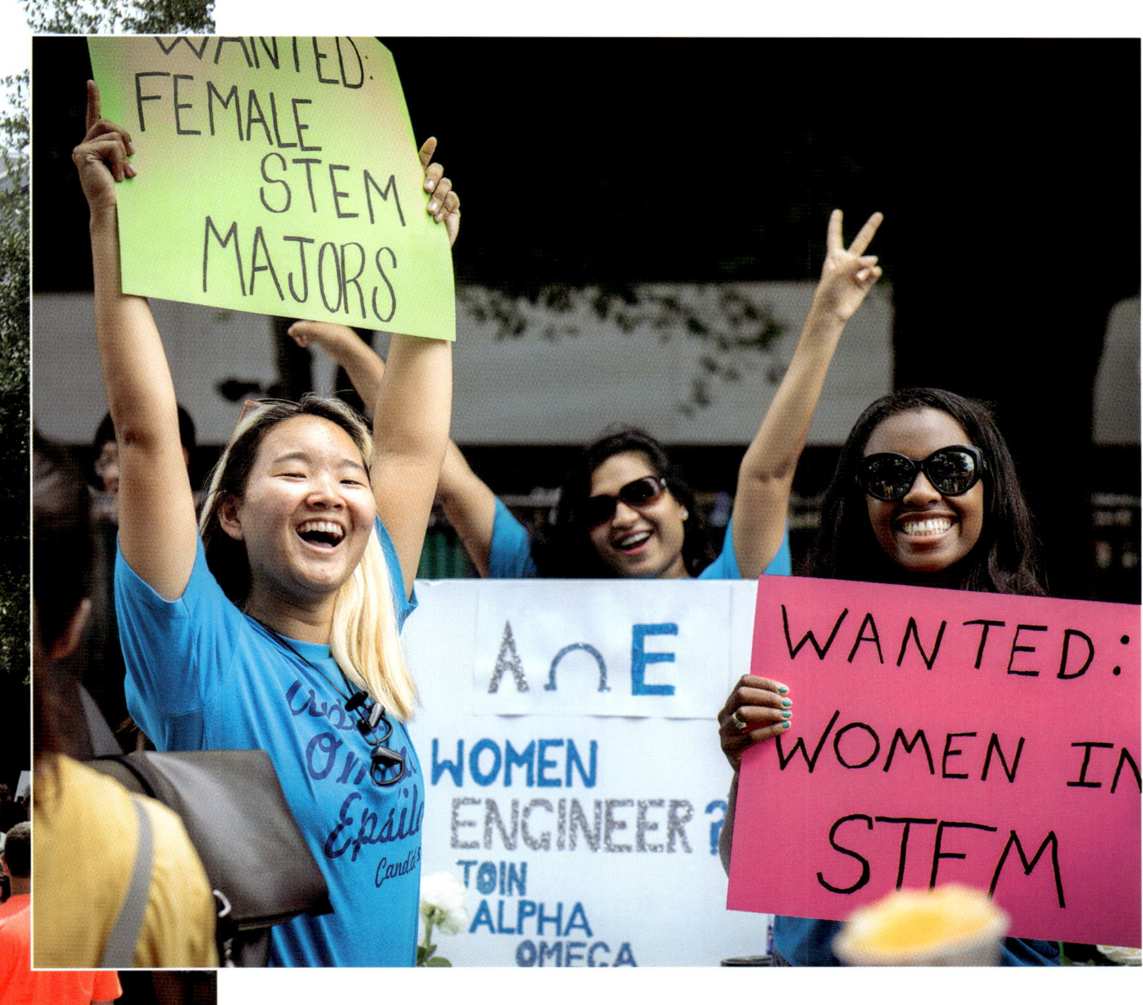

From the Academic Team (quiz bowl competition) to Zeta Phi Eta (a professional fraternity in communication arts and sciences), South Carolina students can join any of the more than 550 student organizations on campus.

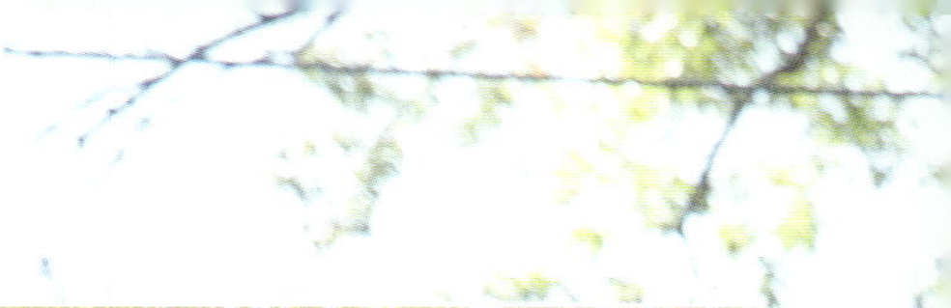

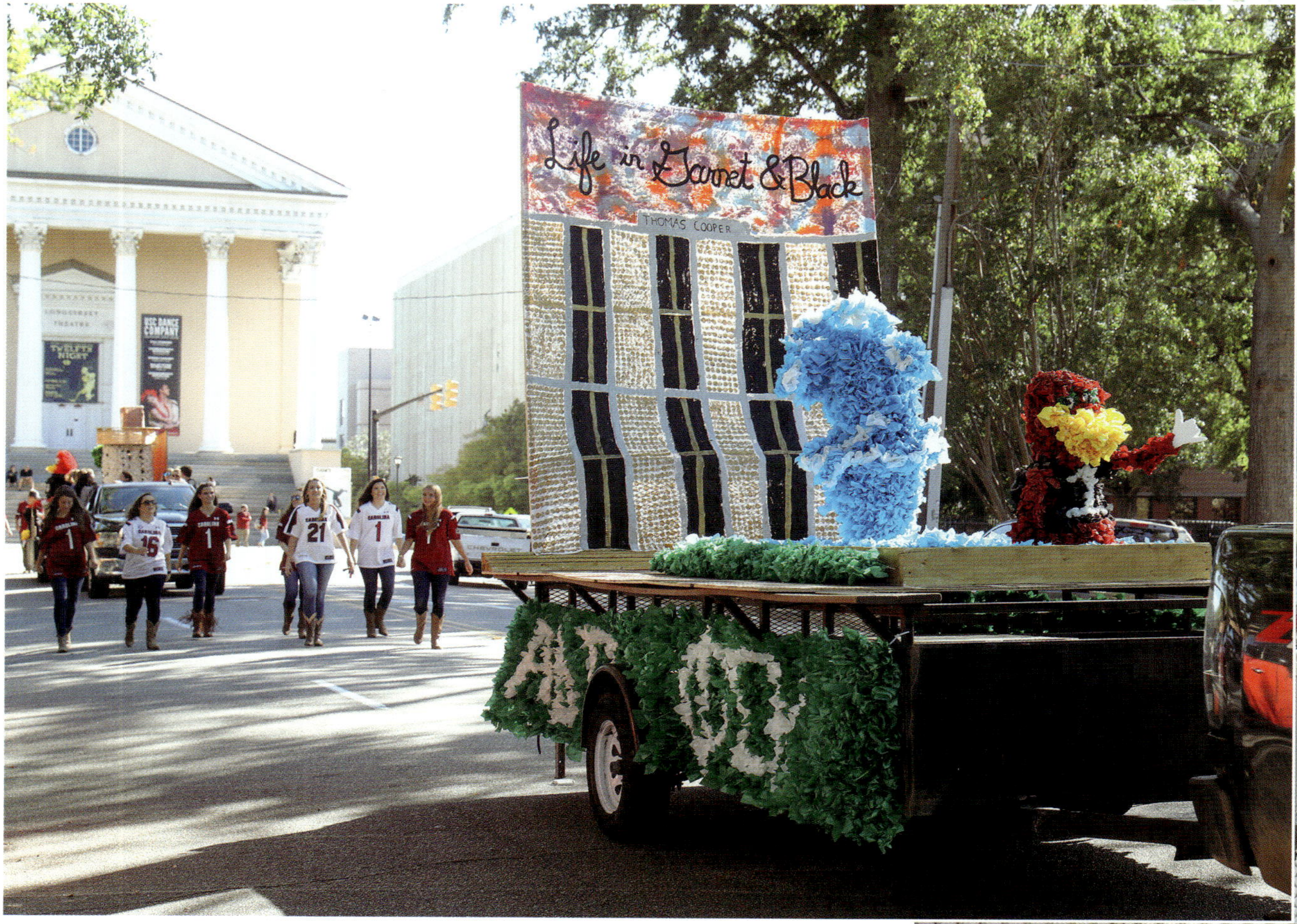

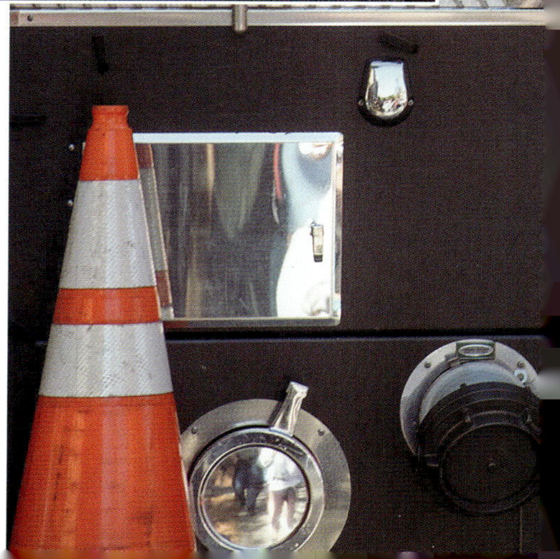

Homecoming festivities include a spirited parade through the heart of campus, with everyone's favorite mascot showing up in unexpected places.

Overleaf: Morning sunlight bathes Williams-Brice Stadium—a warmup for the autumn afternoons when Gamecock fans arrive for tailgating, cheering, and camaraderie.

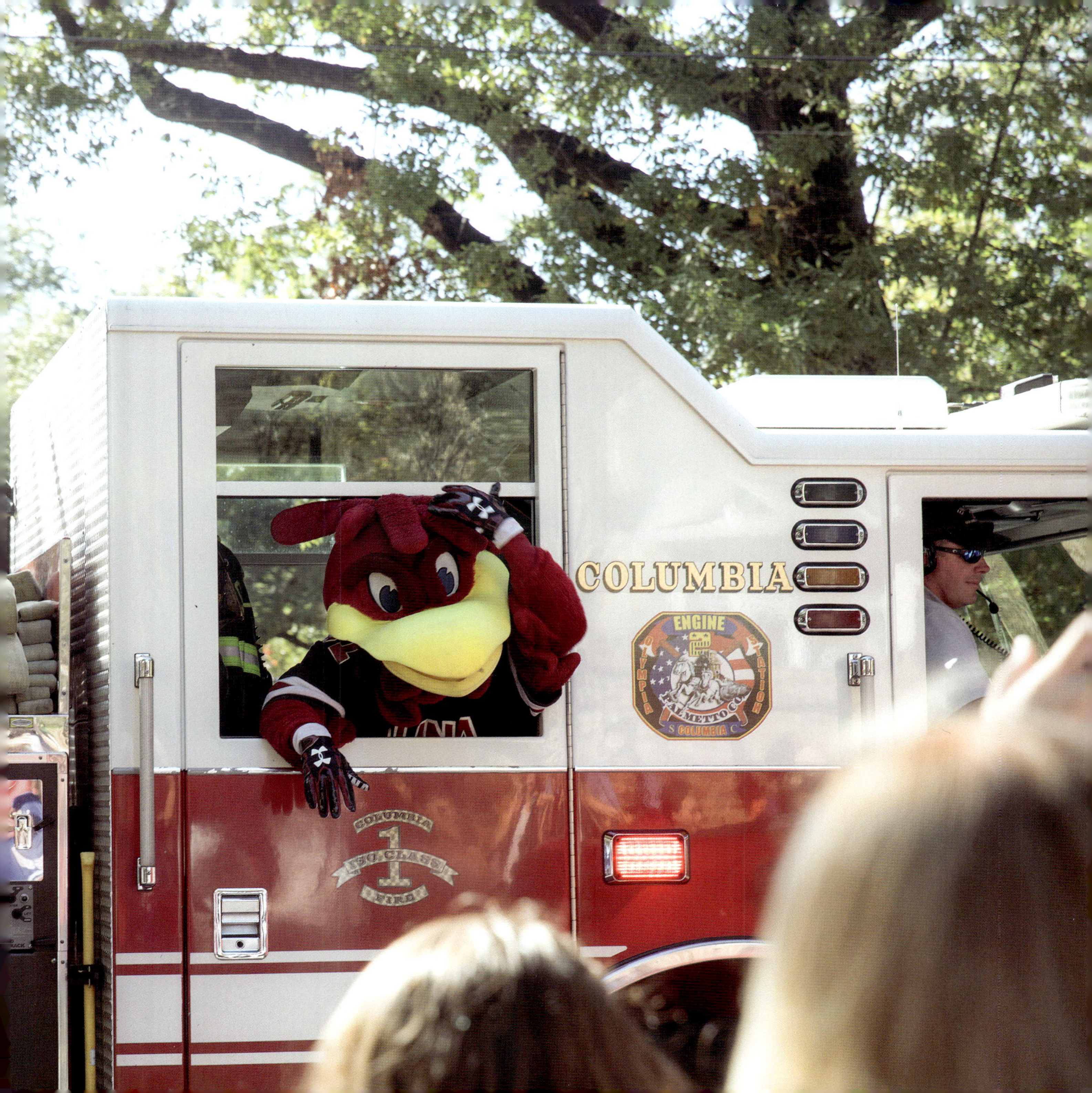

COLUMBIA
ENGINE
OLYMPIA
PALMETTO CO
S COLUMBIA C
COLUMBIA
CLASS
1
FIRE

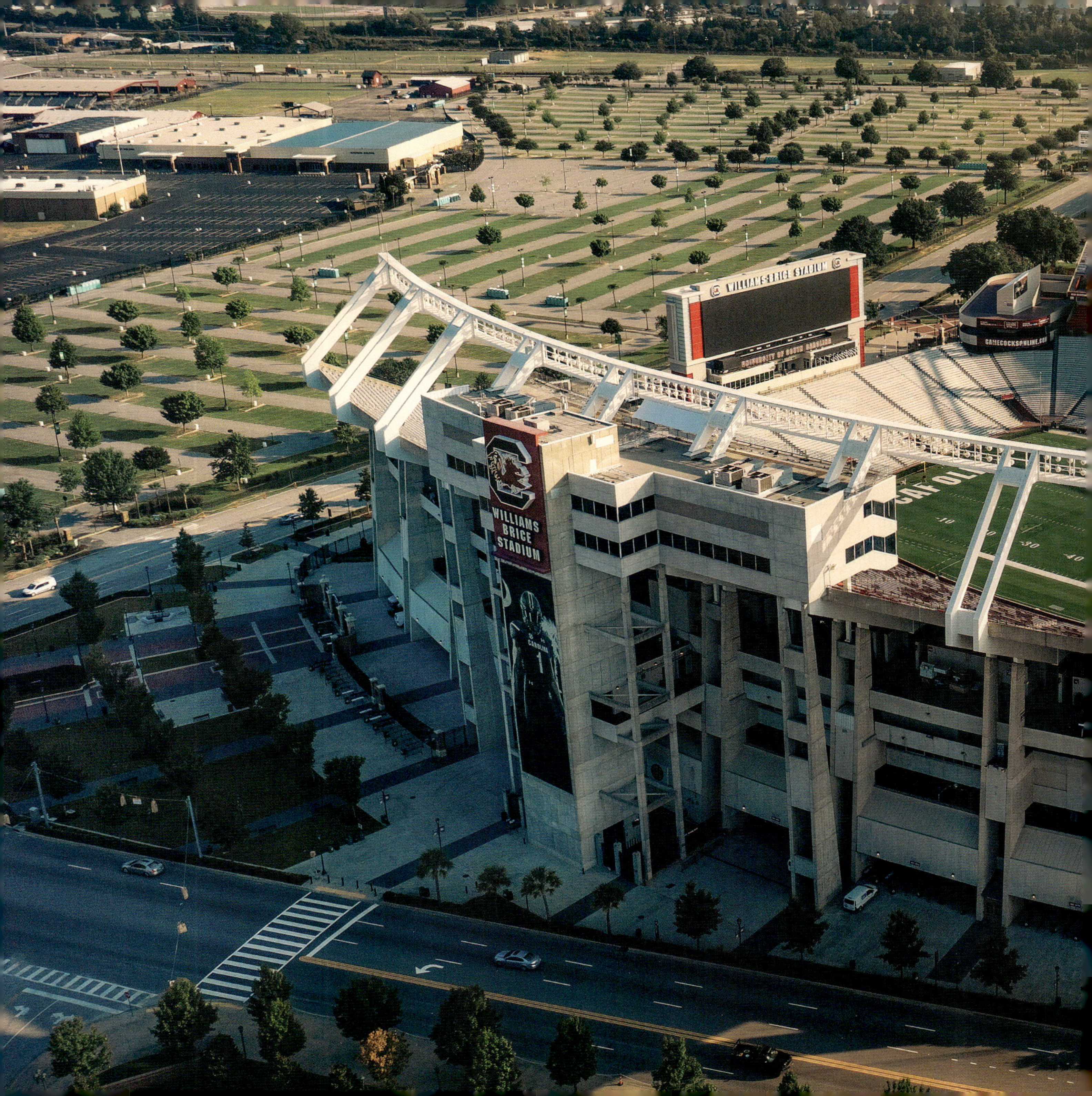

WILLIAMS-BRICE STADIUM
UNIVERSITY OF SOUTH CAROLINA
GAMECOCKSONLINE.COM
WILLIAMS
BRICE
STADIUM

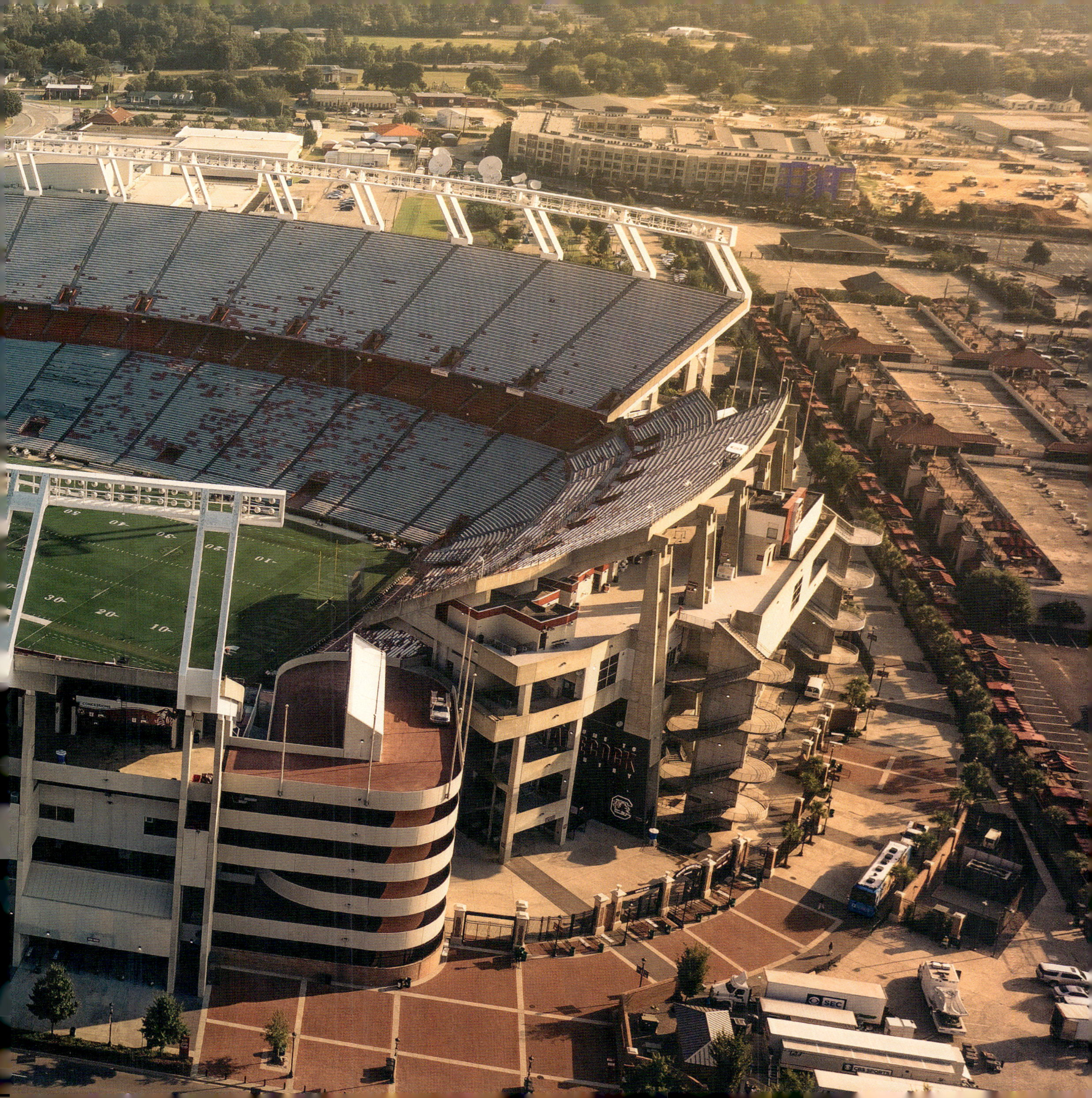

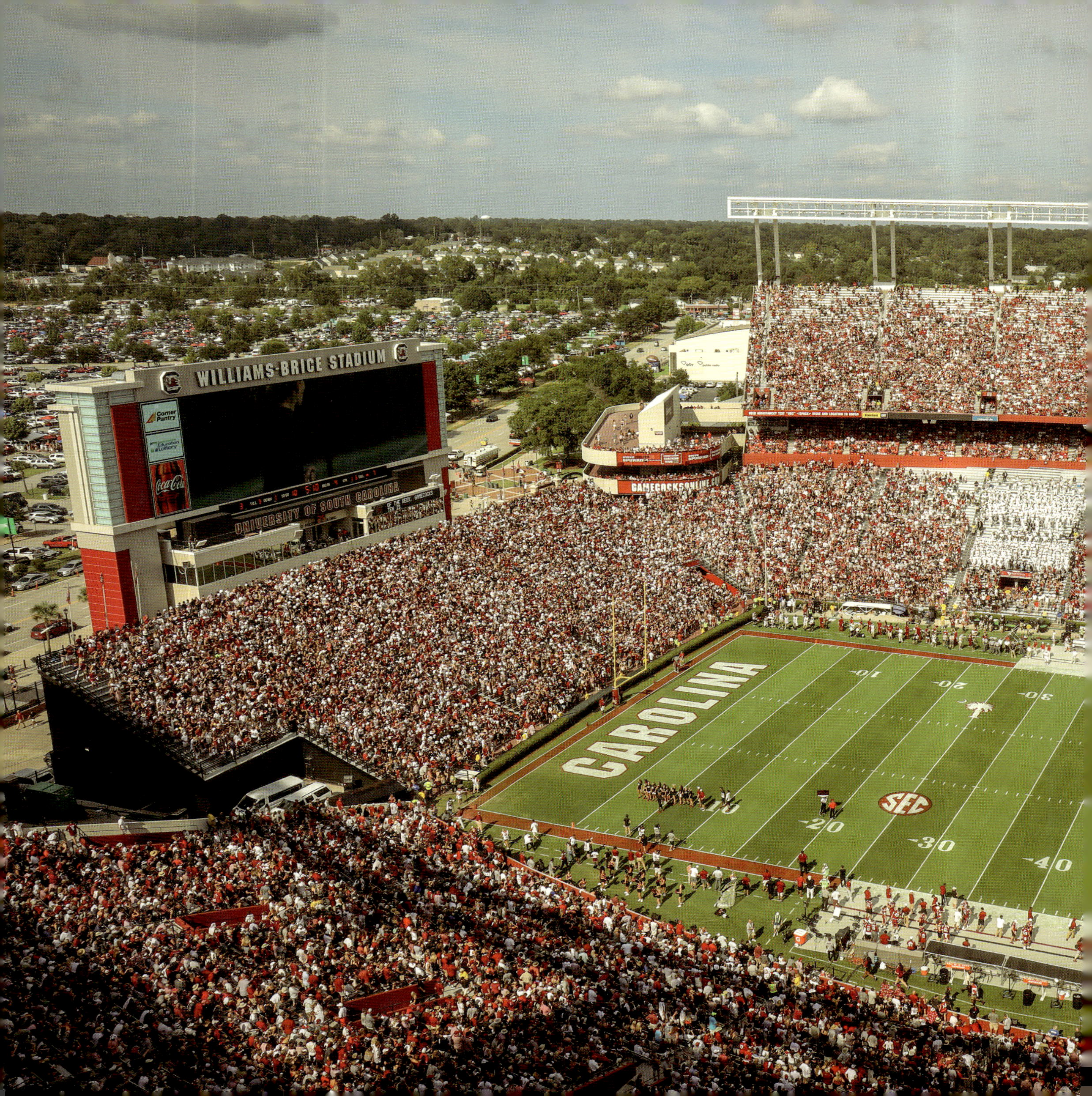

WILLIAMS-BRICE STADIUM
Corner Pantry
SC Education Lottery
Coca-Cola
UNIVERSITY OF SOUTH CAROLINA
GAMECOCKSONLINE
CAROLINA
SEC

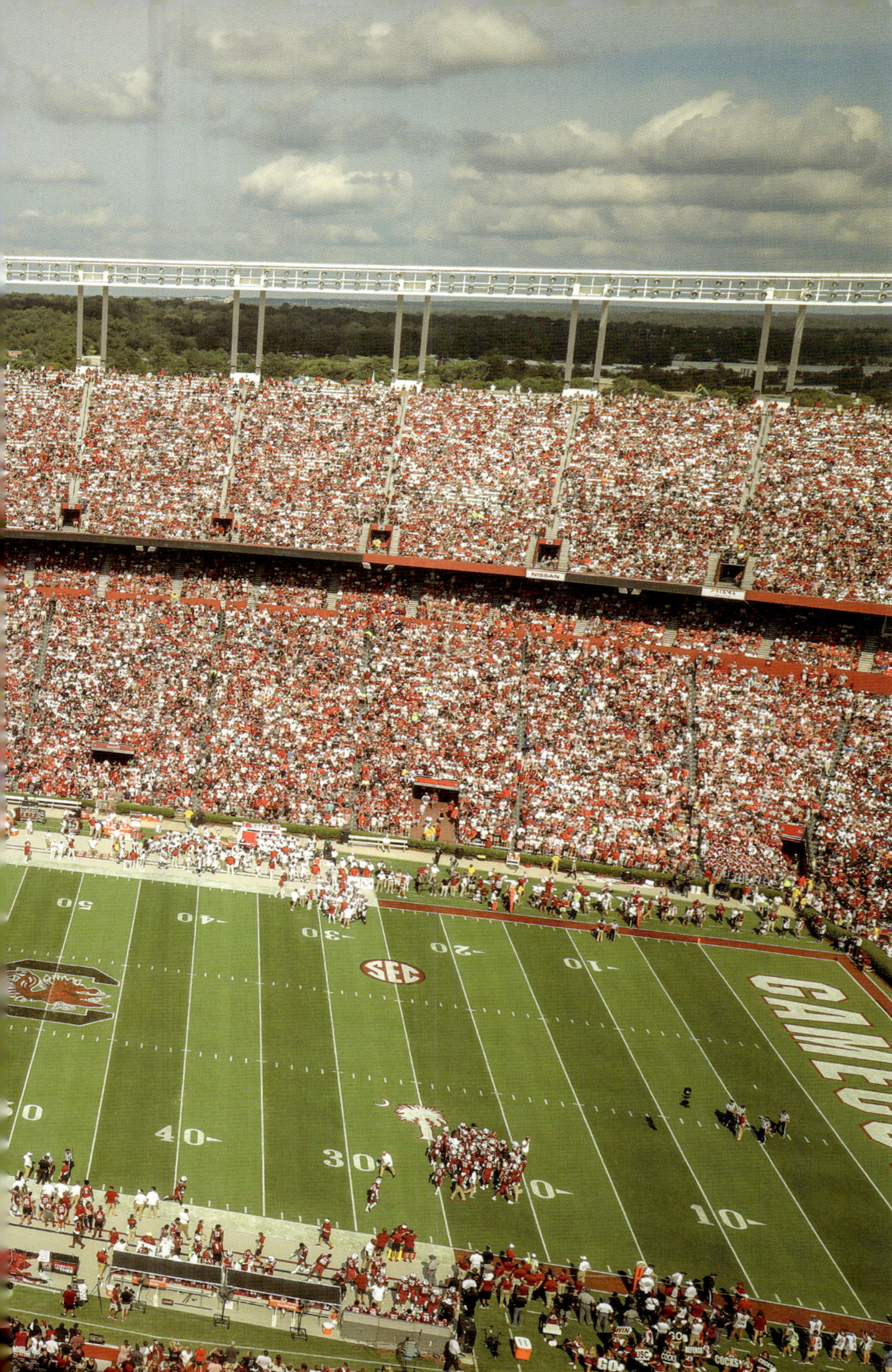

Game day at Williams-Brice Stadium draws upwards of 80,000 Gamecock fans and is considered one of the loudest college football venues in the country.

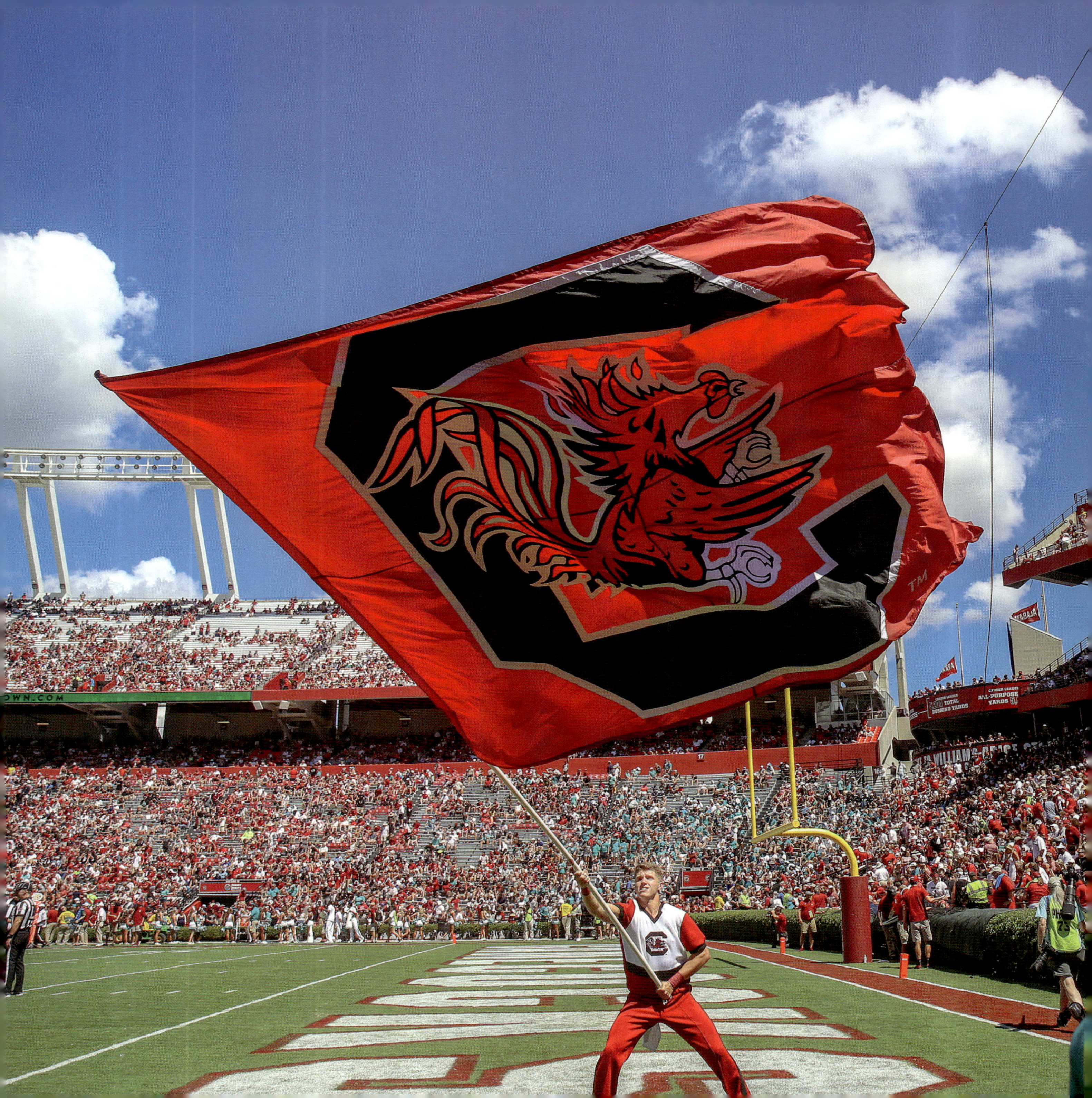

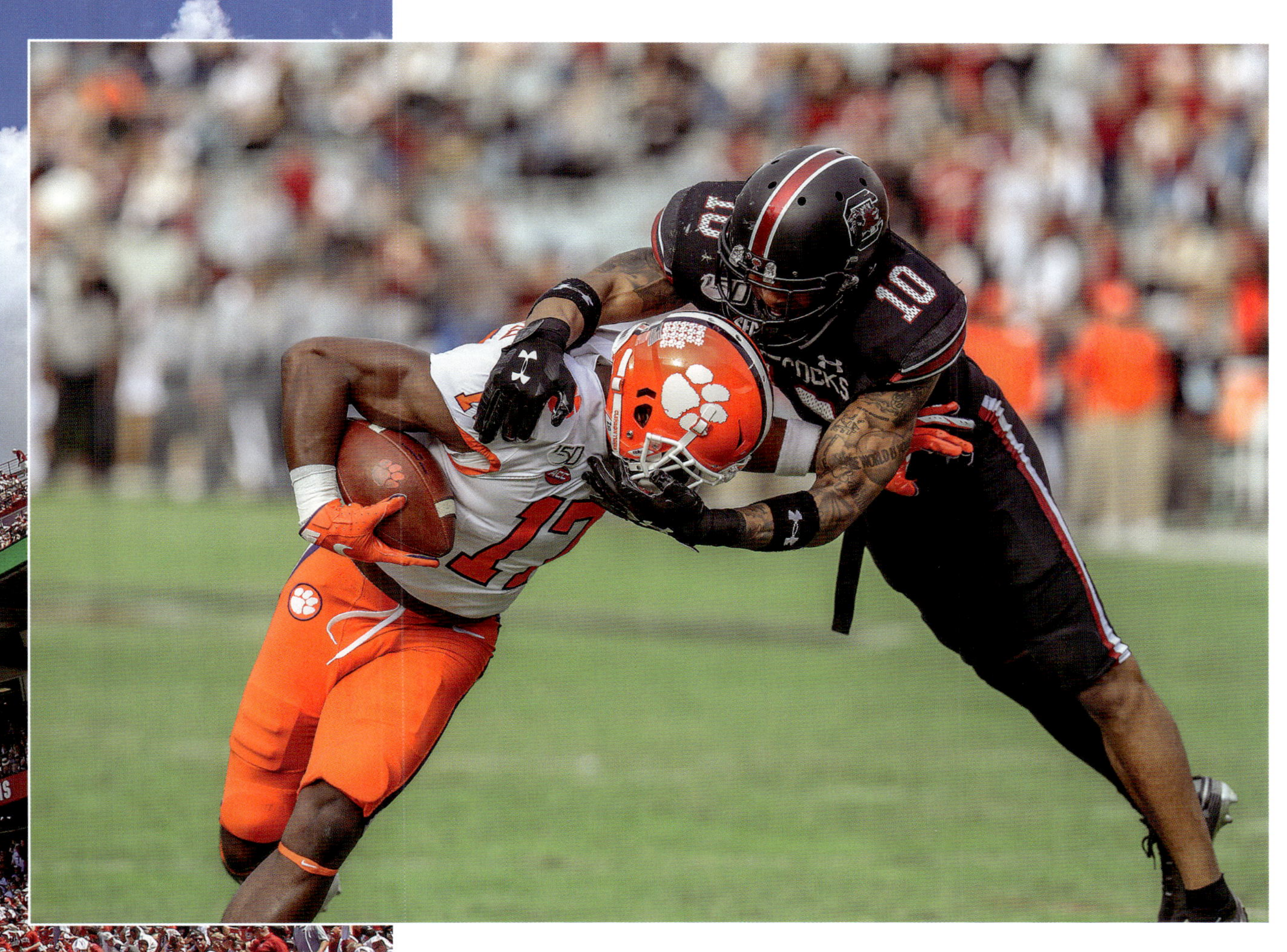

The Gamecocks' in-state football rivalry with the Clemson Tigers is the stuff of legends and attracts one of the largest crowds of the year.

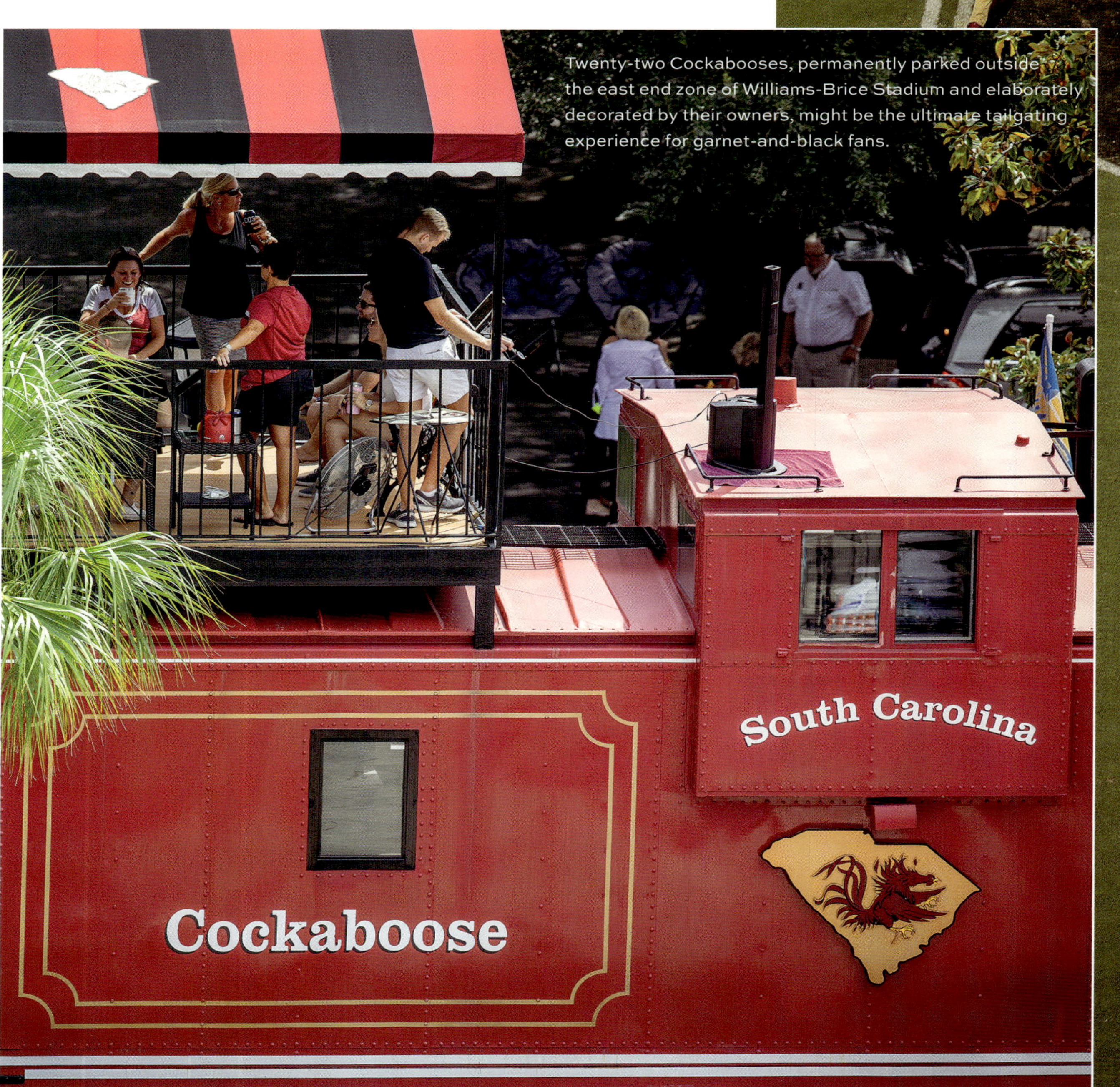

Twenty-two Cockabooses, permanently parked outside the east end zone of Williams-Brice Stadium and elaborately decorated by their owners, might be the ultimate tailgating experience for garnet-and-black fans.

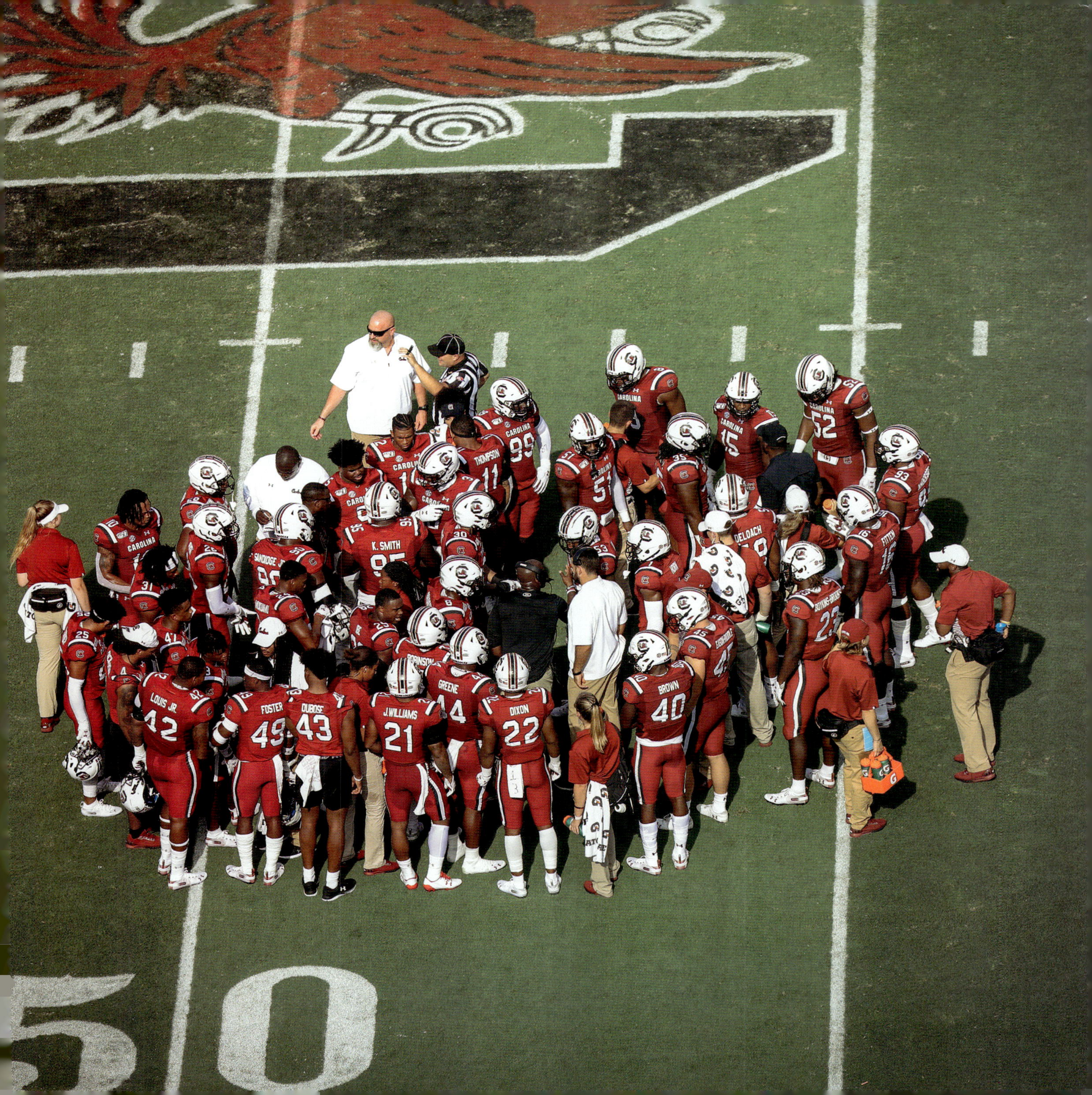

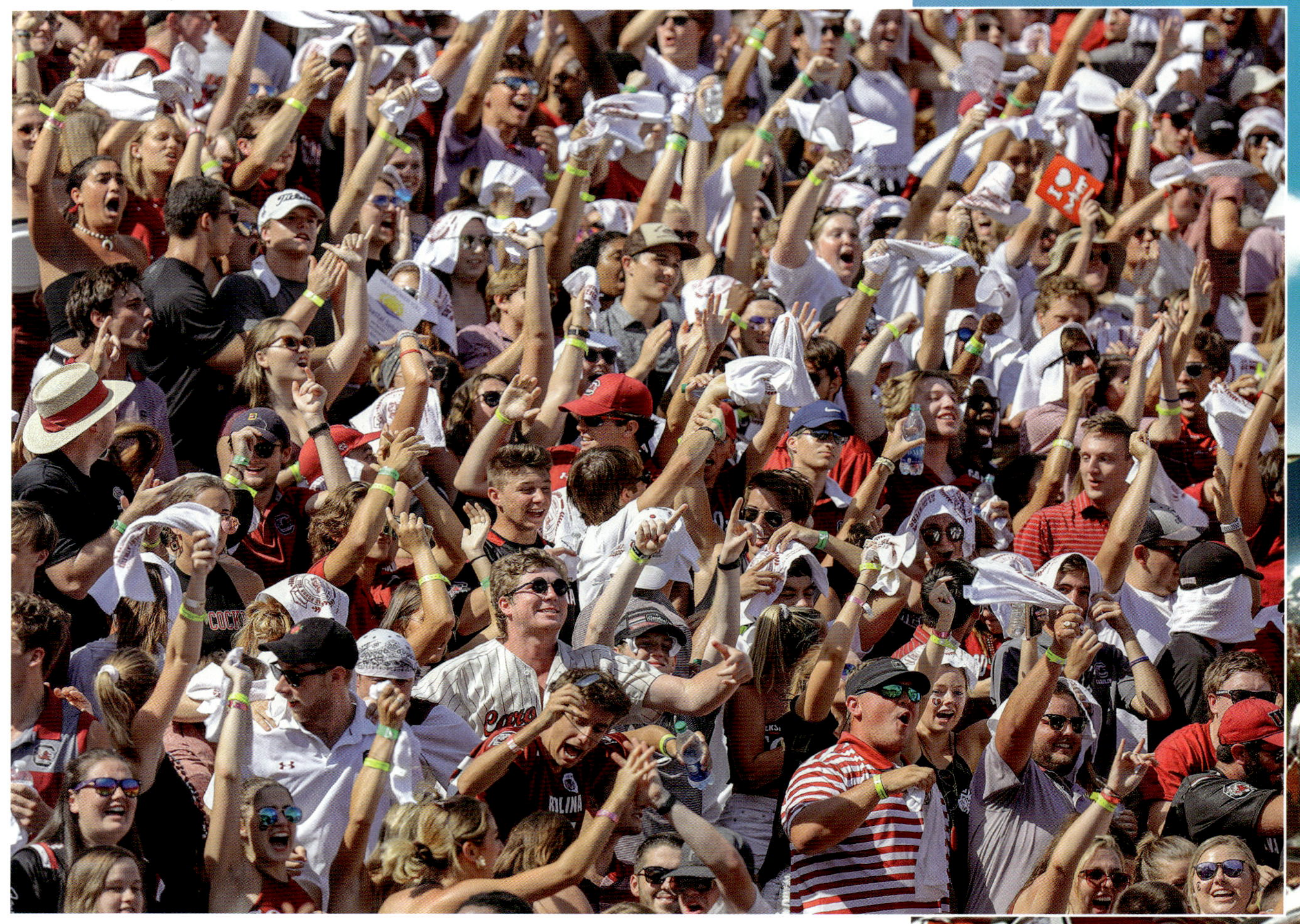

It's hard to match the exuberance of Carolina students who bring high-octane spirit to every football game.

The Mighty Sound of the Southeast, as the university's marching band is known, celebrated its one hundredth anniversary in 2020–21.

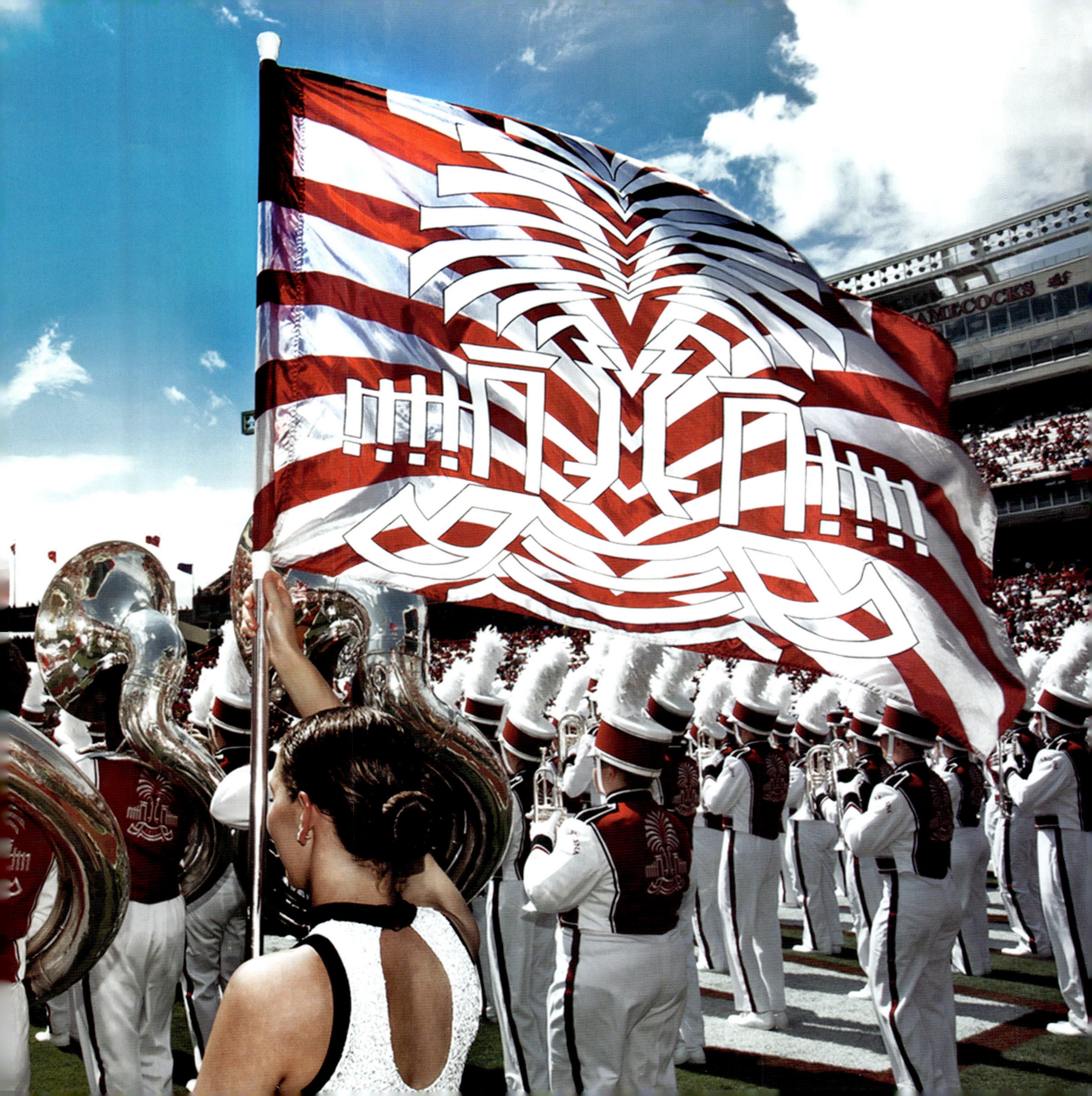

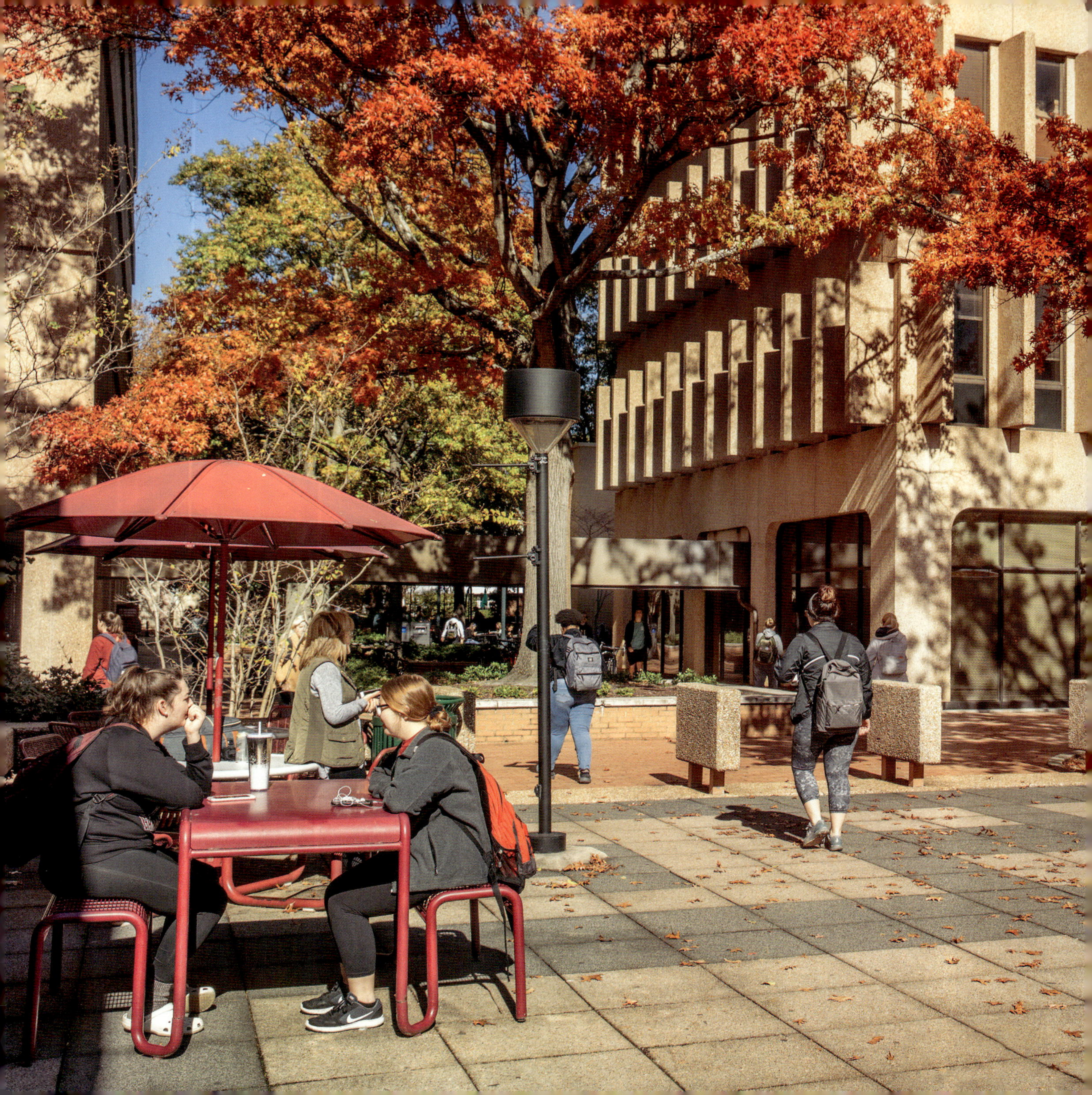

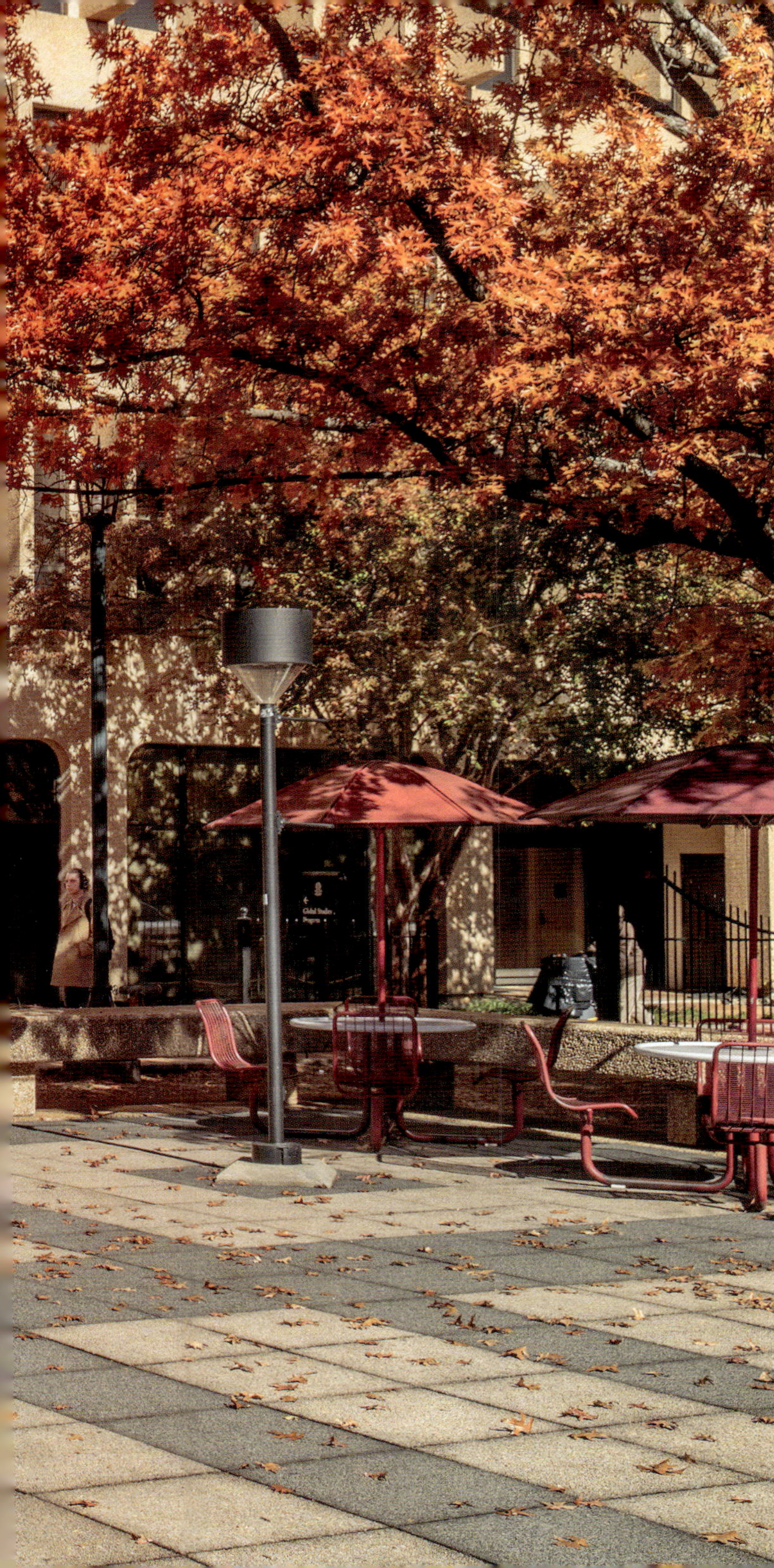

Covered tables provide a cozy place to chat, study, or eat outside the Welsh Humanities Buildings.

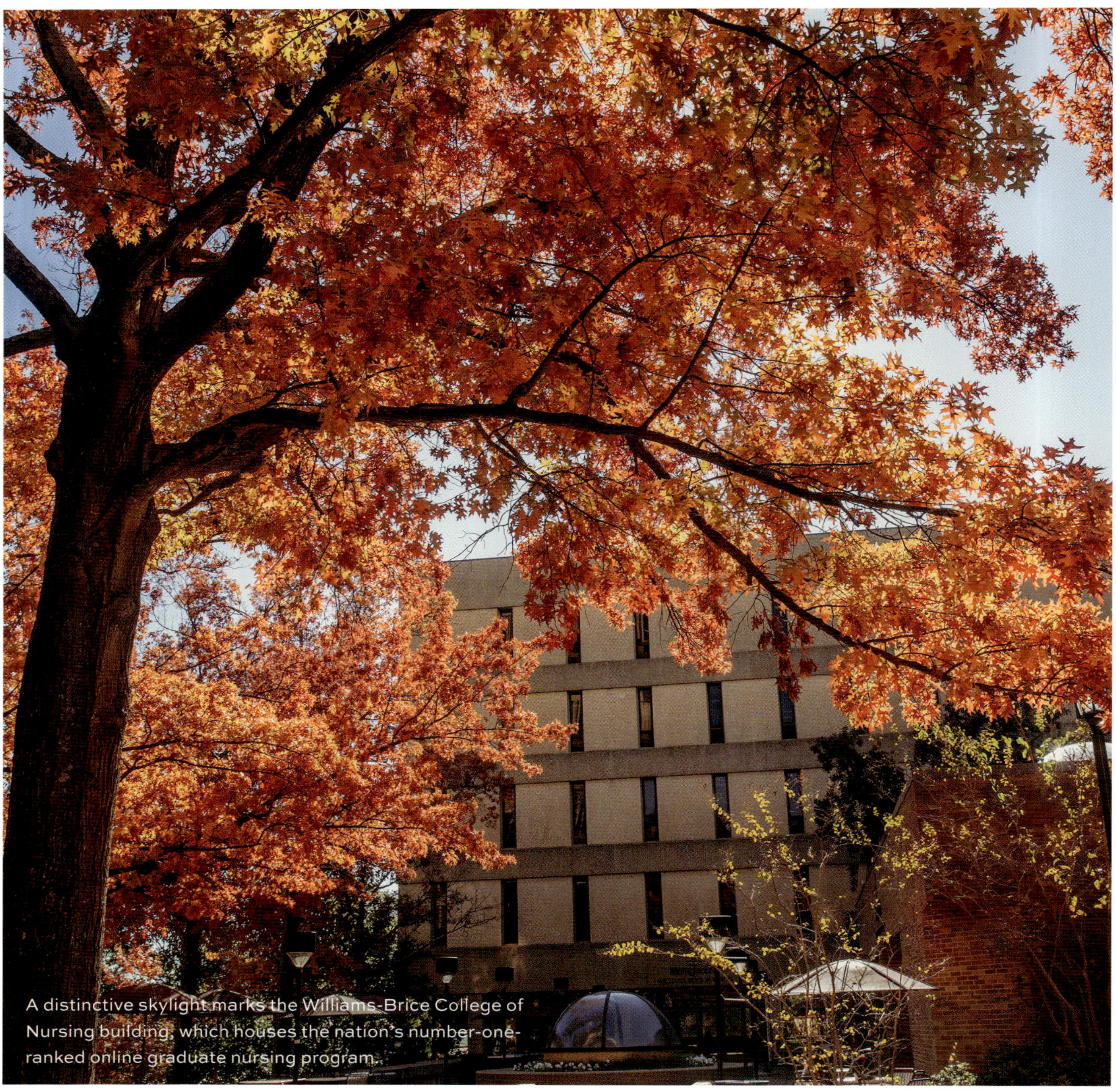

A distinctive skylight marks the Williams-Brice College of
Nursing building, which houses the nation's number-one-
ranked online graduate nursing program.

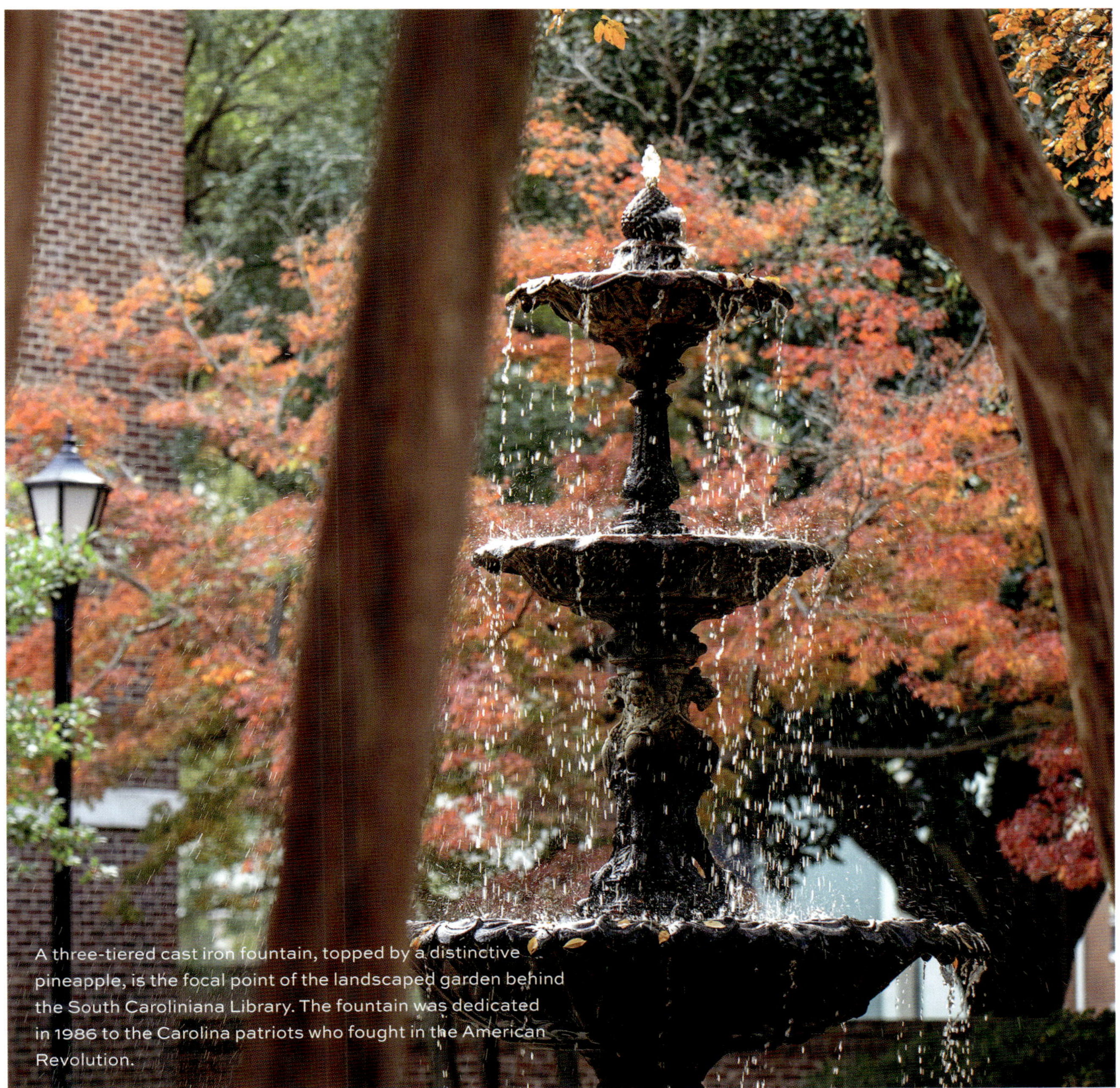

A three-tiered cast iron fountain, topped by a distinctive pineapple, is the focal point of the landscaped garden behind the South Caroliniana Library. The fountain was dedicated in 1986 to the Carolina patriots who fought in the American Revolution.

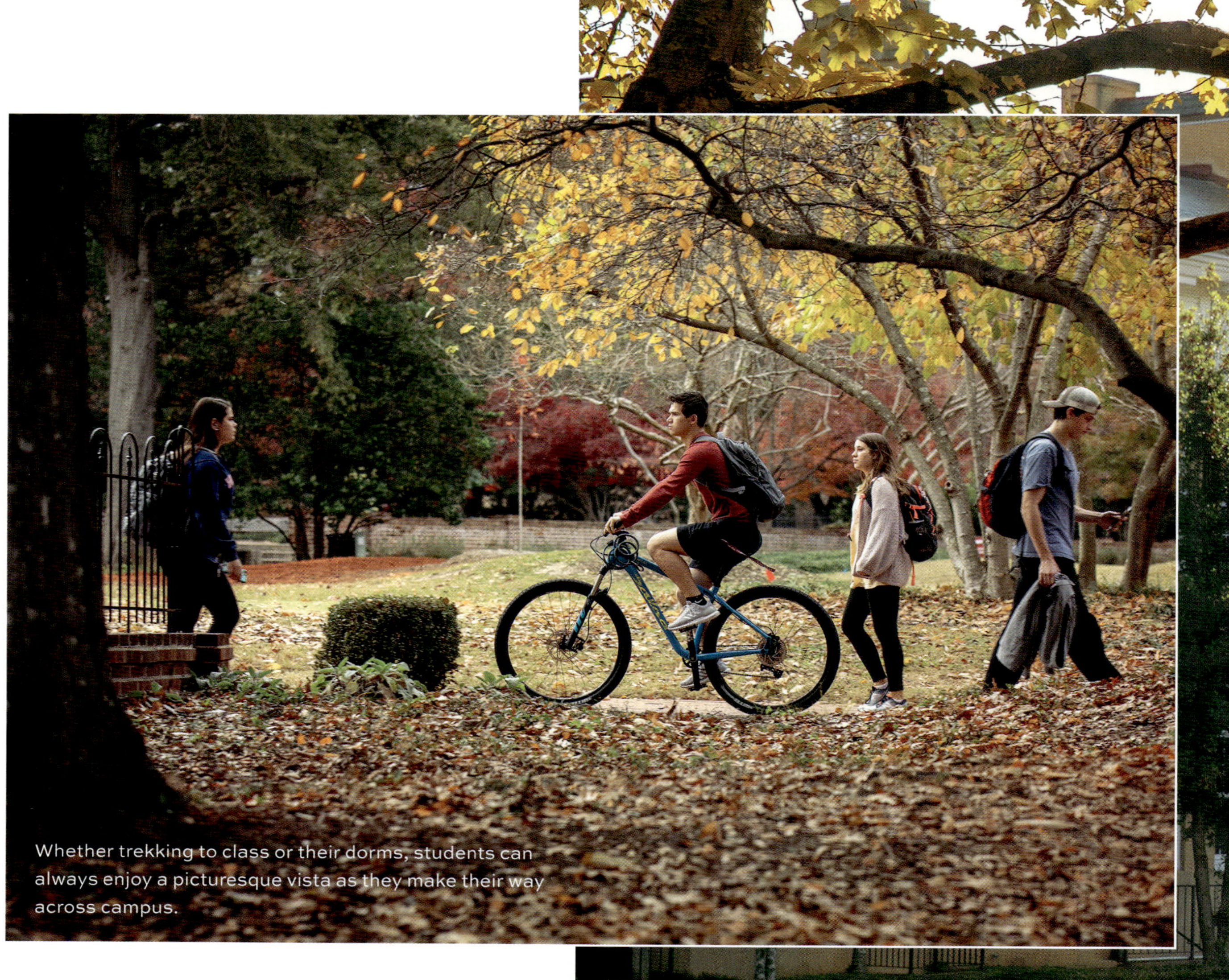

Expansive brick walkways wind across the rolling terrain of Gibbes Green, a lovely section of campus just east of the Horseshoe that includes Davis (pictured), Barnwell, Sloan, LeConte, Petigru, and the Melton Memorial Observatory. Autumn brings a fresh palette of color to campus as crepe myrtles, maples, hickories, and scarlet oaks exhibit a brilliant foliar display.

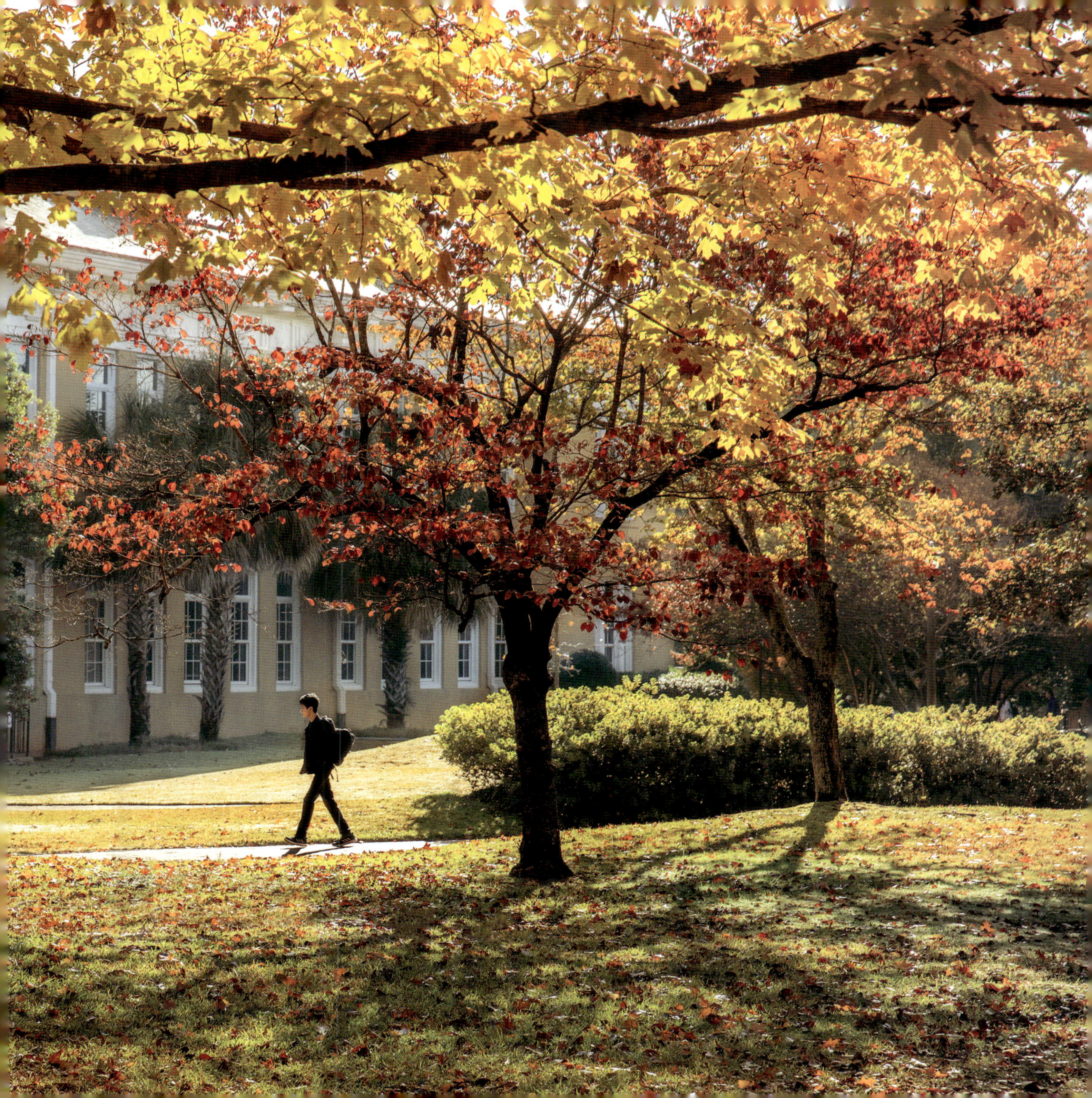

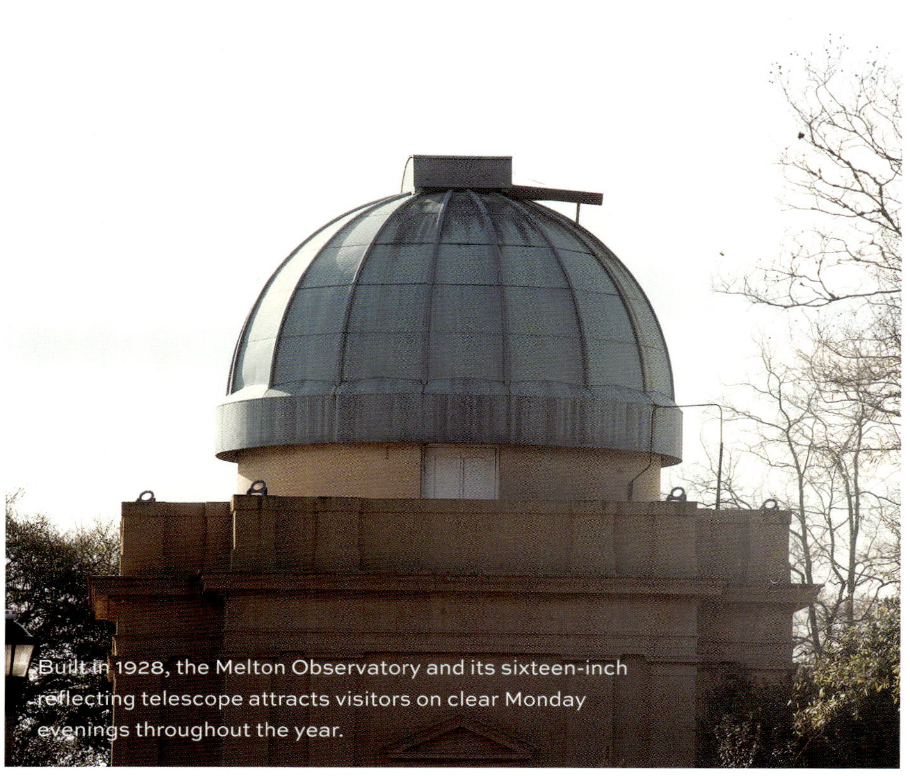

Built in 1928, the Melton Observatory and its sixteen-inch reflecting telescope attracts visitors on clear Monday evenings throughout the year.

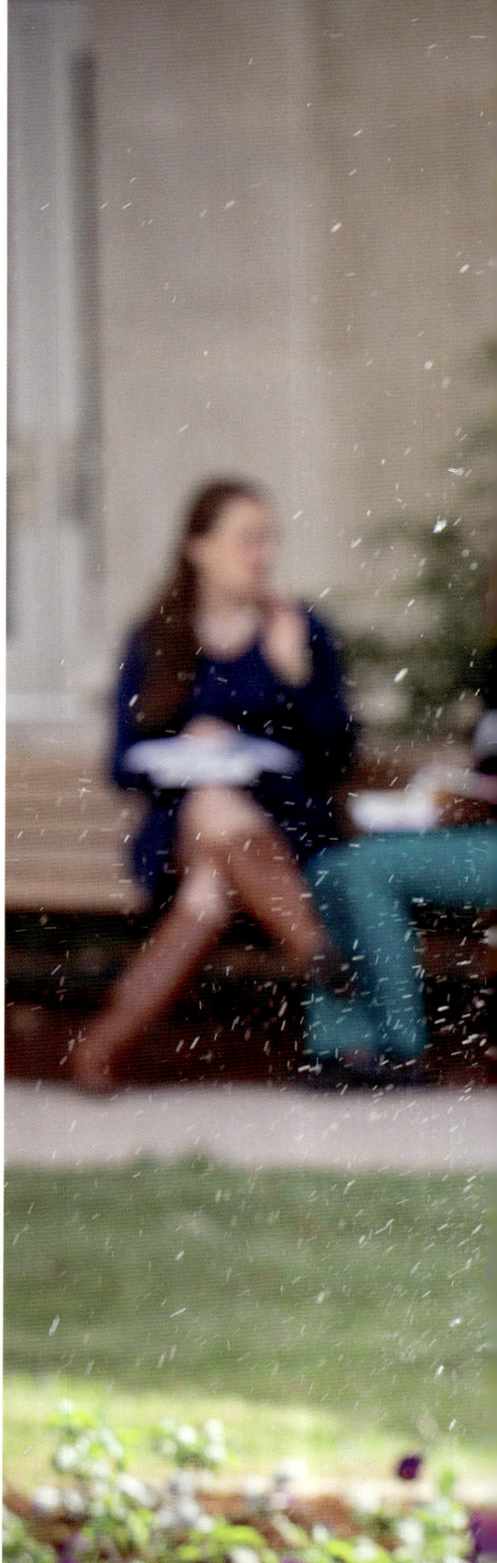

Las Palomas, a bronze water fountain designed by wildlife sculptor Sandy Scott, featuring doves in flight, is the center-piece of Anne's Garden, located behind the Arnold School of Public Health Research Center. The fountain and landscaping for the quiet respite were donated by the late John Rainey in honor of his wife, Anne Edens Rainey, a 1961 graduate of the university.

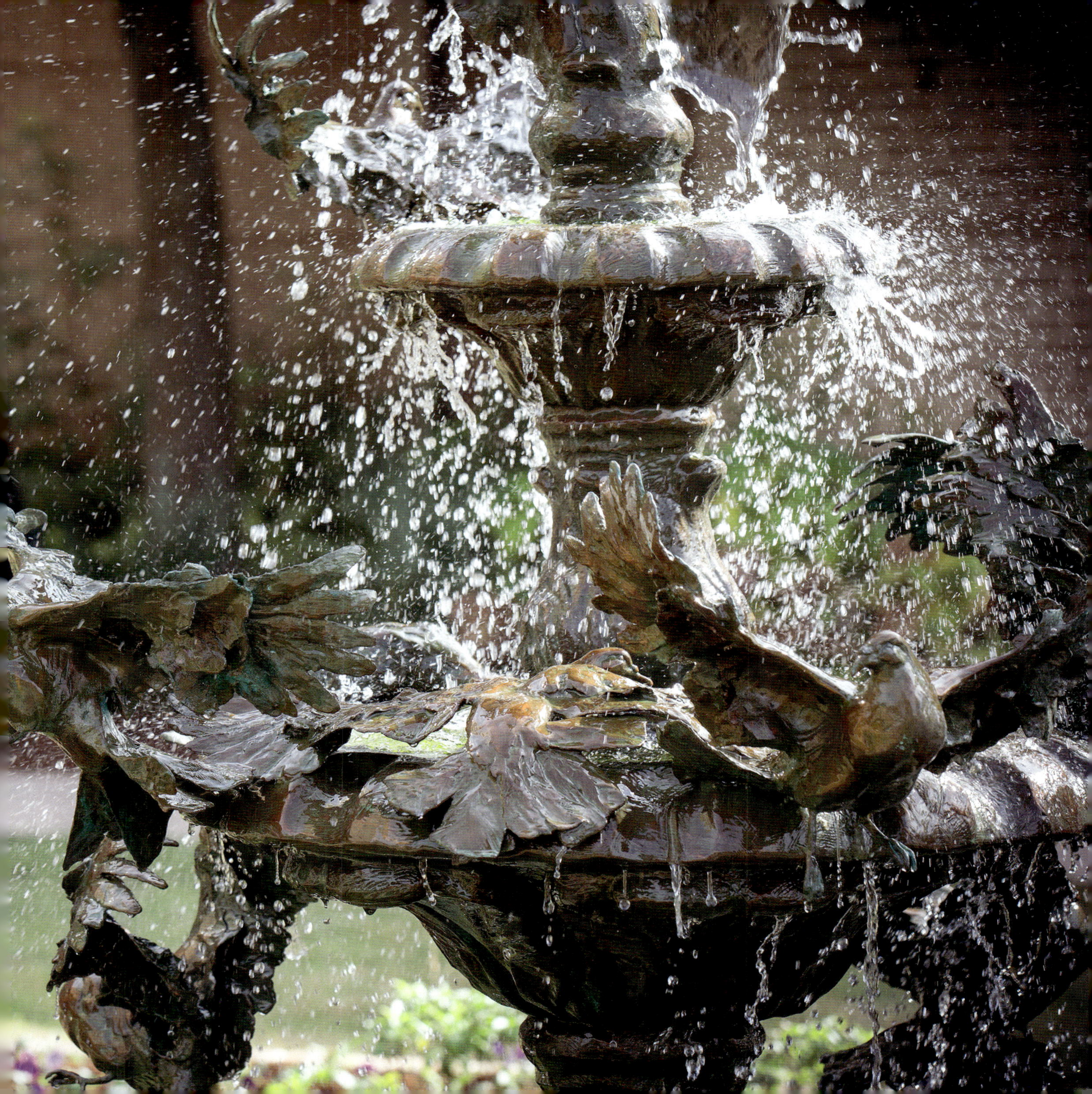

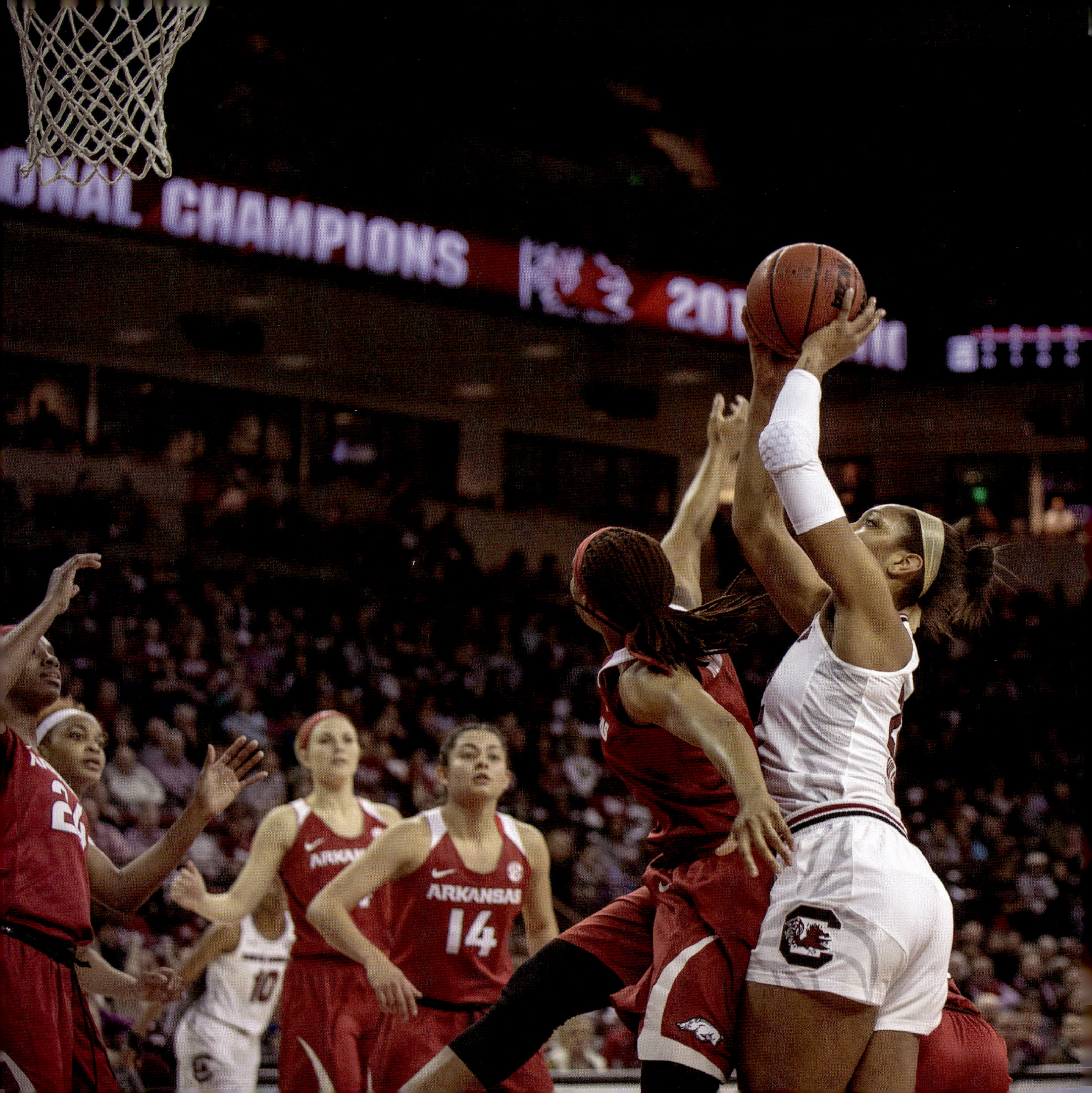

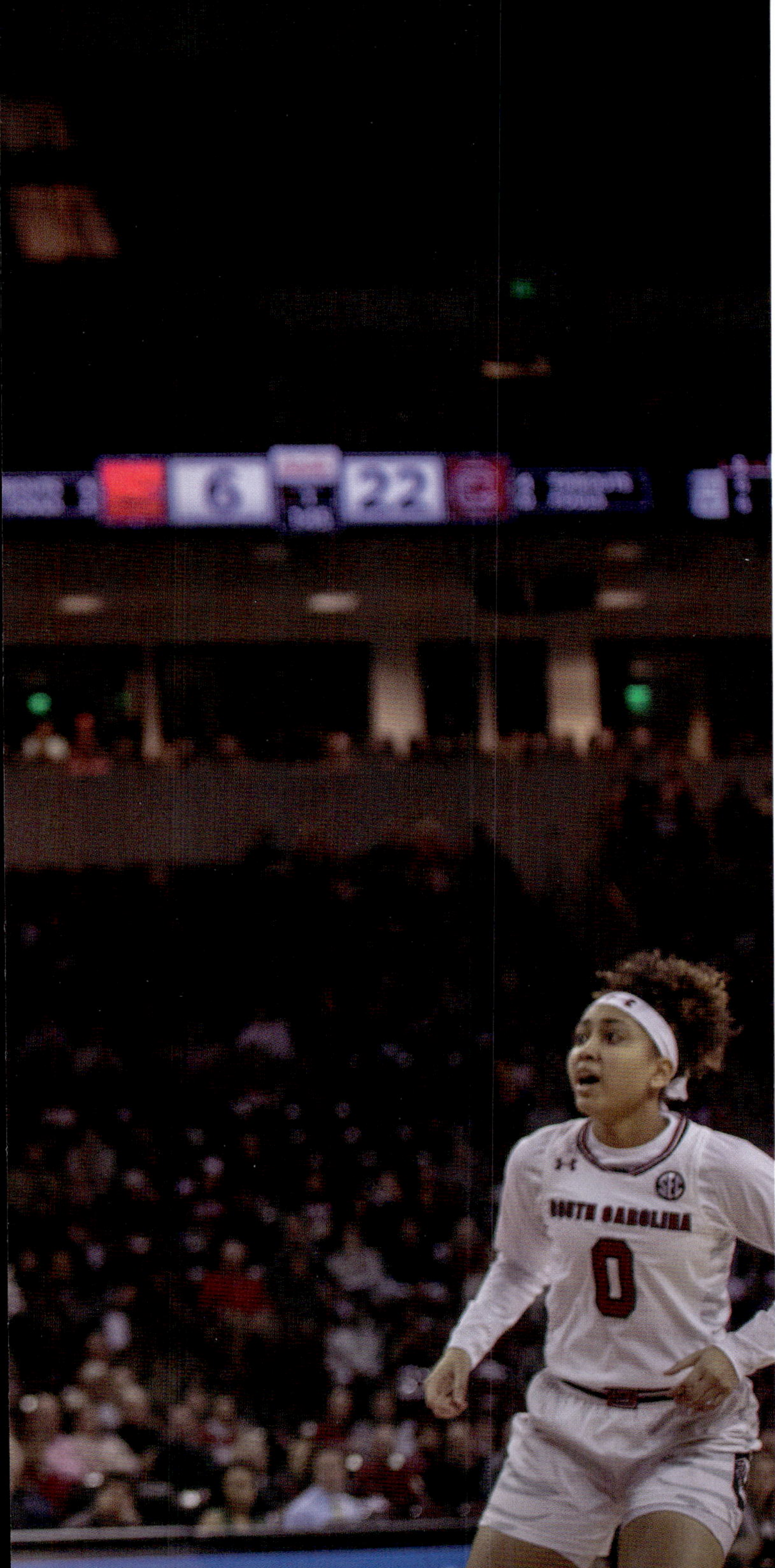

The women's basketball team has grown accustomed to winning with a long string of standcut players thriving under the tutelage of Head Coach Dawn Staley.

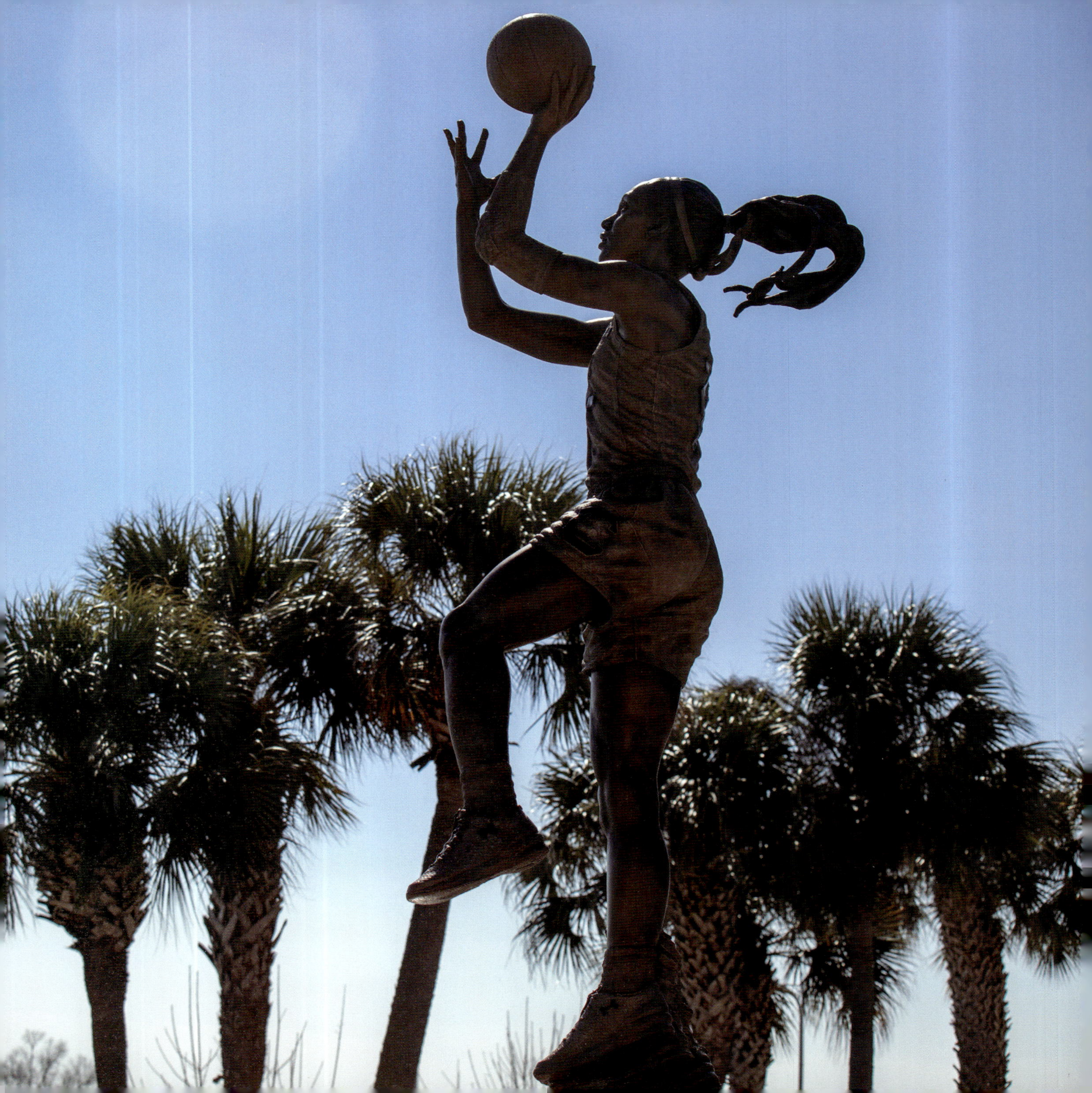

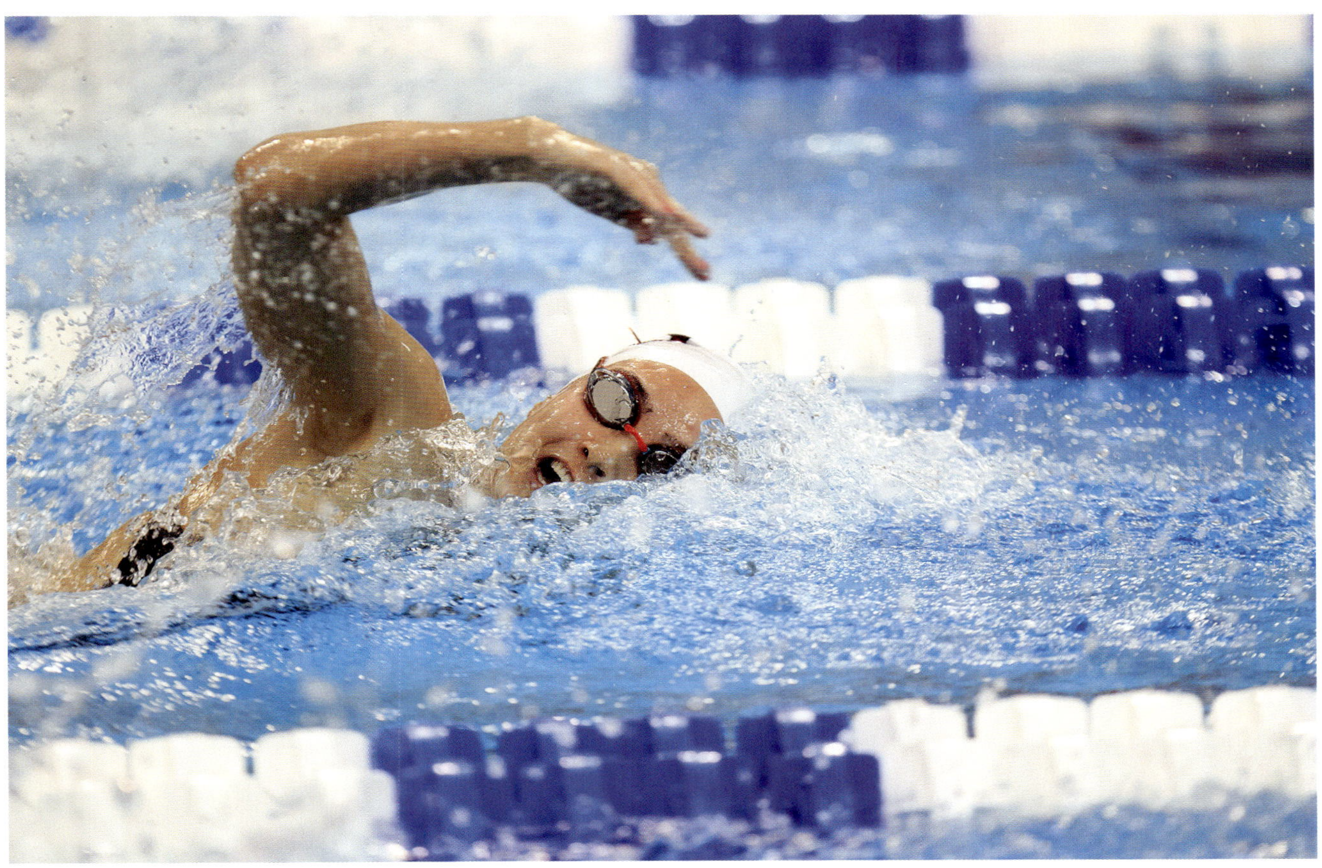

Above and overleaf: They might not generate big headlines in the intercollegiate sporting world, but swimming, track and field, and volleyball attract their own fervent fans and generate memorable moments in the water and high in the air.

"It is truly a beautiful thing when someone believes in you," said former Gamecock standout A'ja Wilson when a statue in her likeness, created by sculptor Julie Rotblatt-Amrany, was dedicated outside Colonial Life Arena in January 2021. Wilson helped lead the team to its first NCAA basketball championship in 2017 and was the first player selected in the 2018 WNBA draft.

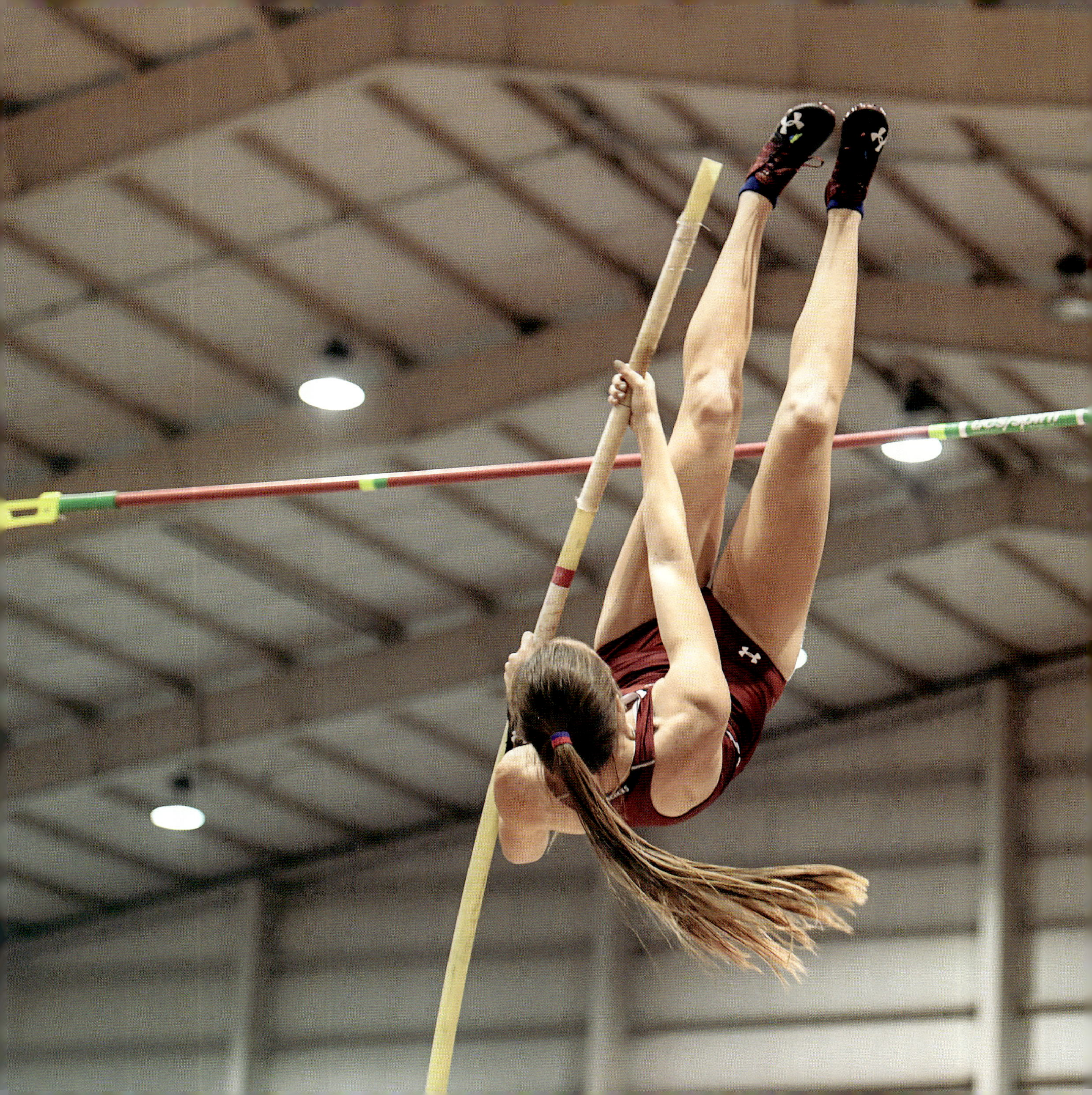

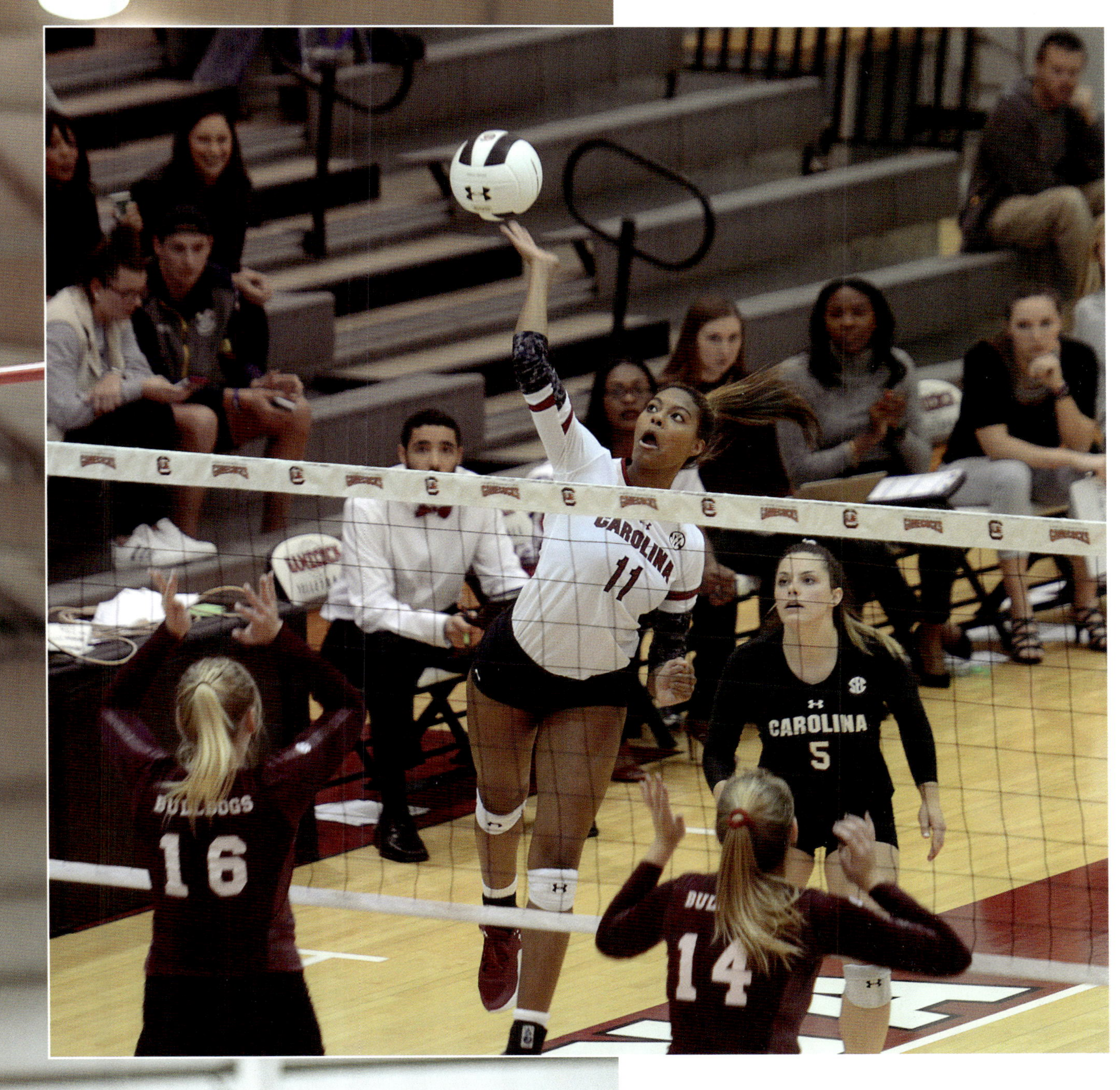

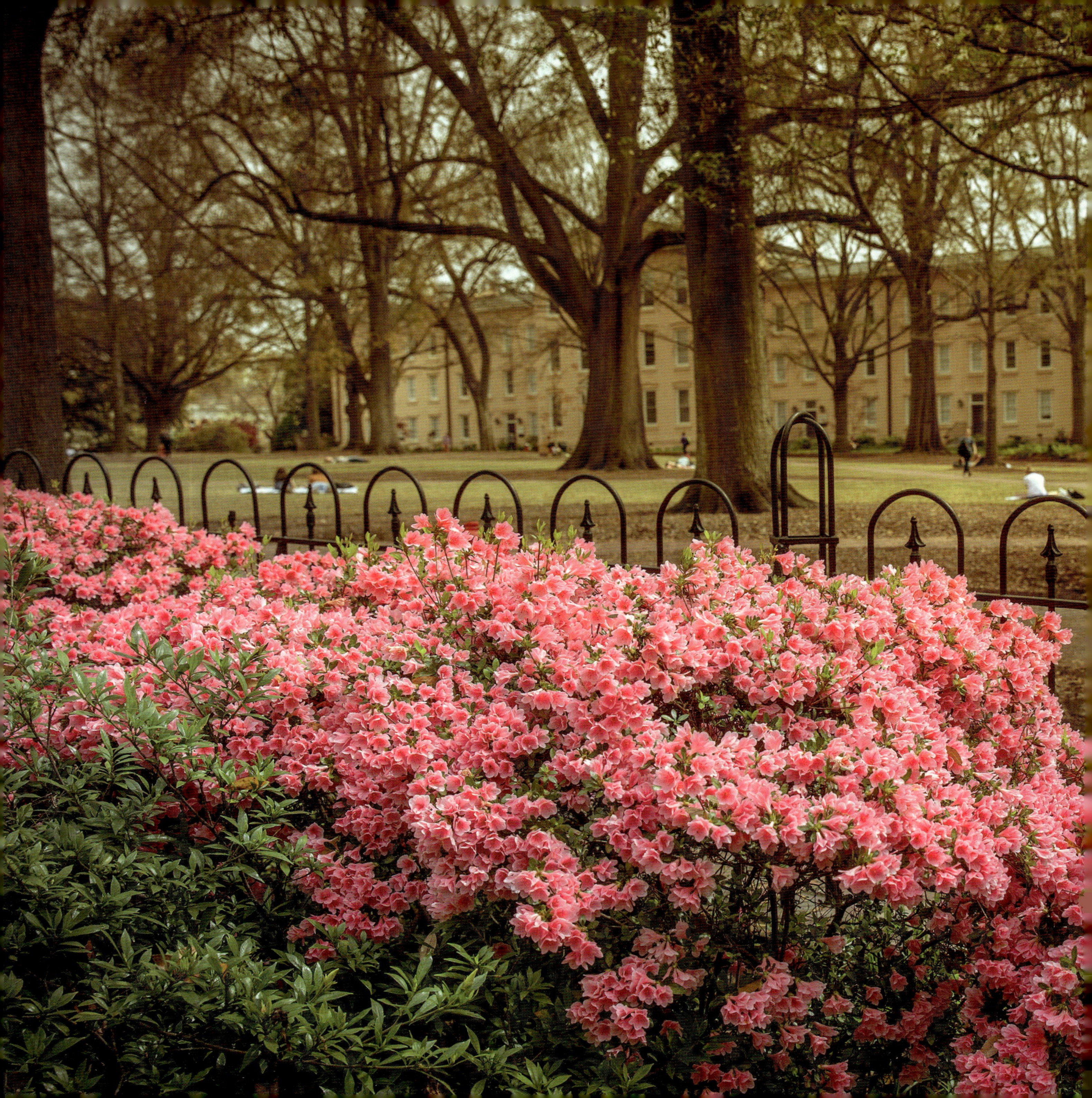

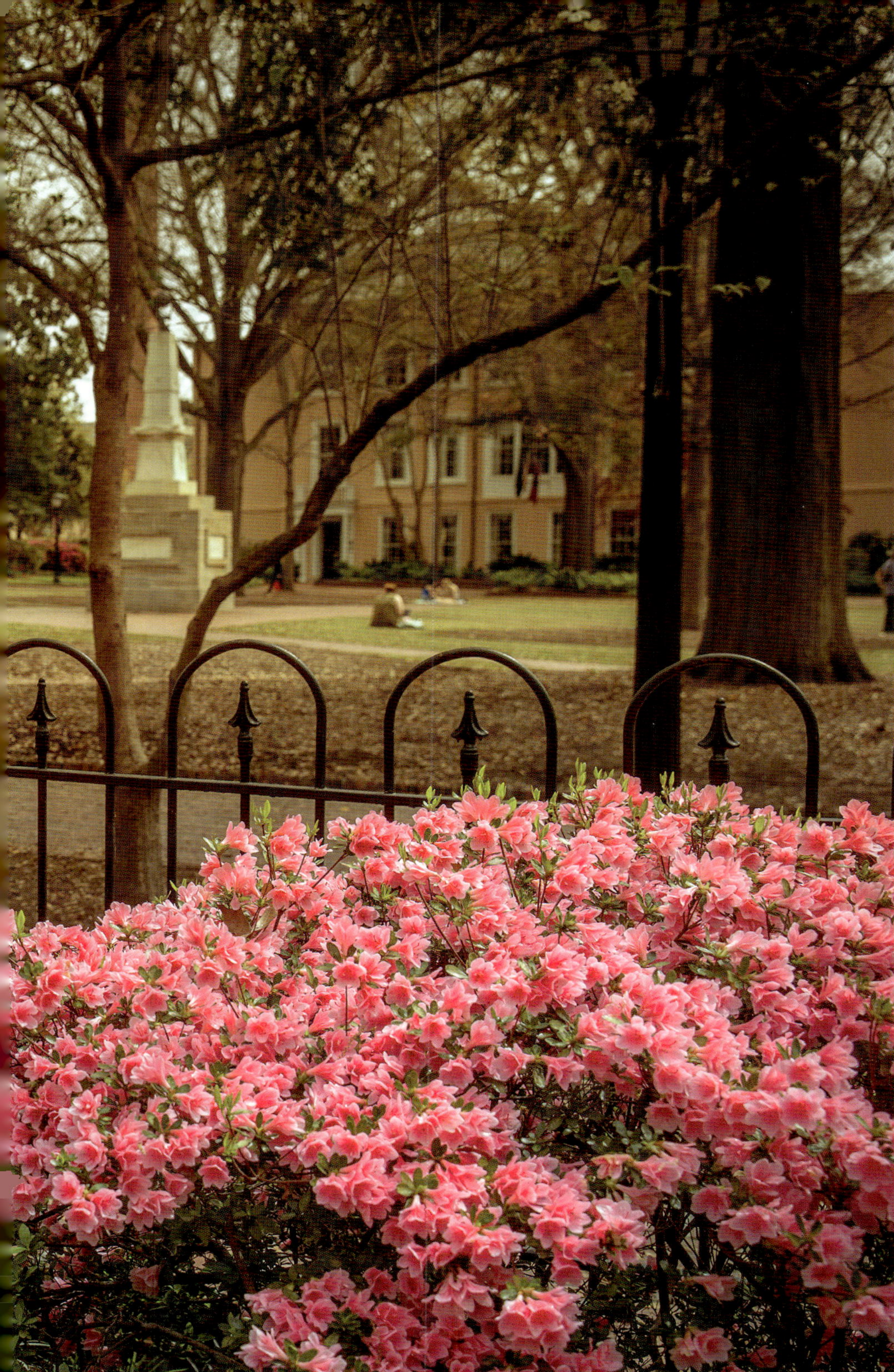

It's a sure sign of spring when scores of azaleas break into bloom across the campus, including these on the Horseshoe.

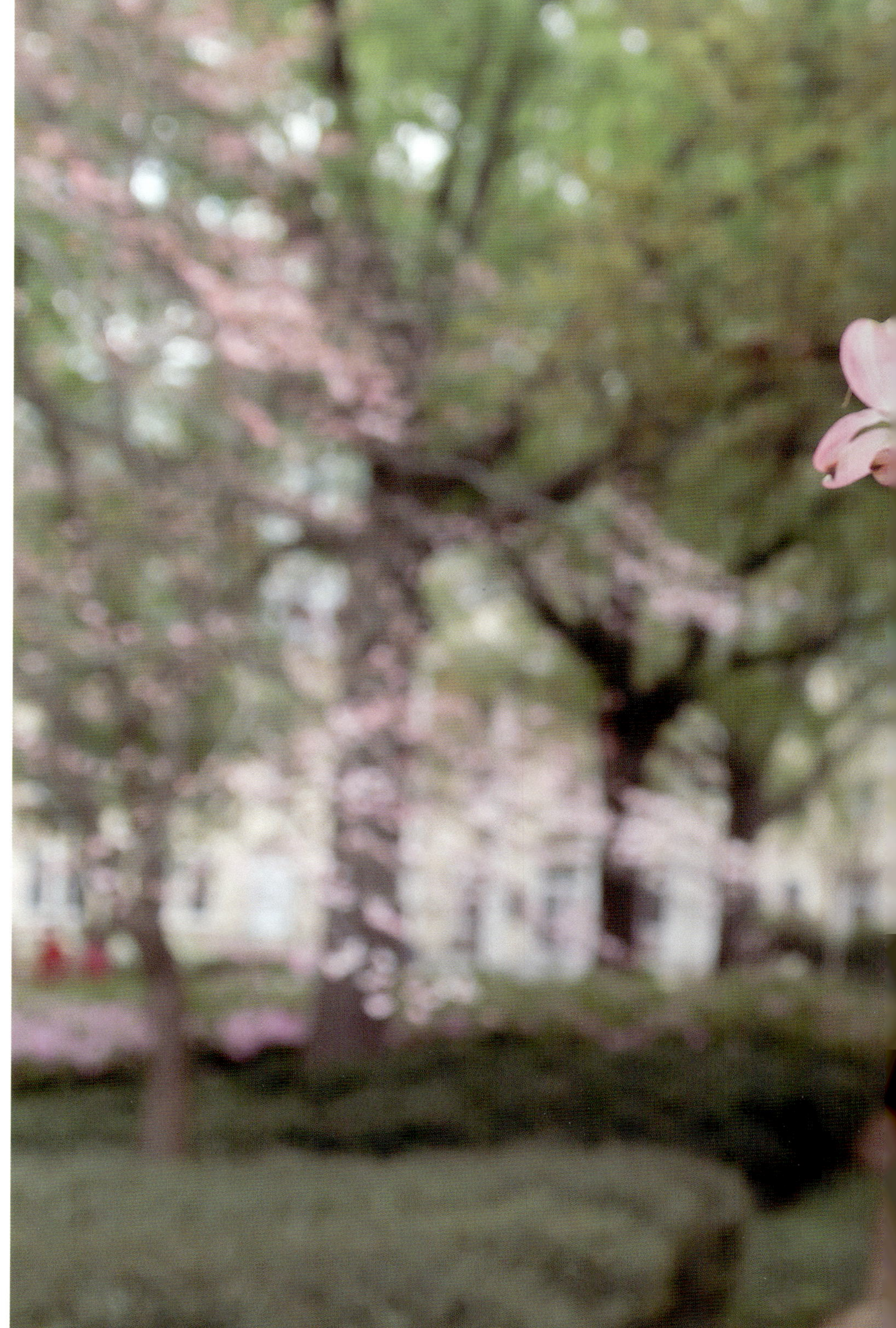

The Women's Quad looks pretty in pink dogwoods on a spring morning.

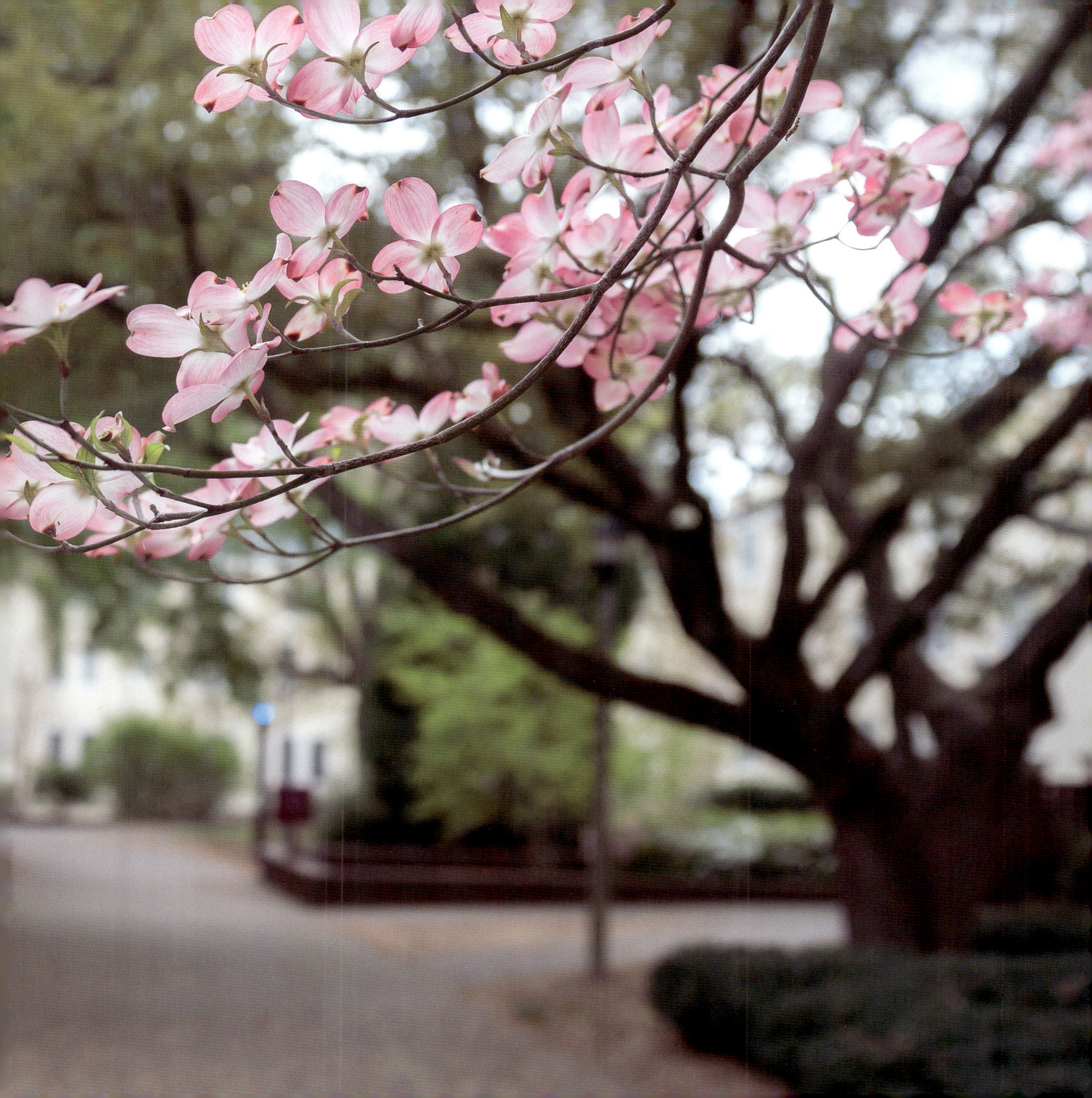

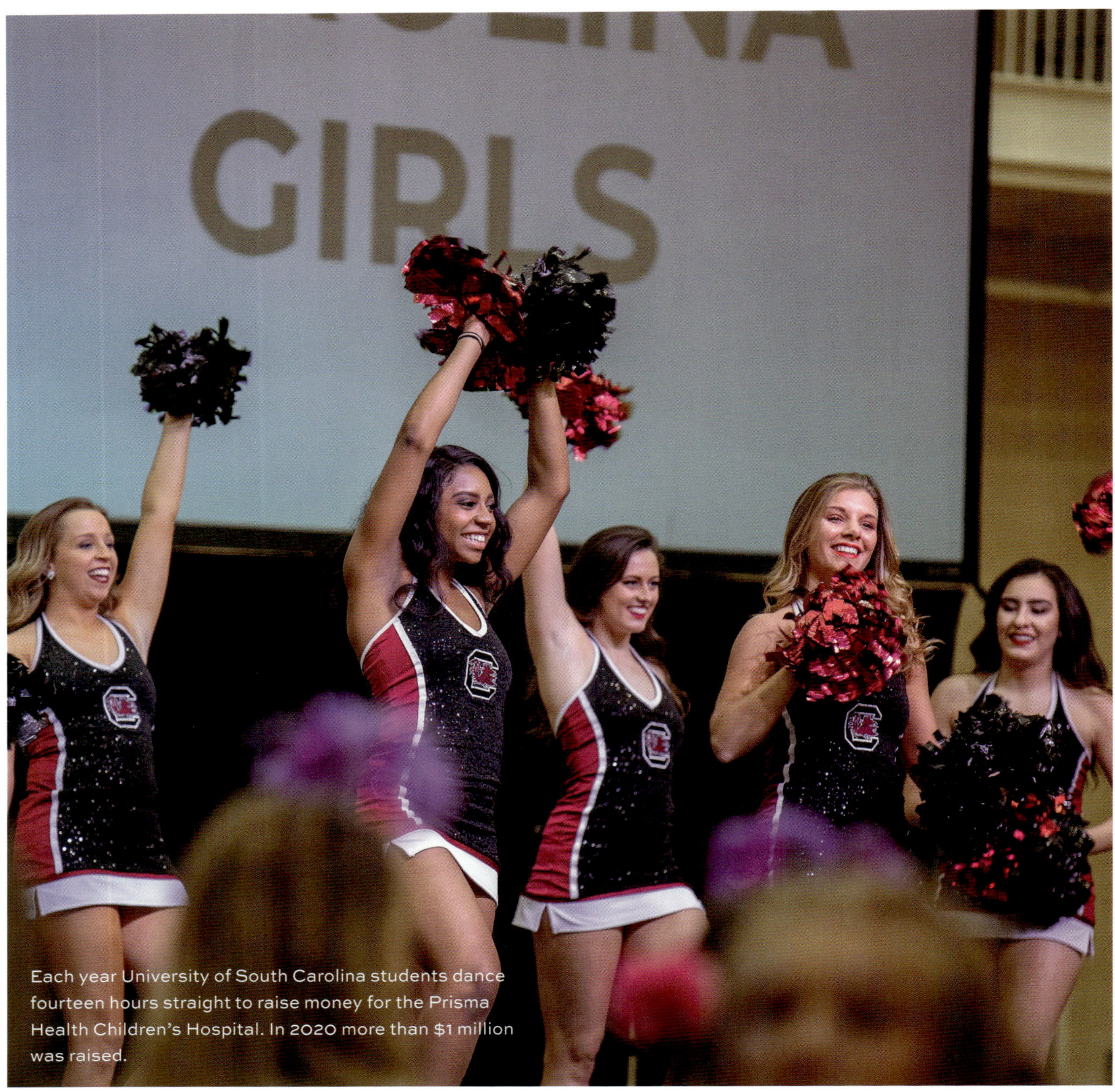

Each year University of South Carolina students dance fourteen hours straight to raise money for the Prisma Health Children's Hospital. In 2020 more than $1 million was raised.

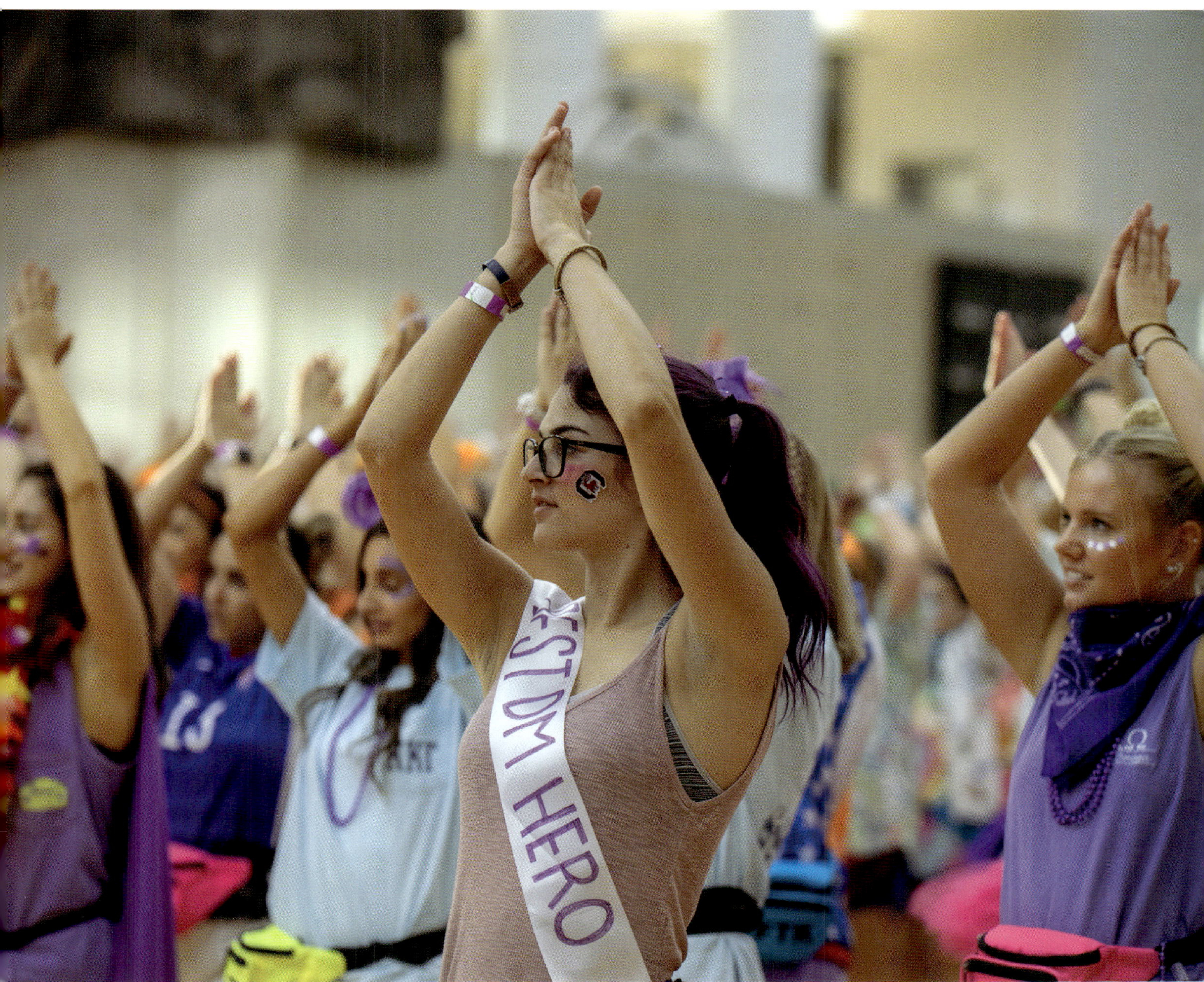
ESTDM HERO

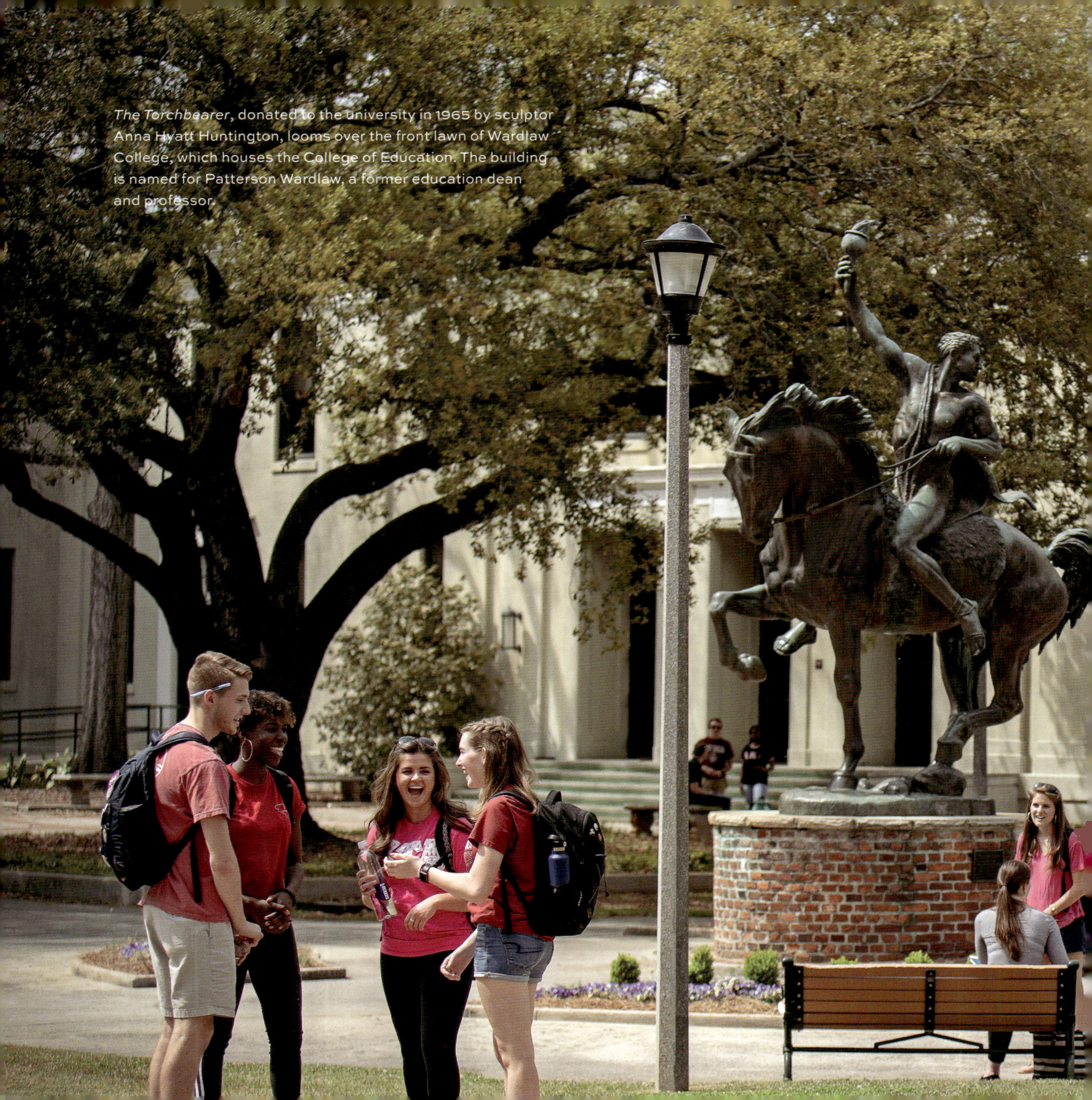

The Torchbearer, donated to the university in 1965 by sculptor Anna Hyatt Huntington, looms over the front lawn of Wardlaw College, which houses the College of Education. The building is named for Patterson Wardlaw, a former education dean and professor.

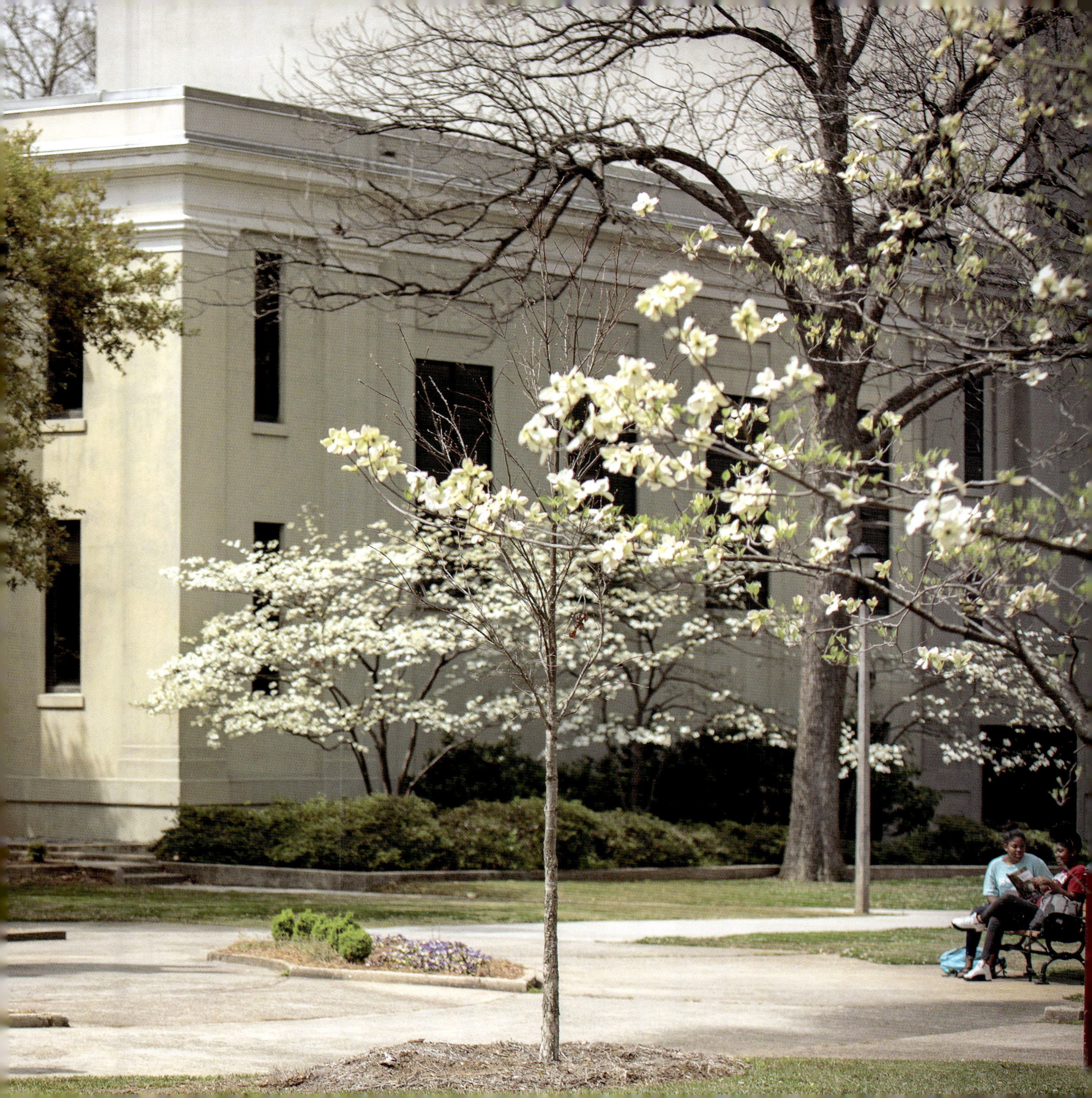

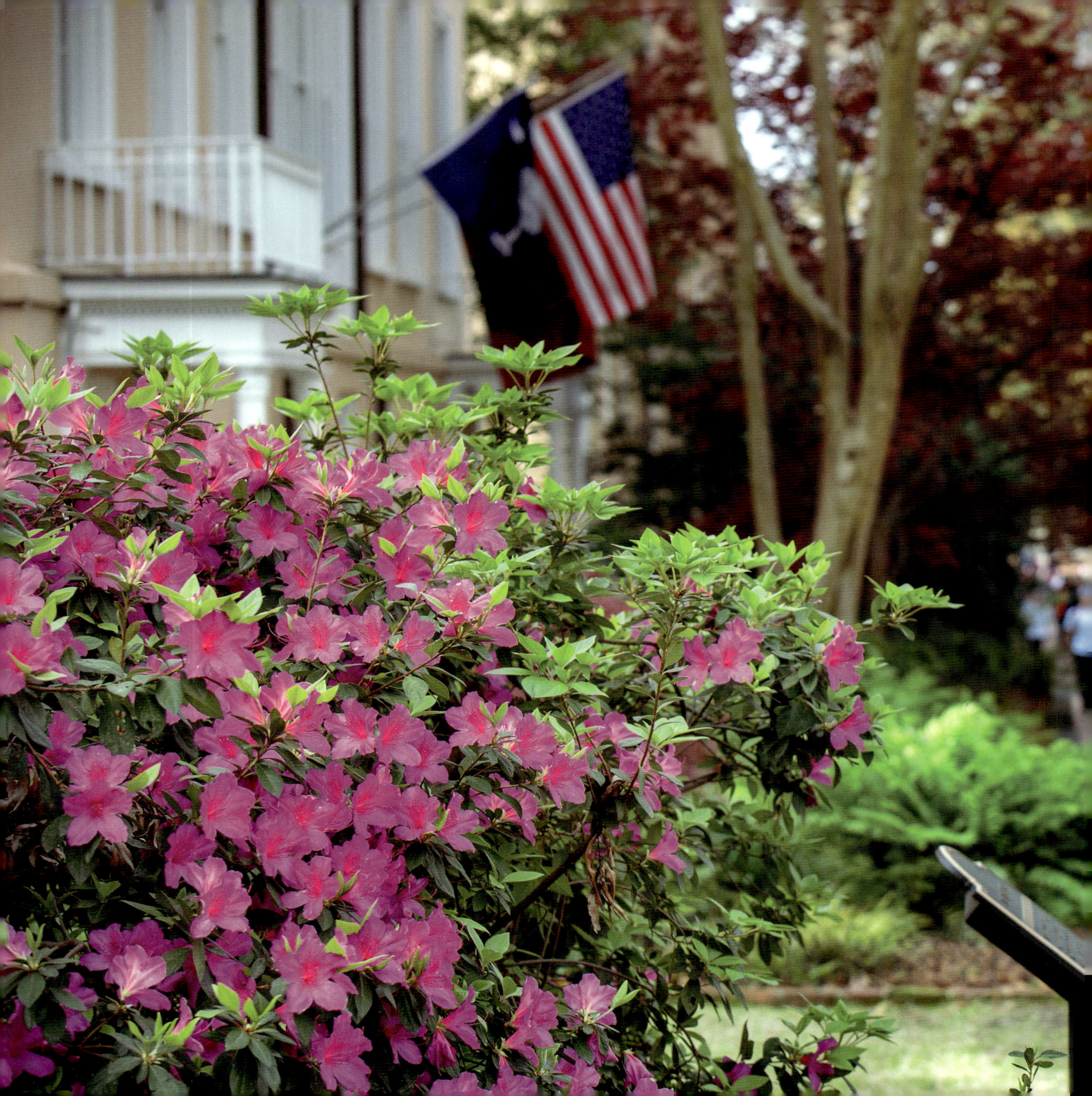

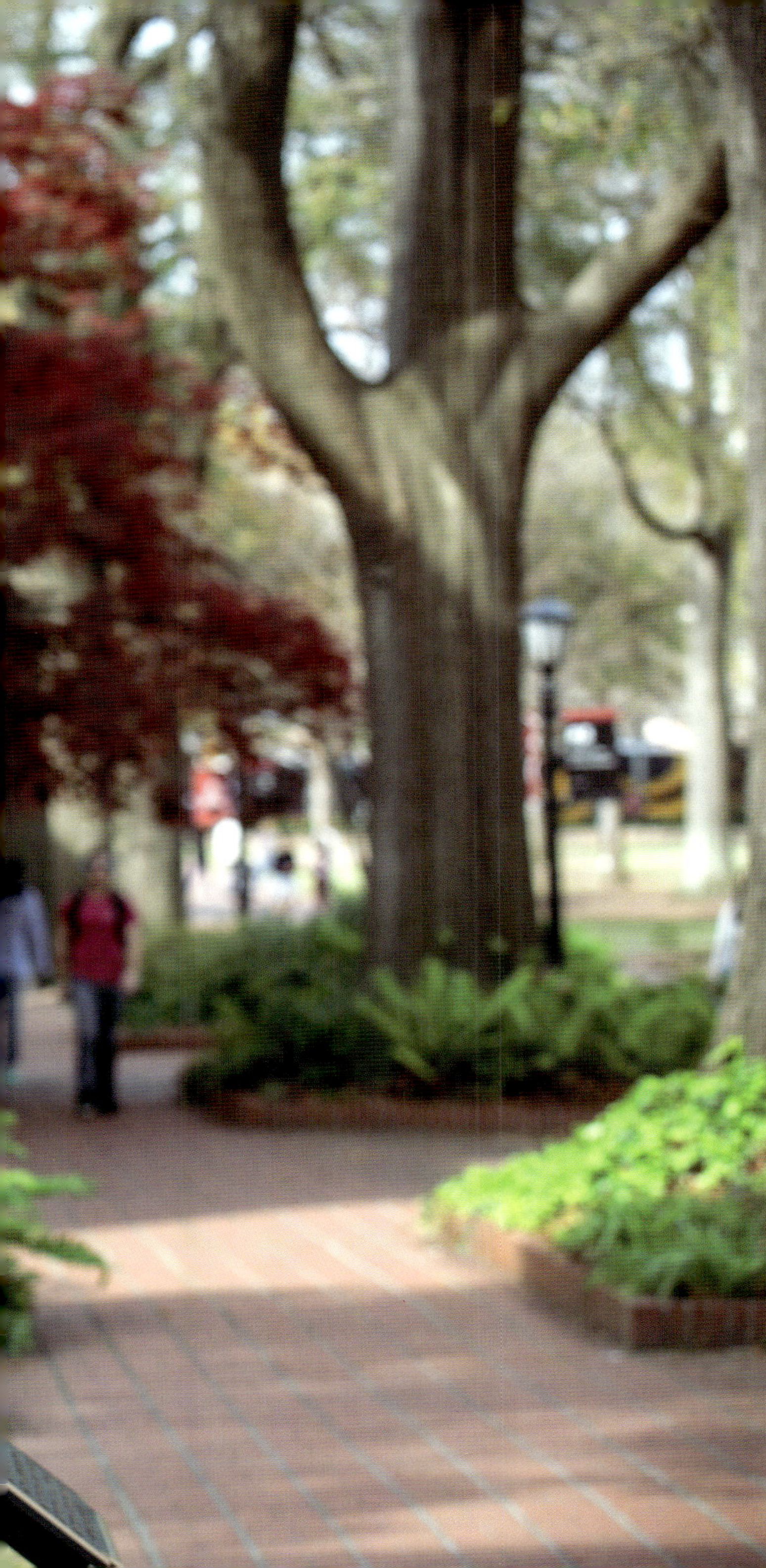

Stately oaks; lush and colorful plantings; and the state, national, and university flags mark the front of the President's House, home to every university president since 1952.

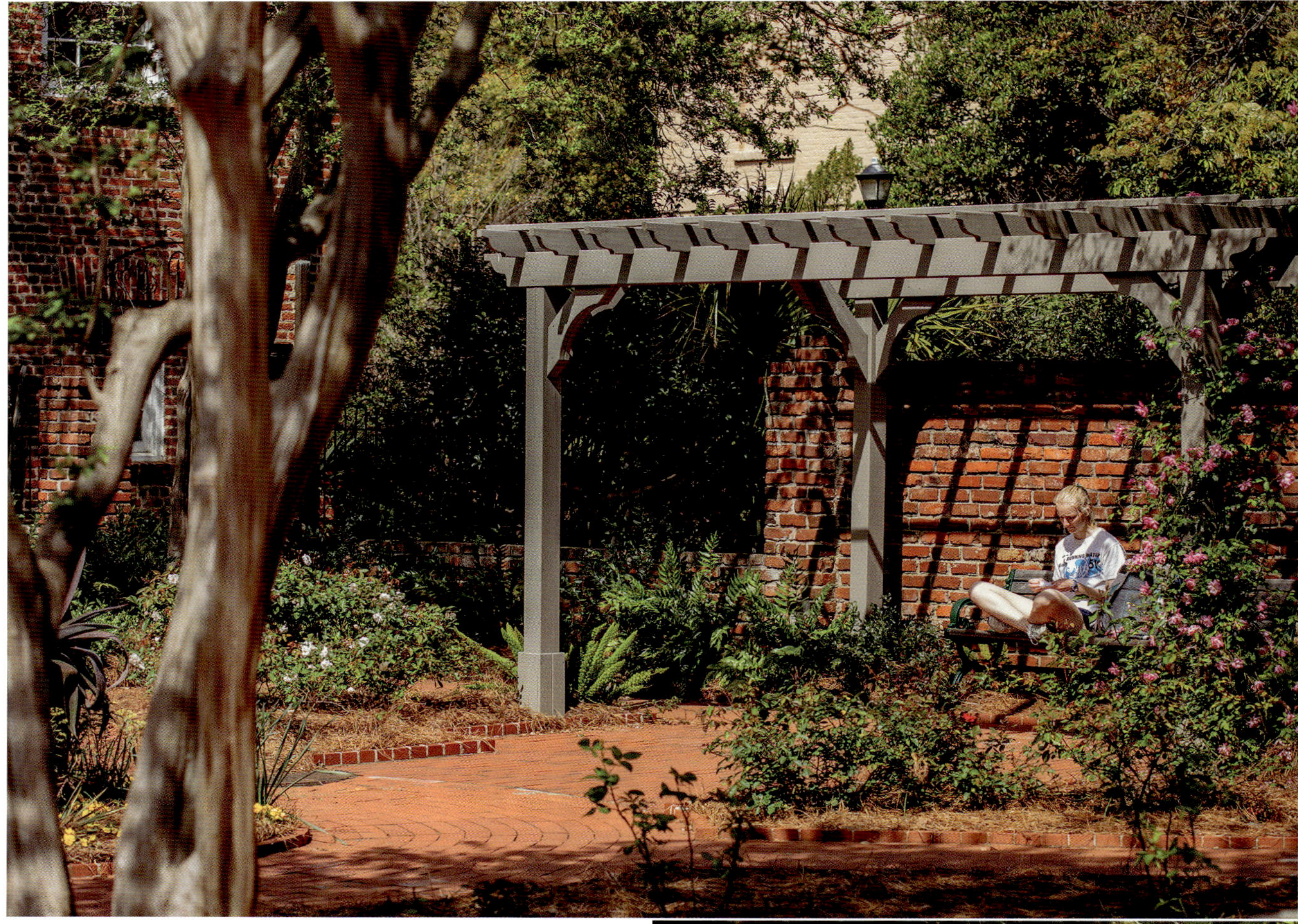

A pergola tucked between Lieber College and the School of Journalism and Mass Communications offers a contemplative spot for reading and relaxation.

A sculpted pineapple, the Southern symbol of welcome, adorns a column framed by crepe myrtles.

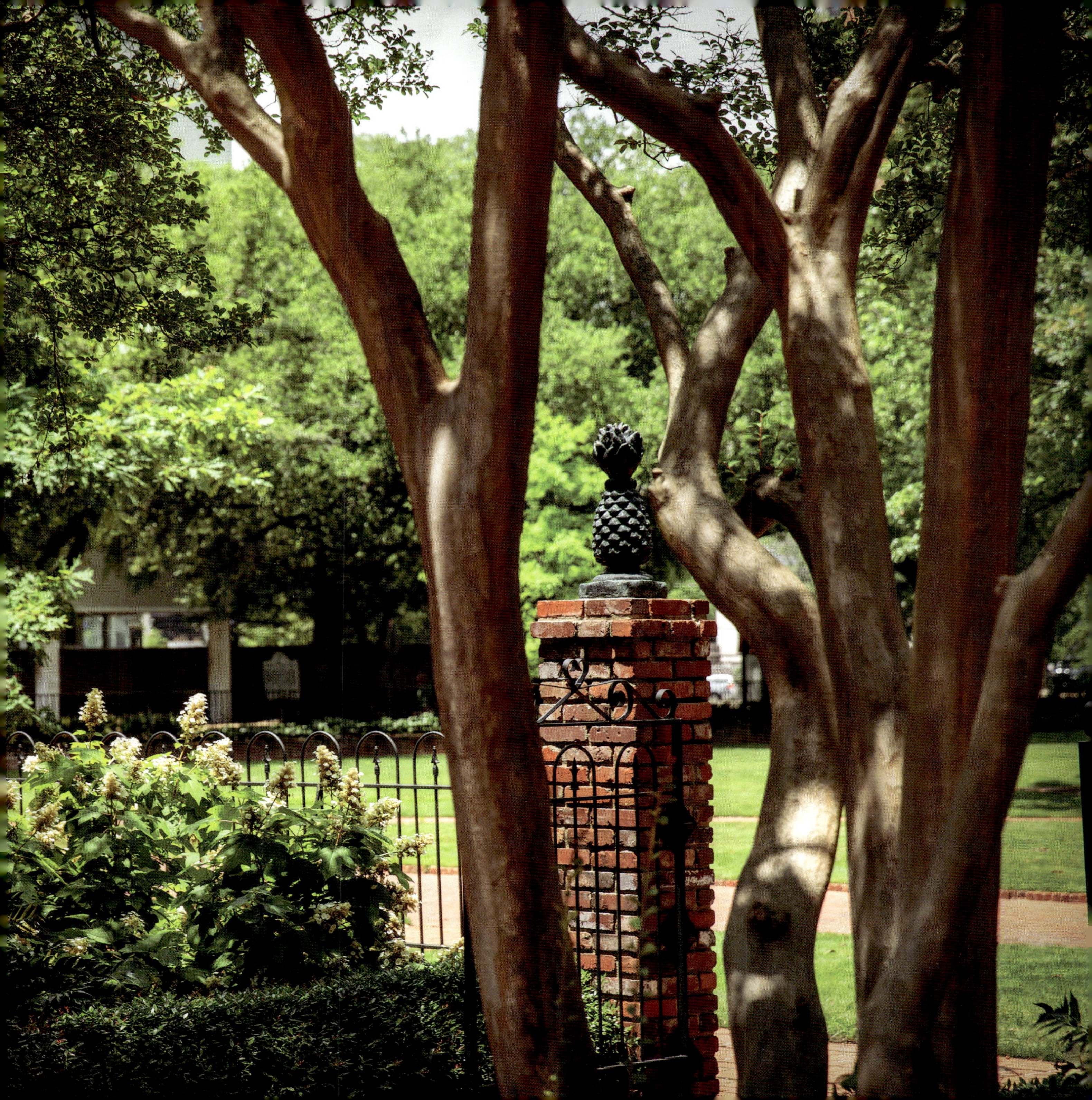

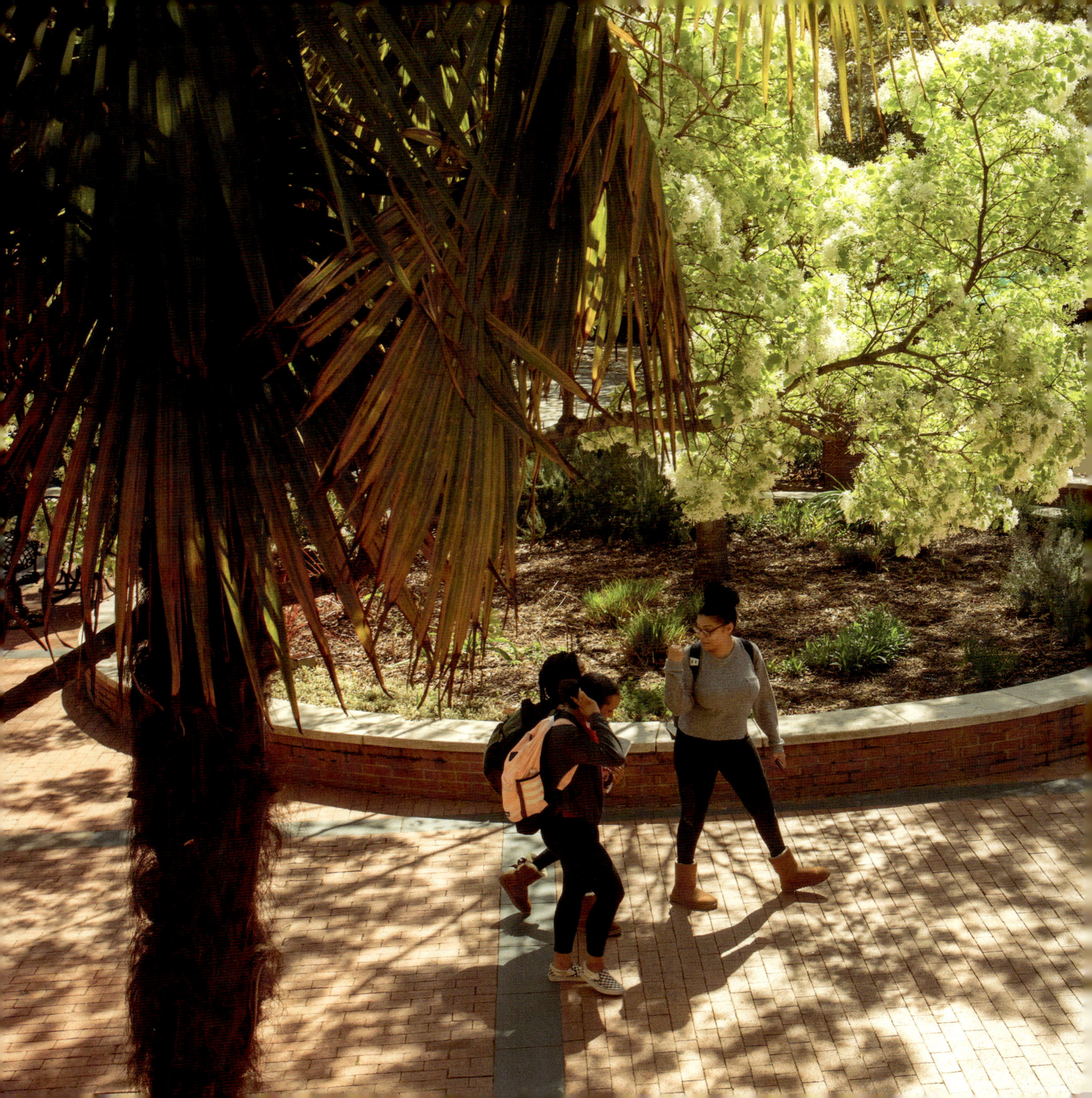

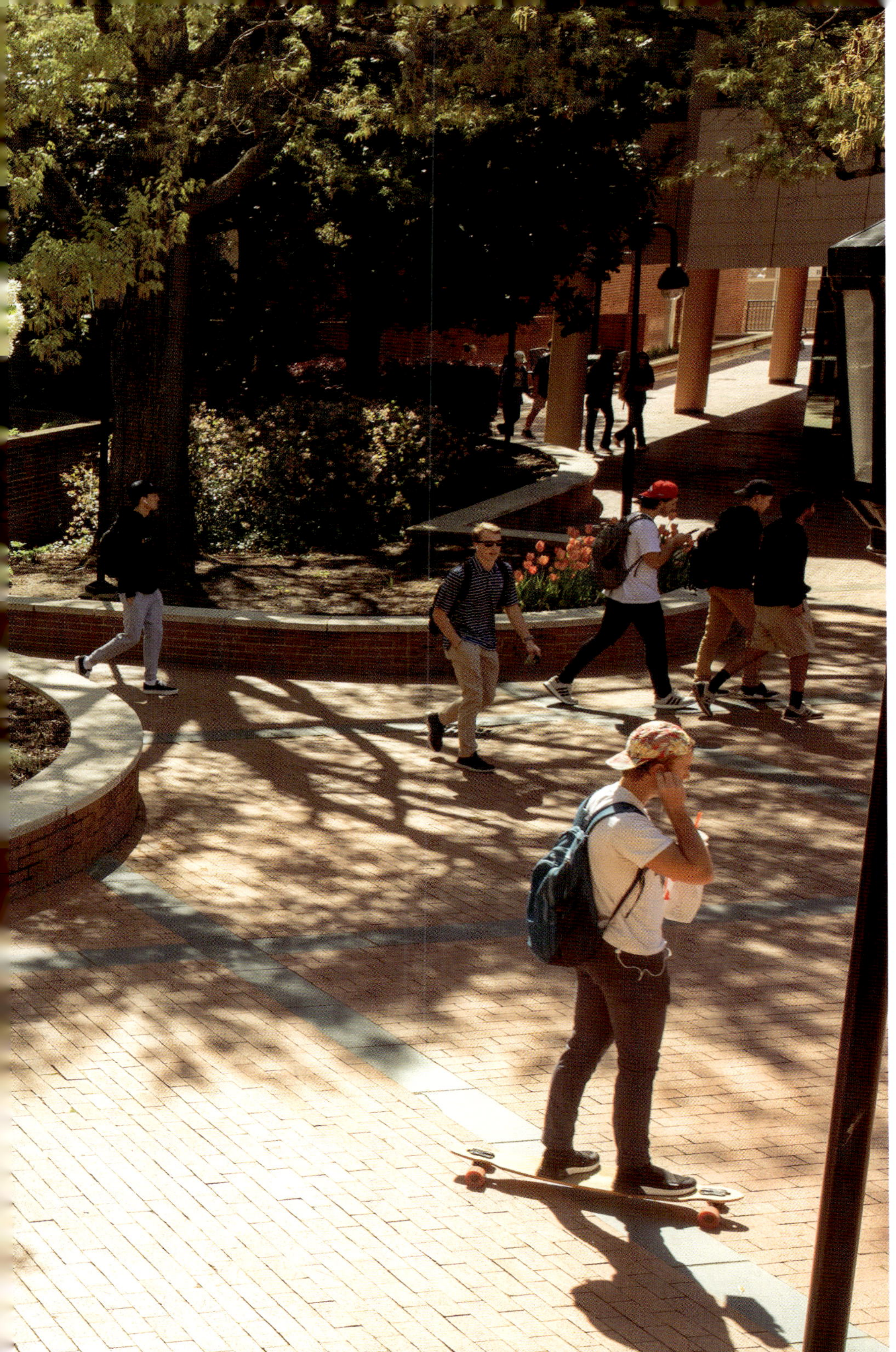

The plaza outside of the Russell House Student Union building is a nexus for walkways in every direction.

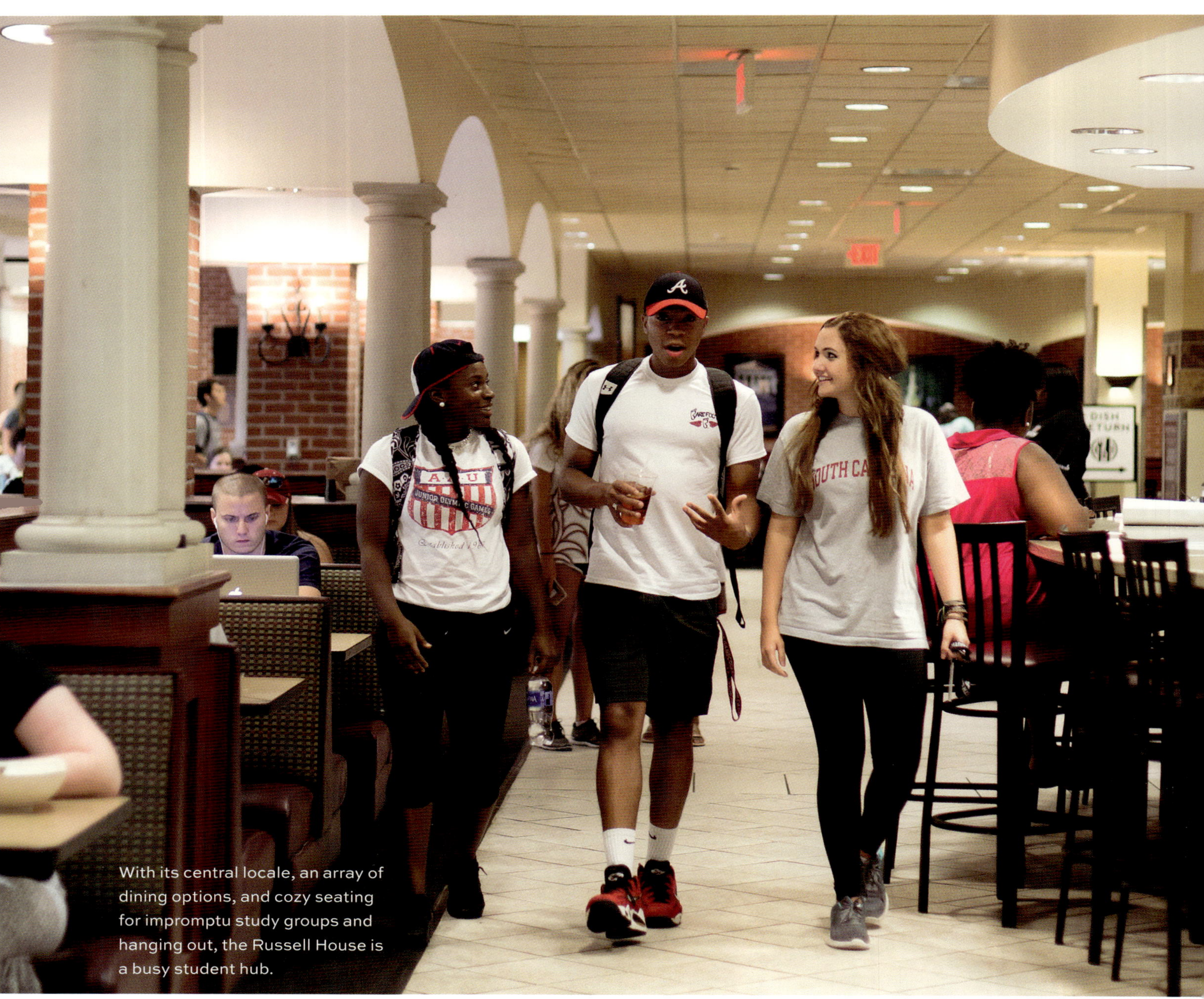

With its central locale, an array of dining options, and cozy seating for impromptu study groups and hanging out, the Russell House is a busy student hub.

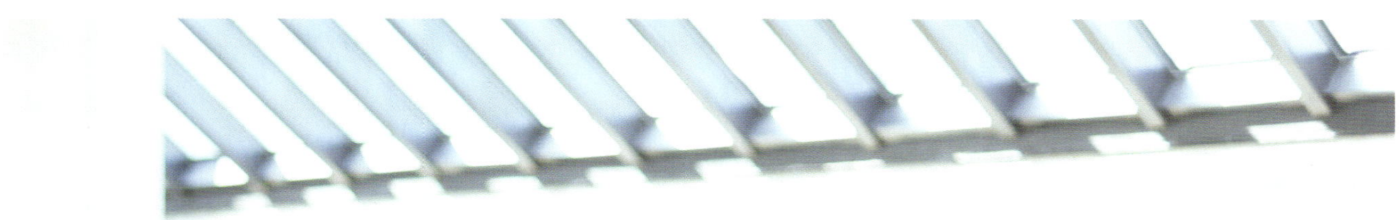

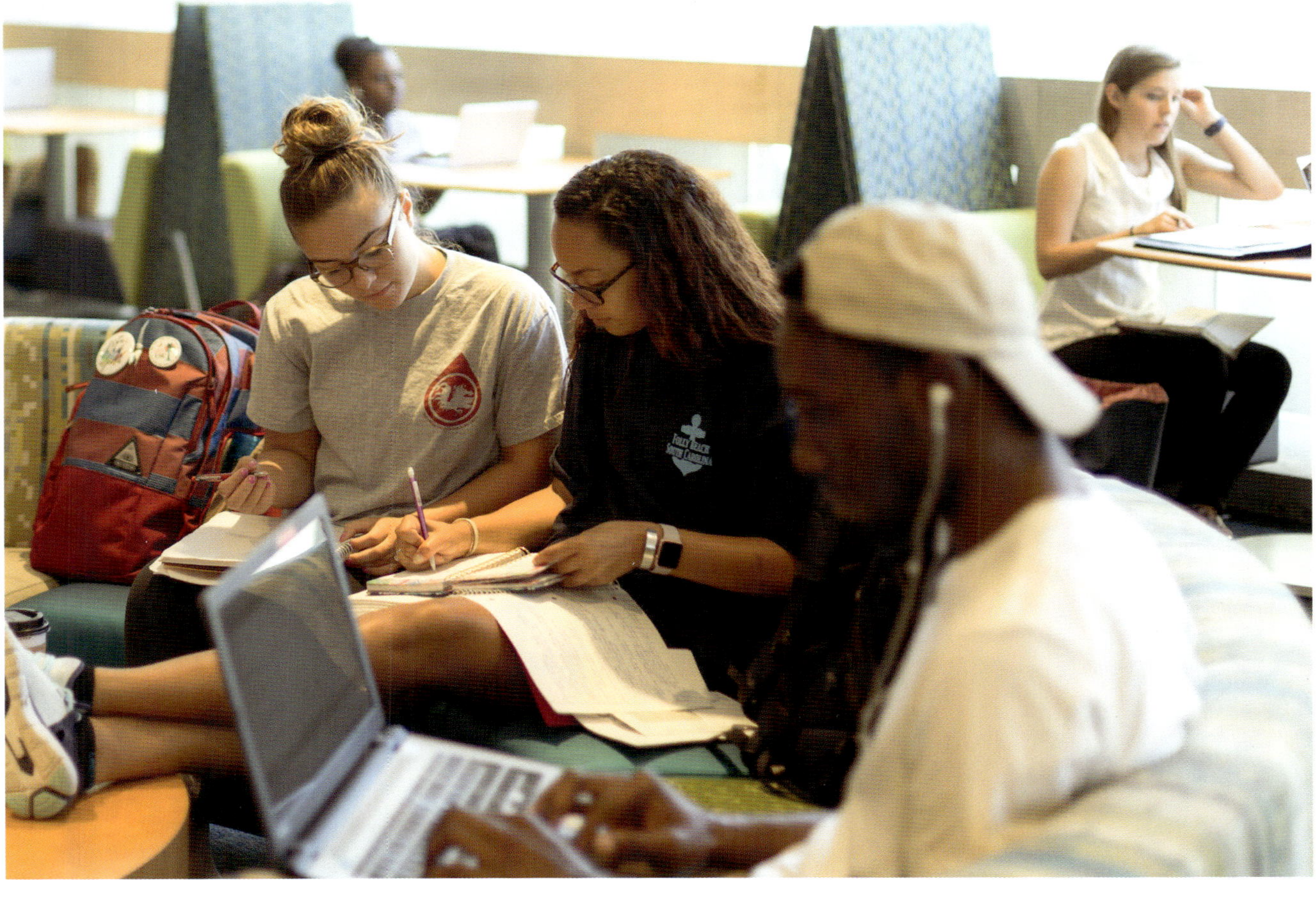

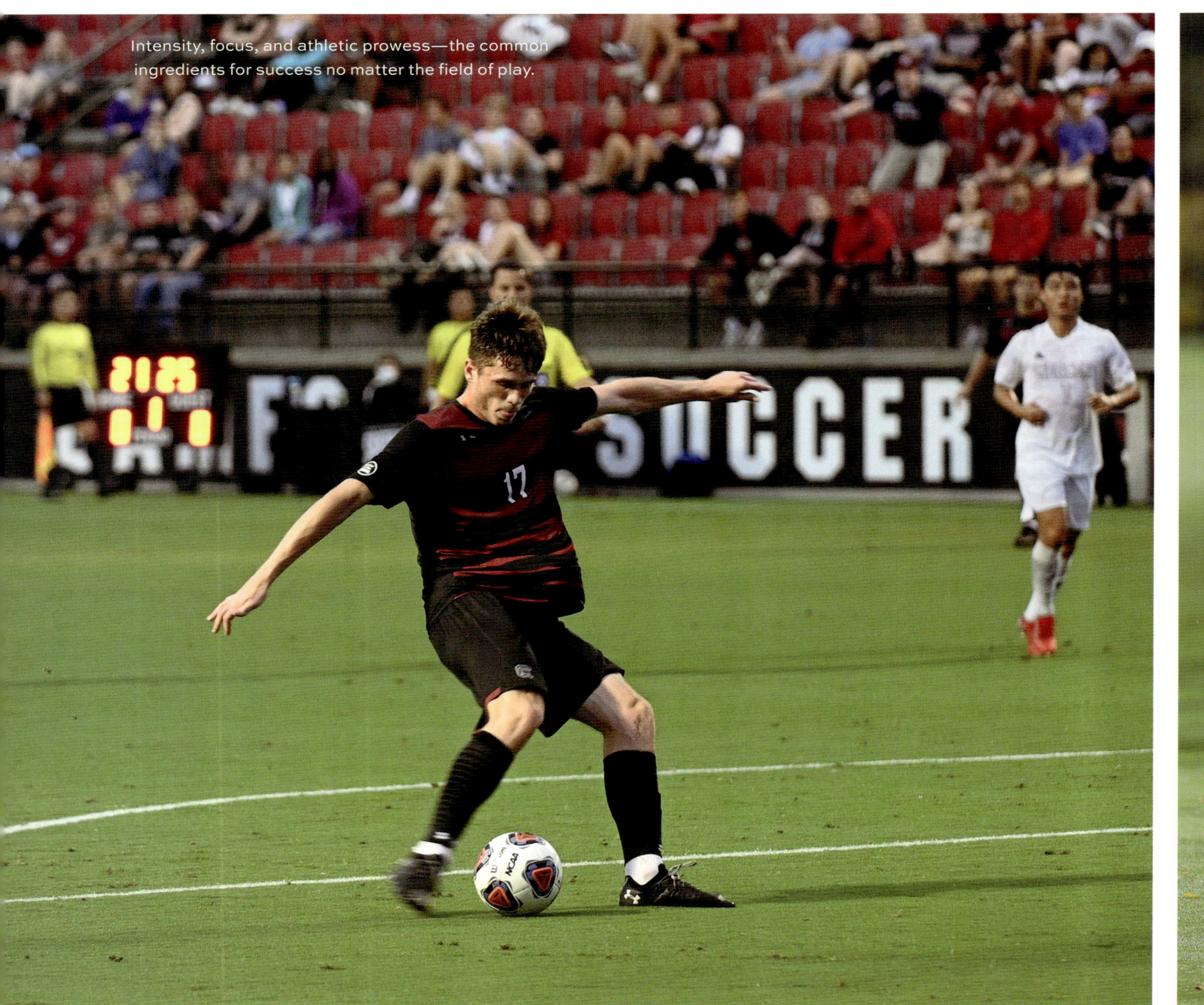

Intensity, focus, and athletic prowess—the common
ingredients for success no matter the field of play.

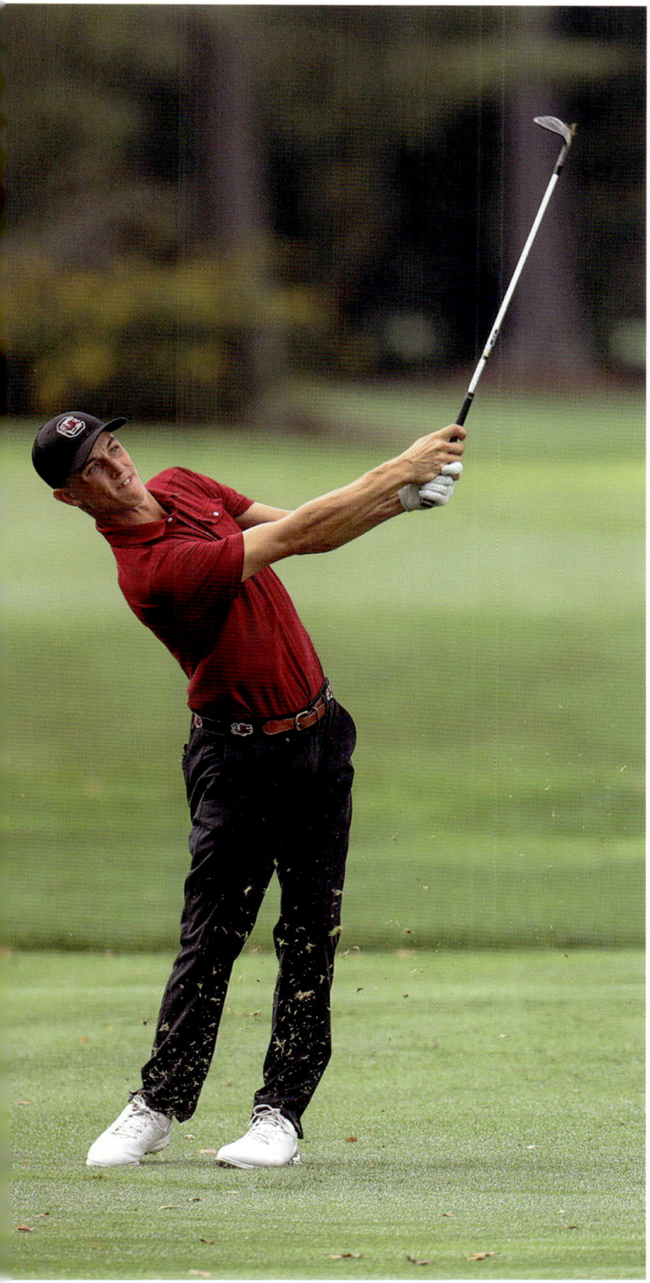

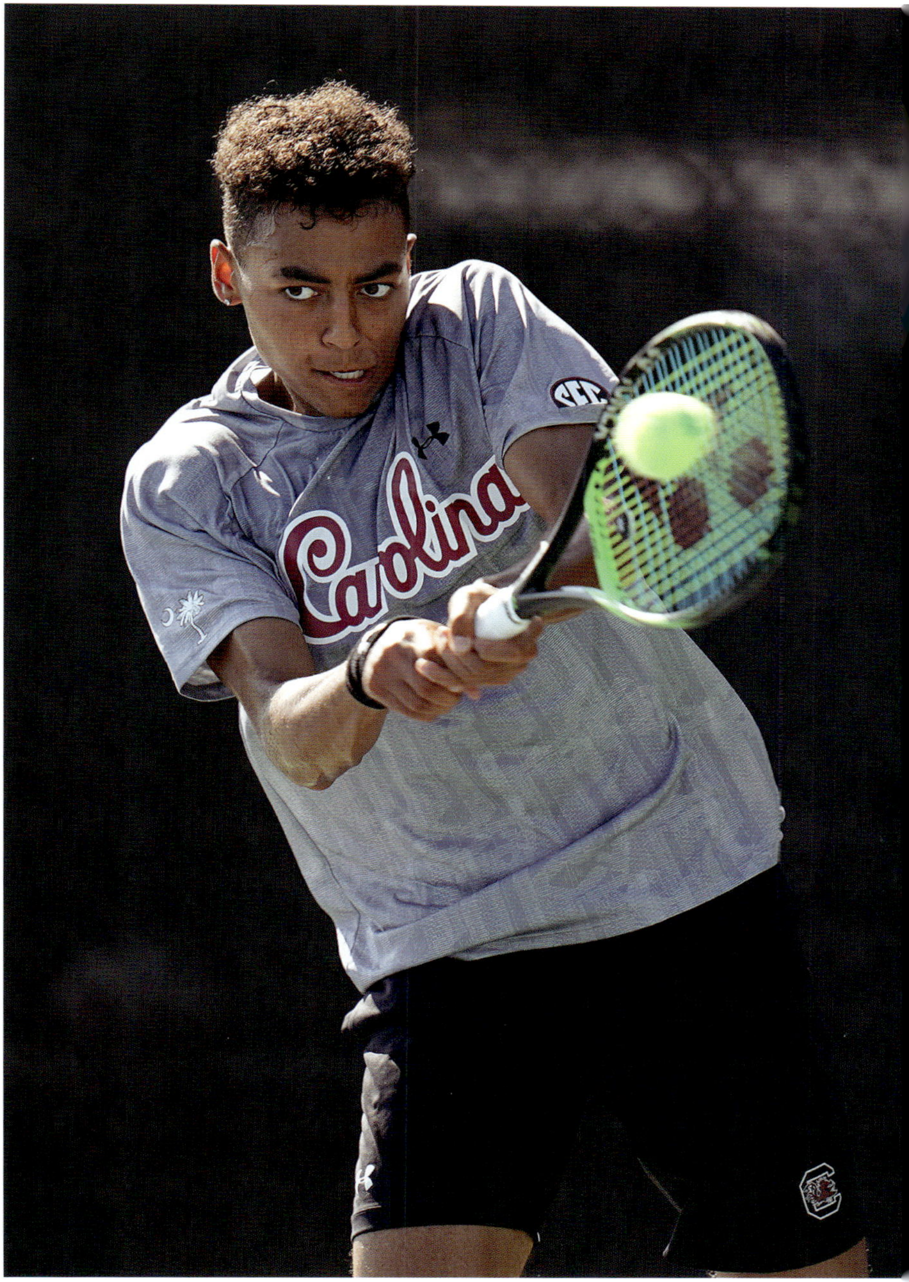

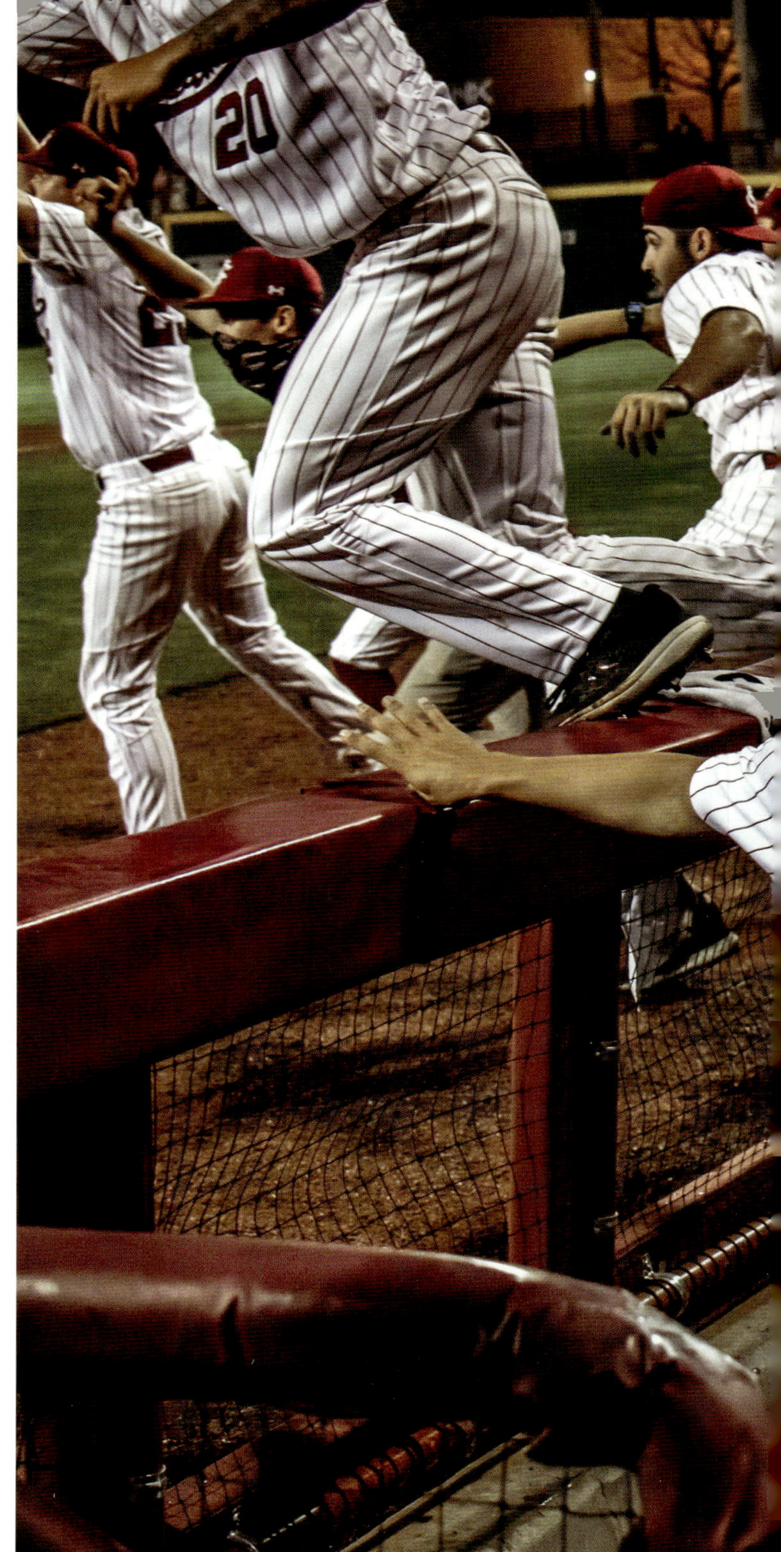

Whether it's the final out in a close game or a homer in the bottom of the ninth, the energy is palpable in Founders Park, home of the Gamecocks baseball team.

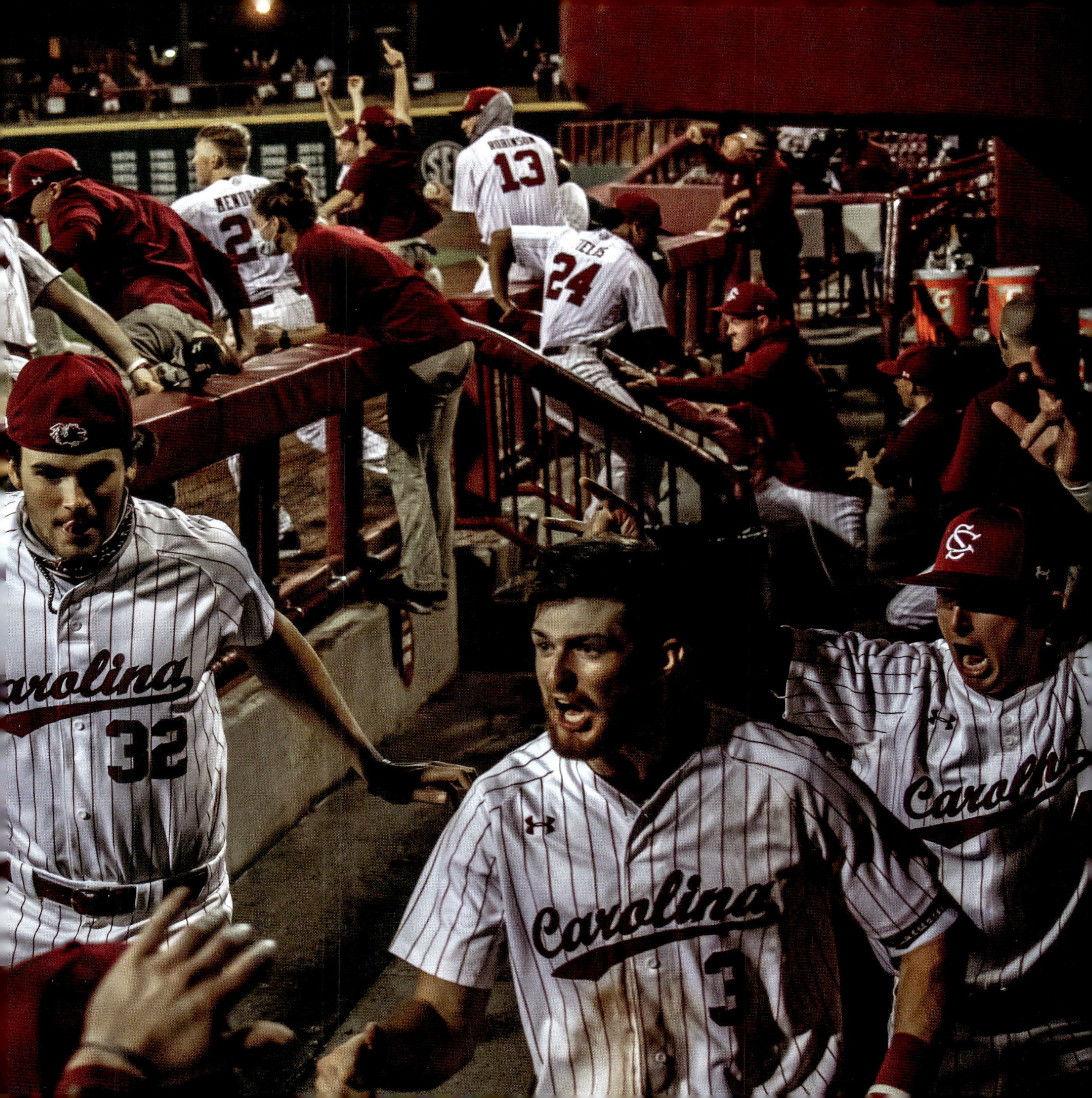

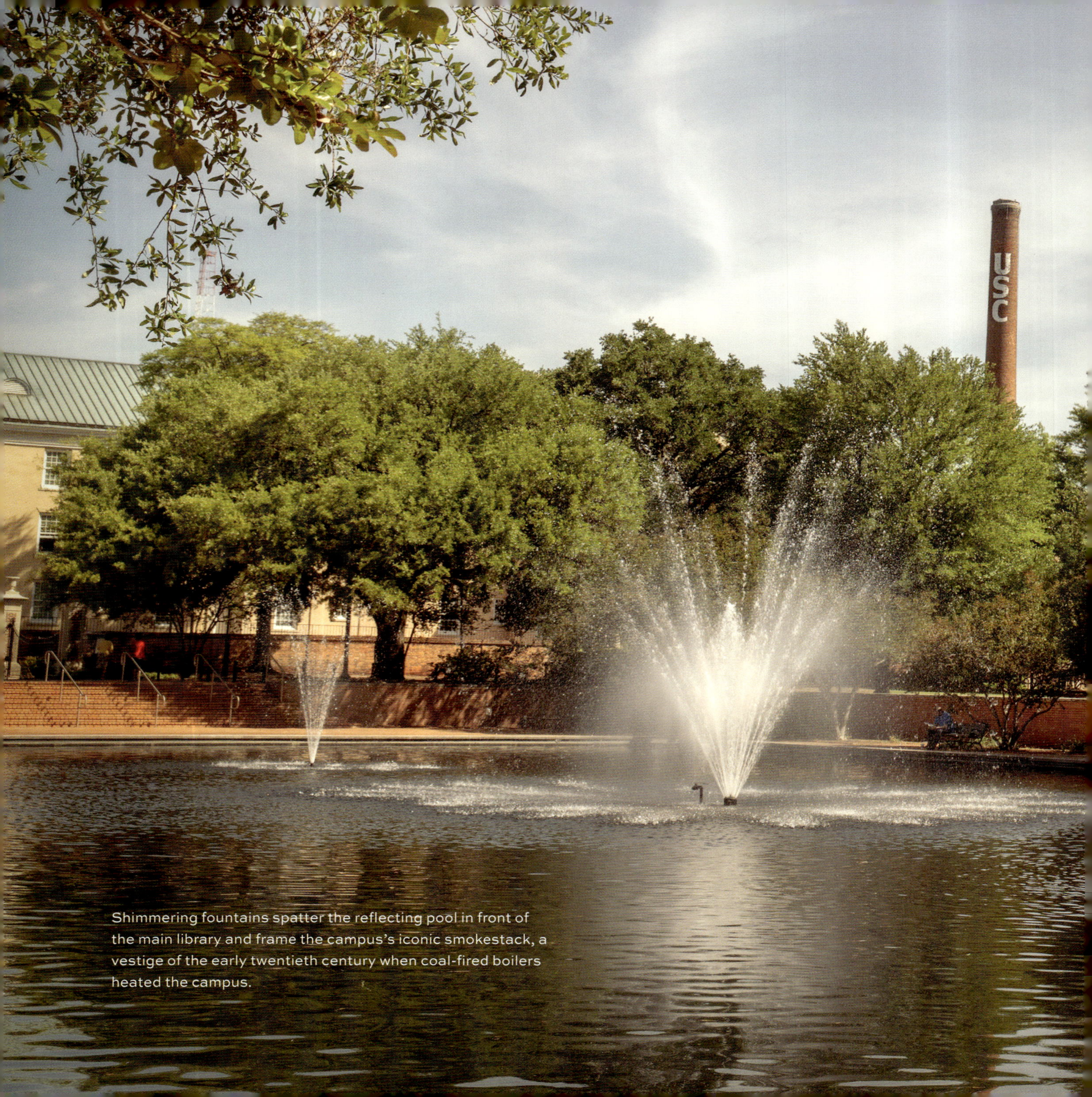

Shimmering fountains spatter the reflecting pool in front of the main library and frame the campus's iconic smokestack, a vestige of the early twentieth century when coal-fired boilers heated the campus.

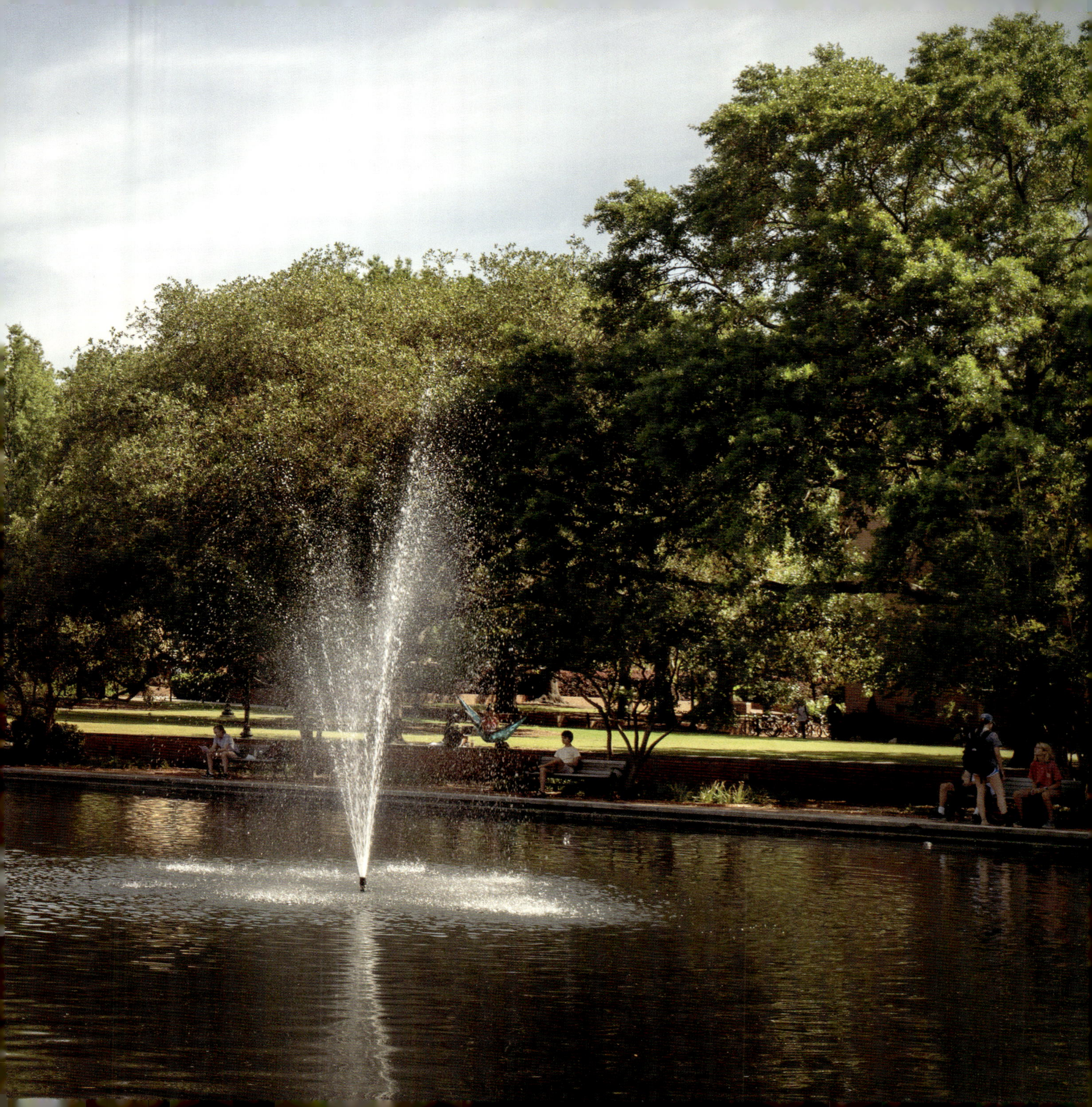

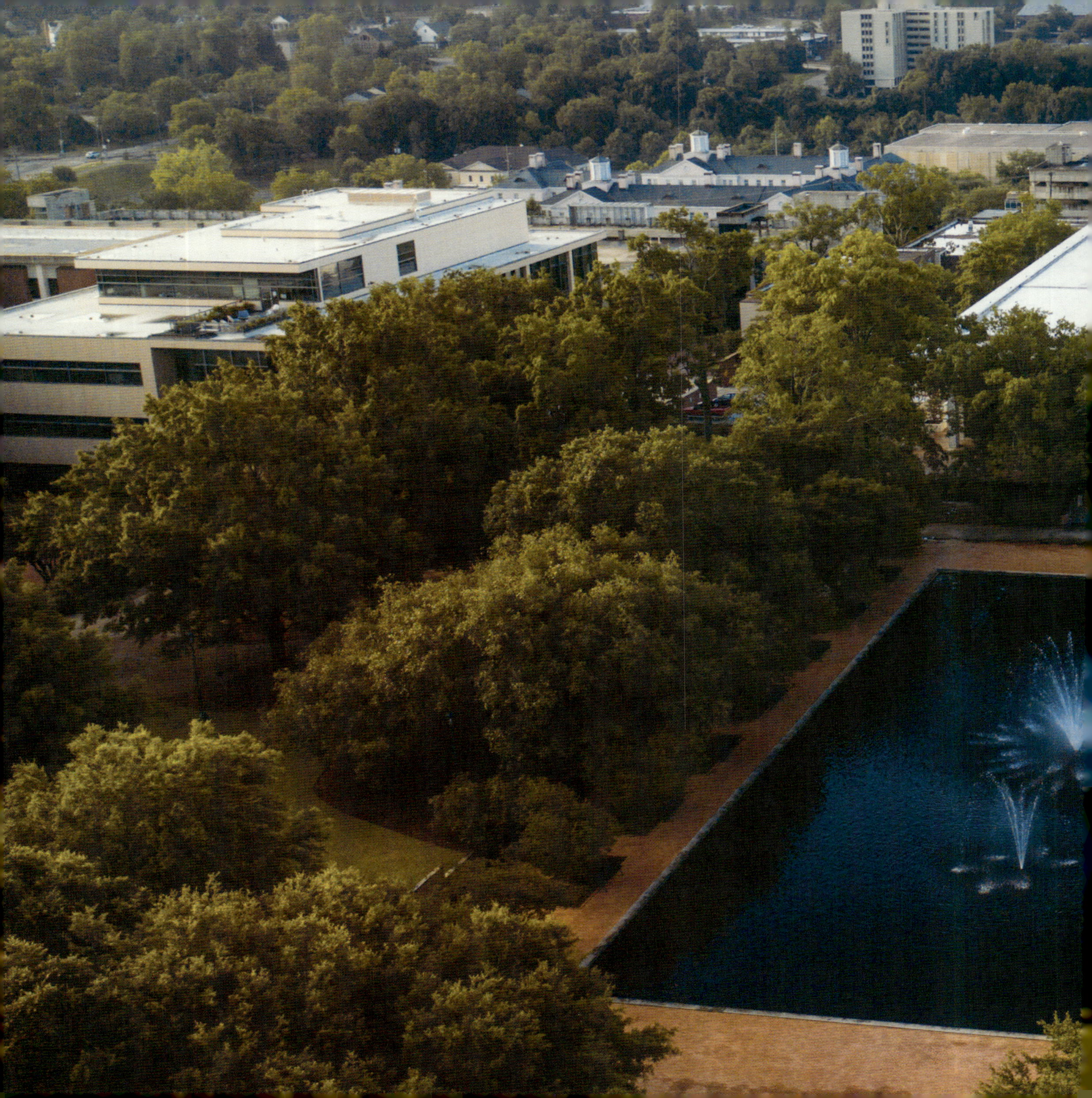

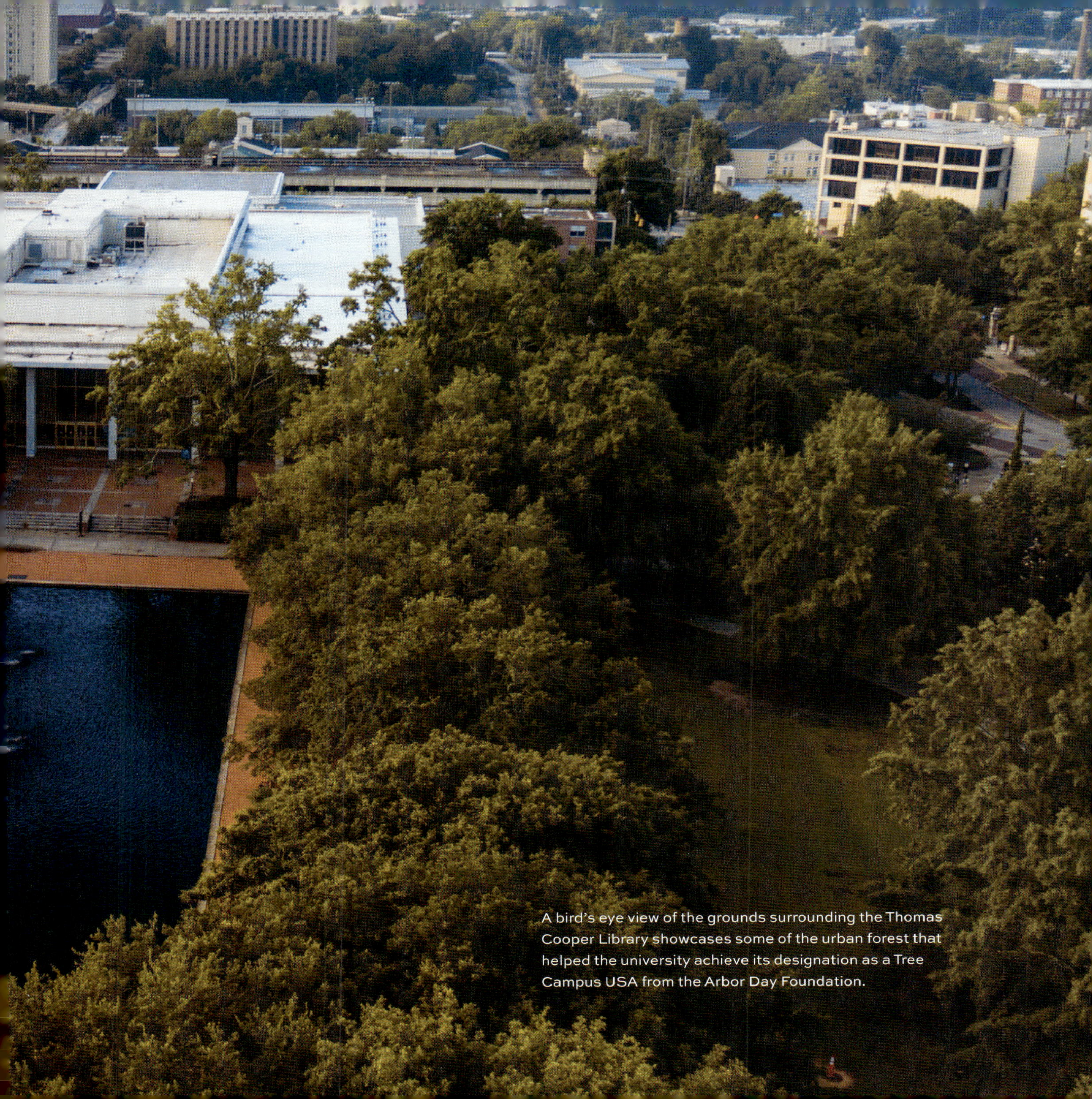

A bird's eye view of the grounds surrounding the Thomas Cooper Library showcases some of the urban forest that helped the university achieve its designation as a Tree Campus USA from the Arbor Day Foundation.

The Thomas Cooper Library's
expansive collections attract
scholars of every level, from
undergraduates to senior pro-
fessors and visiting academics.
Designed by Edward Durell
Stone, the first phase of the
Thomas Cooper Library in 1959
was relatively small—just 30,000
square feet. A massive expansion
project completed in 1976 added
to the rear of the library and created four underground levels and
enough space—286,000 square
feet—to accommodate 1.5 million
volumes and seating for 2,500.

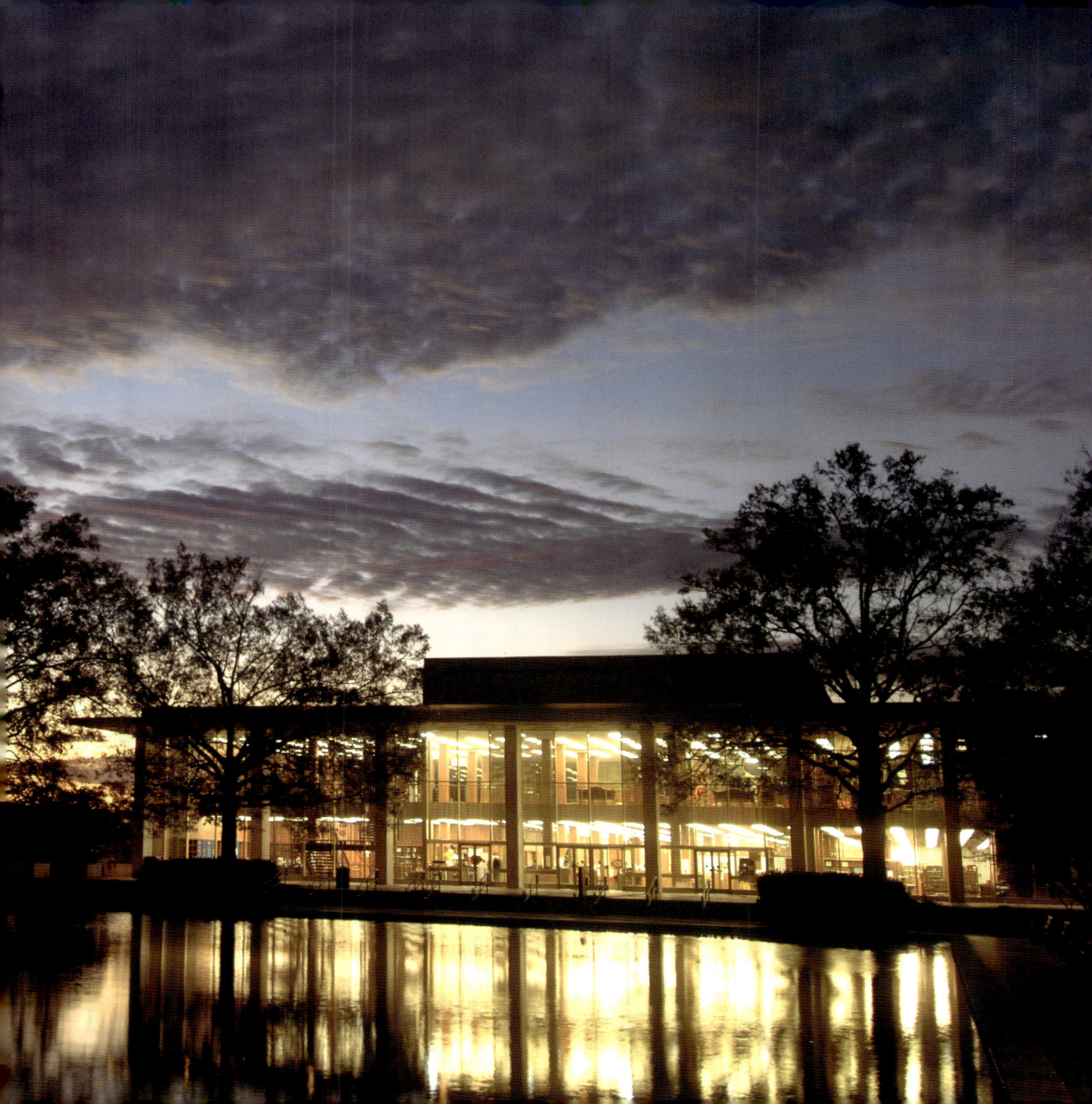

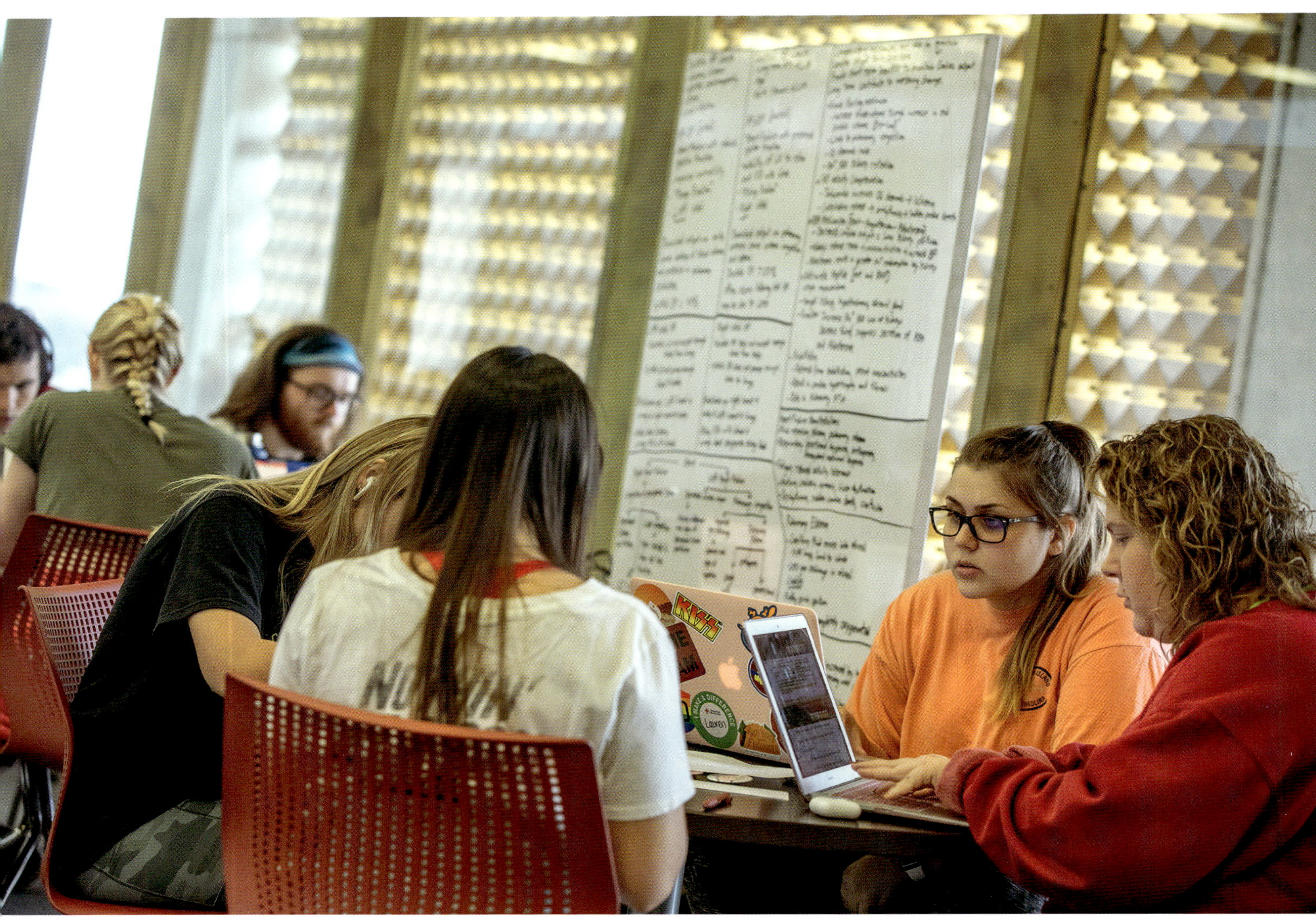

By providing more study nooks and relaxing restrictions on
food and drink, the Thomas Cooper Library has become one
of the most popular places on campus for students to crack
open textbooks and laptops to study—or just hang out with
friends.

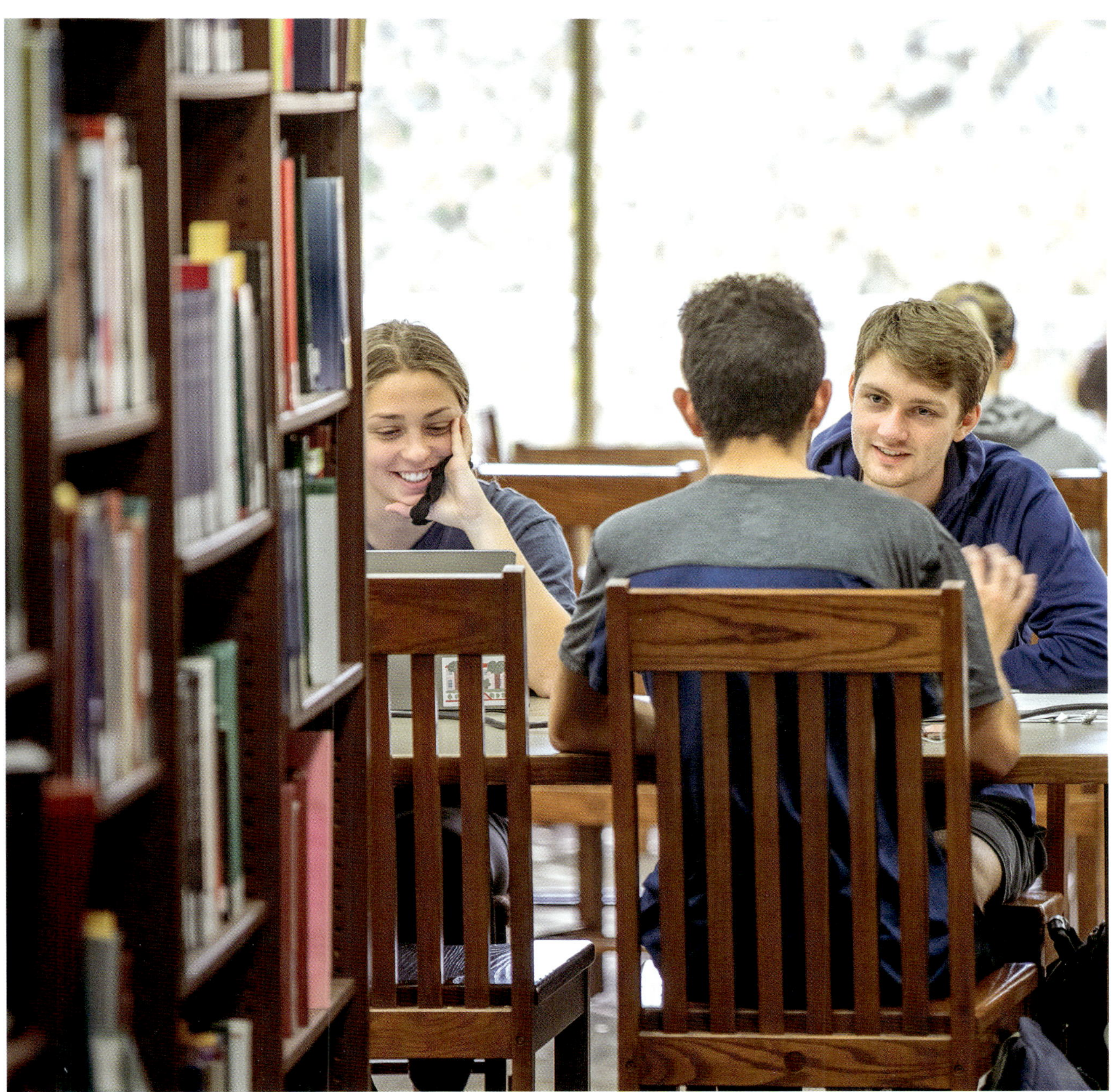

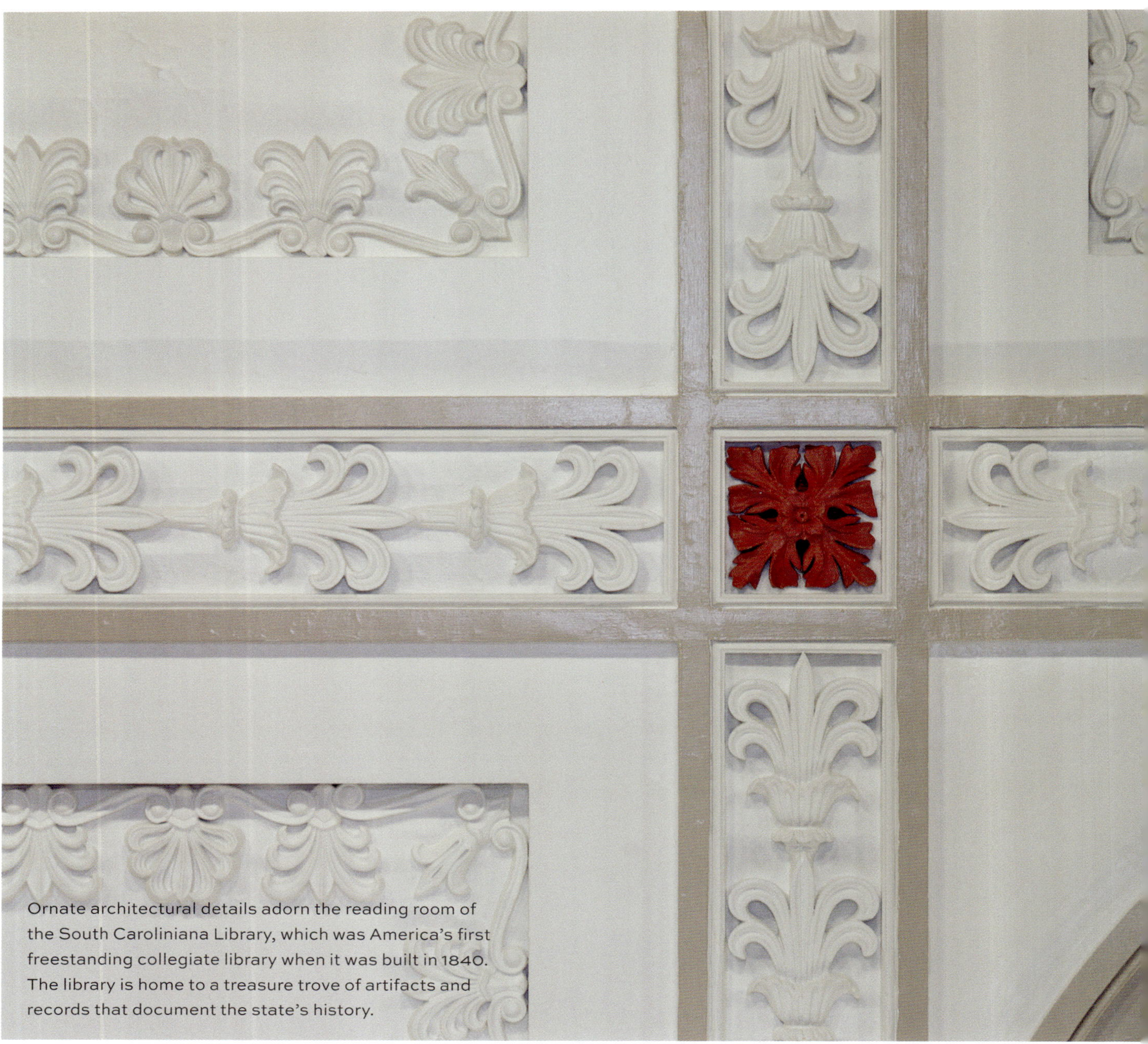

Ornate architectural details adorn the reading room of the South Caroliniana Library, which was America's first freestanding collegiate library when it was built in 1840. The library is home to a treasure trove of artifacts and records that document the state's history.

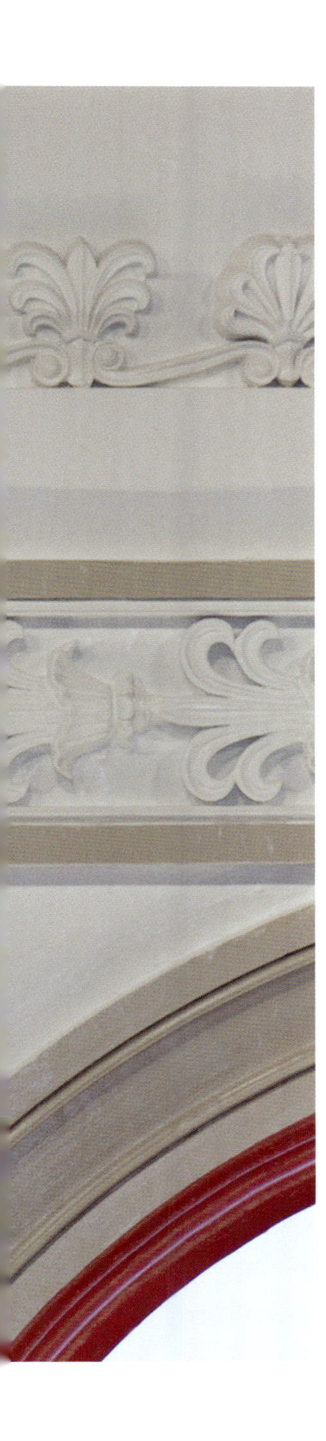

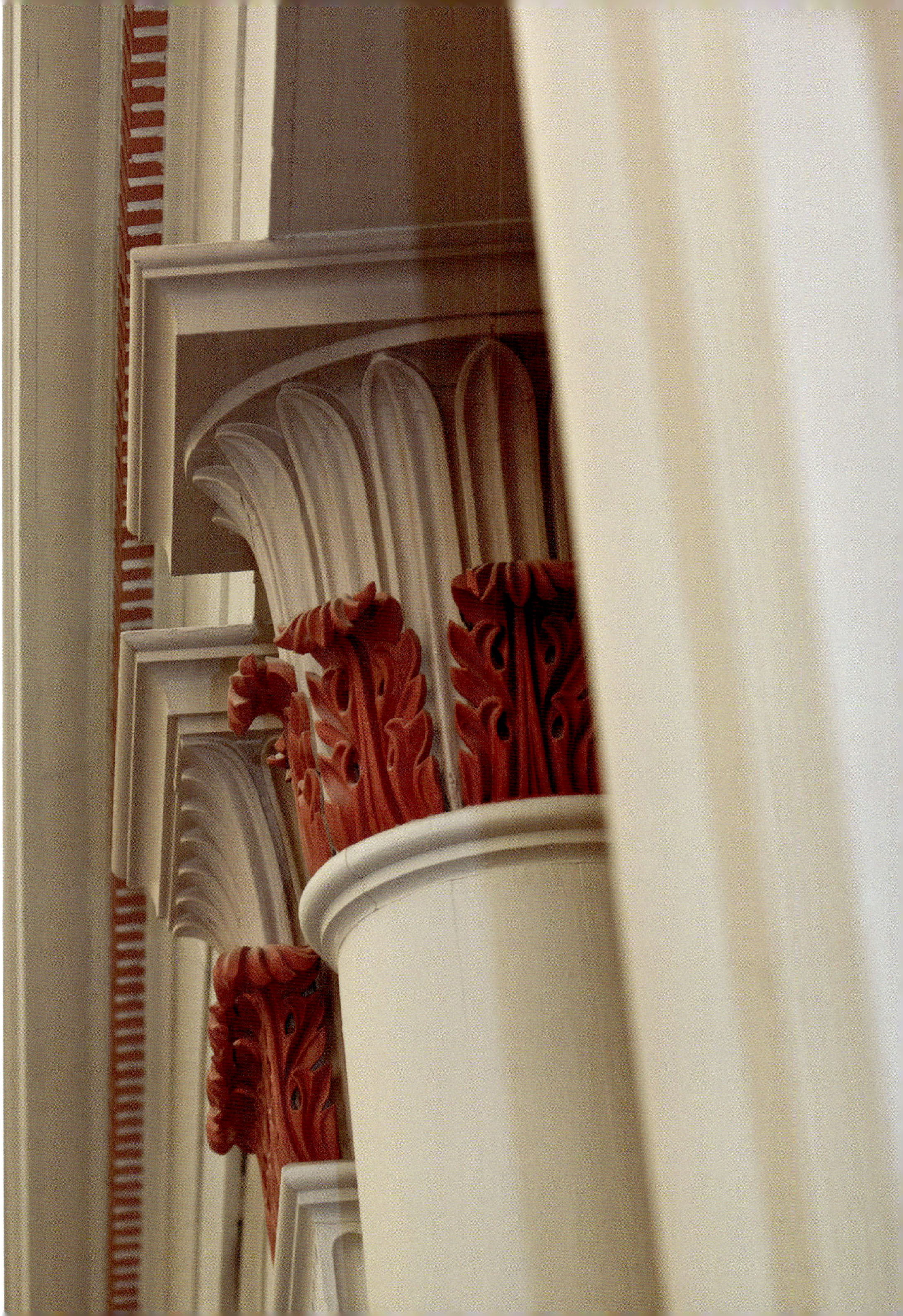

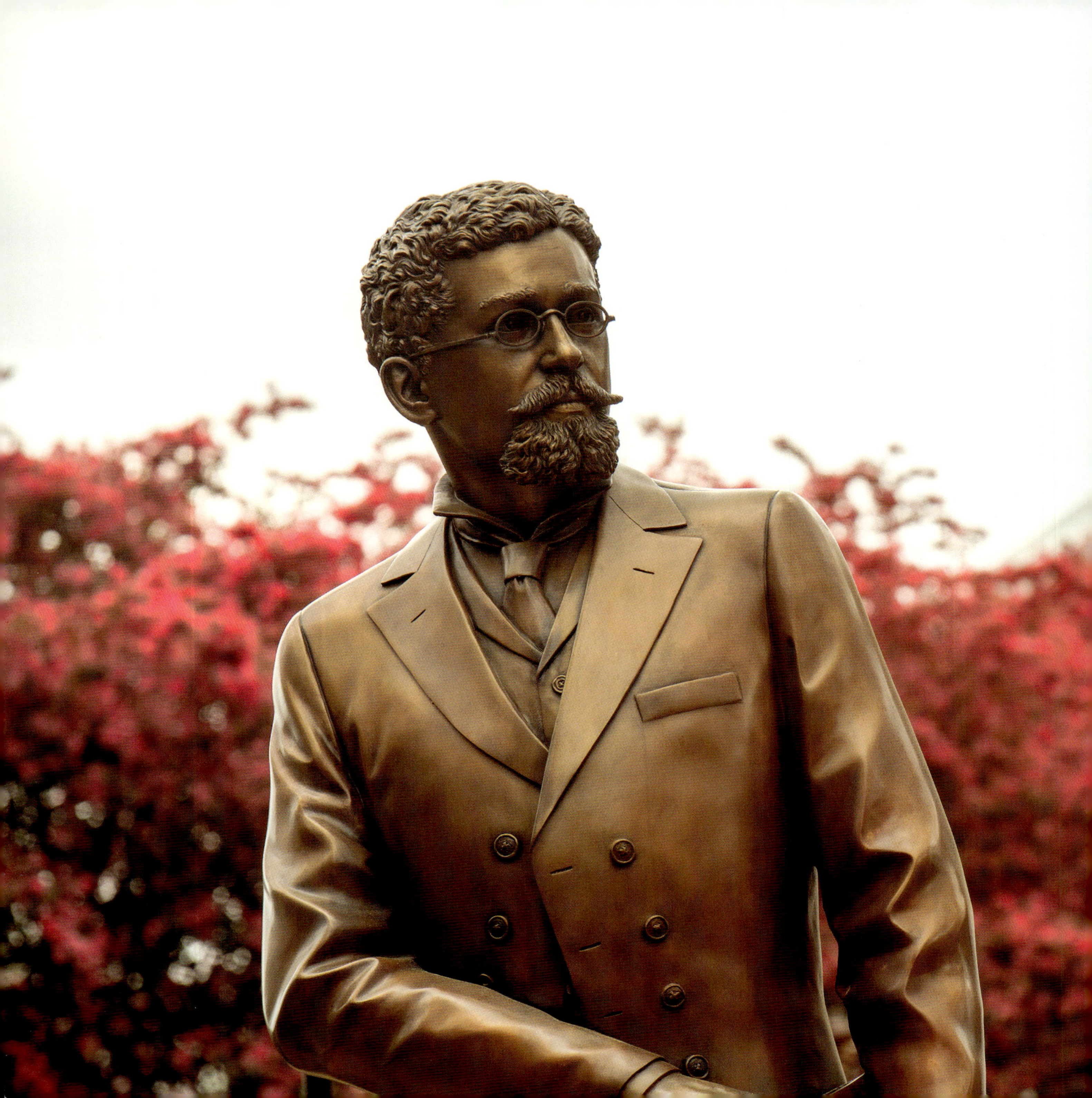

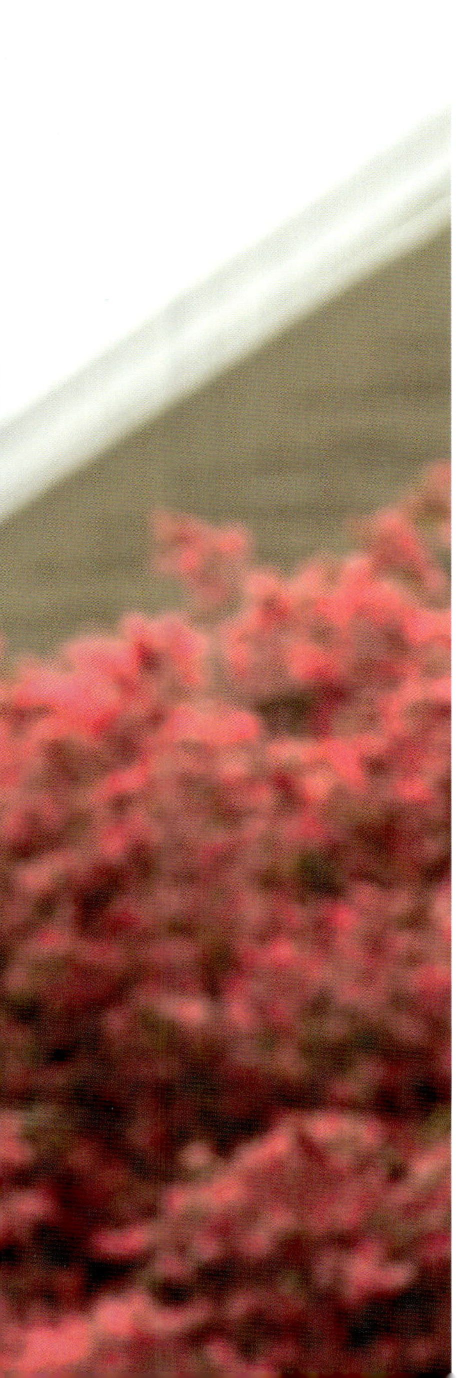

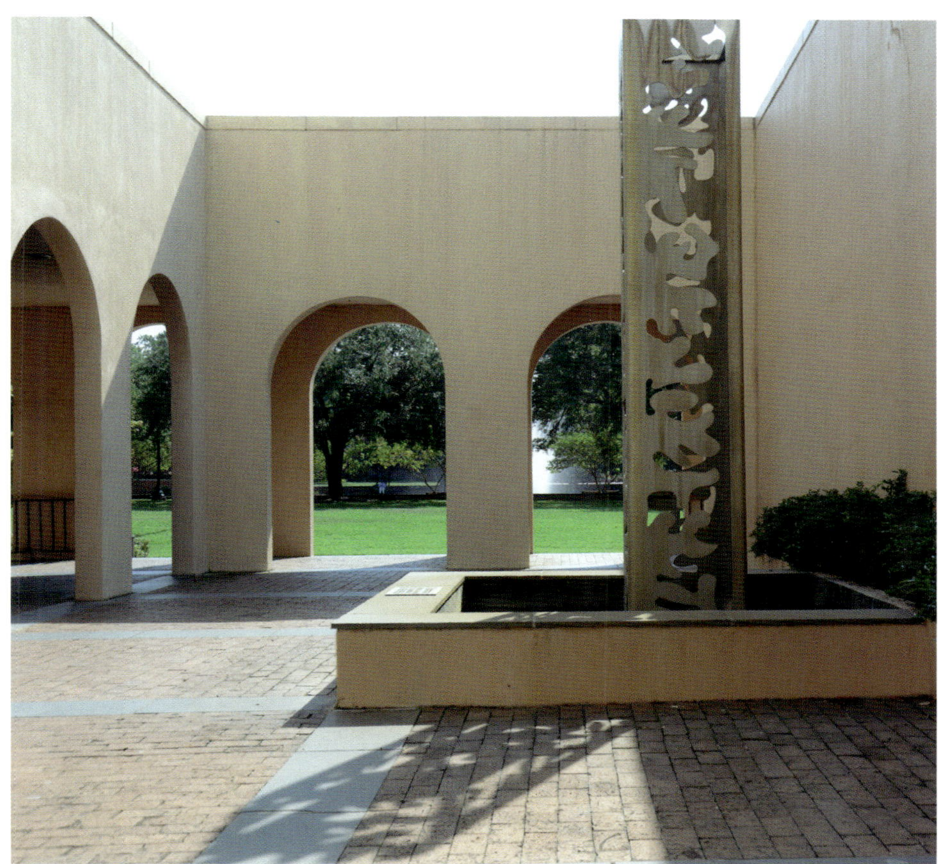

The Longstreet Fountain is based on a design concept by Robert LaForce and was interpreted in stainless steel by university alumnus and sculptor Allan J. Sindler.

A statue of Richard T. Greener, sculpted by Jon Hair and mounted on a pedestal beside the Thomas Cooper Library, pays homage to the university's first African American professor (1873–77) who was also Harvard College's first Black graduate.

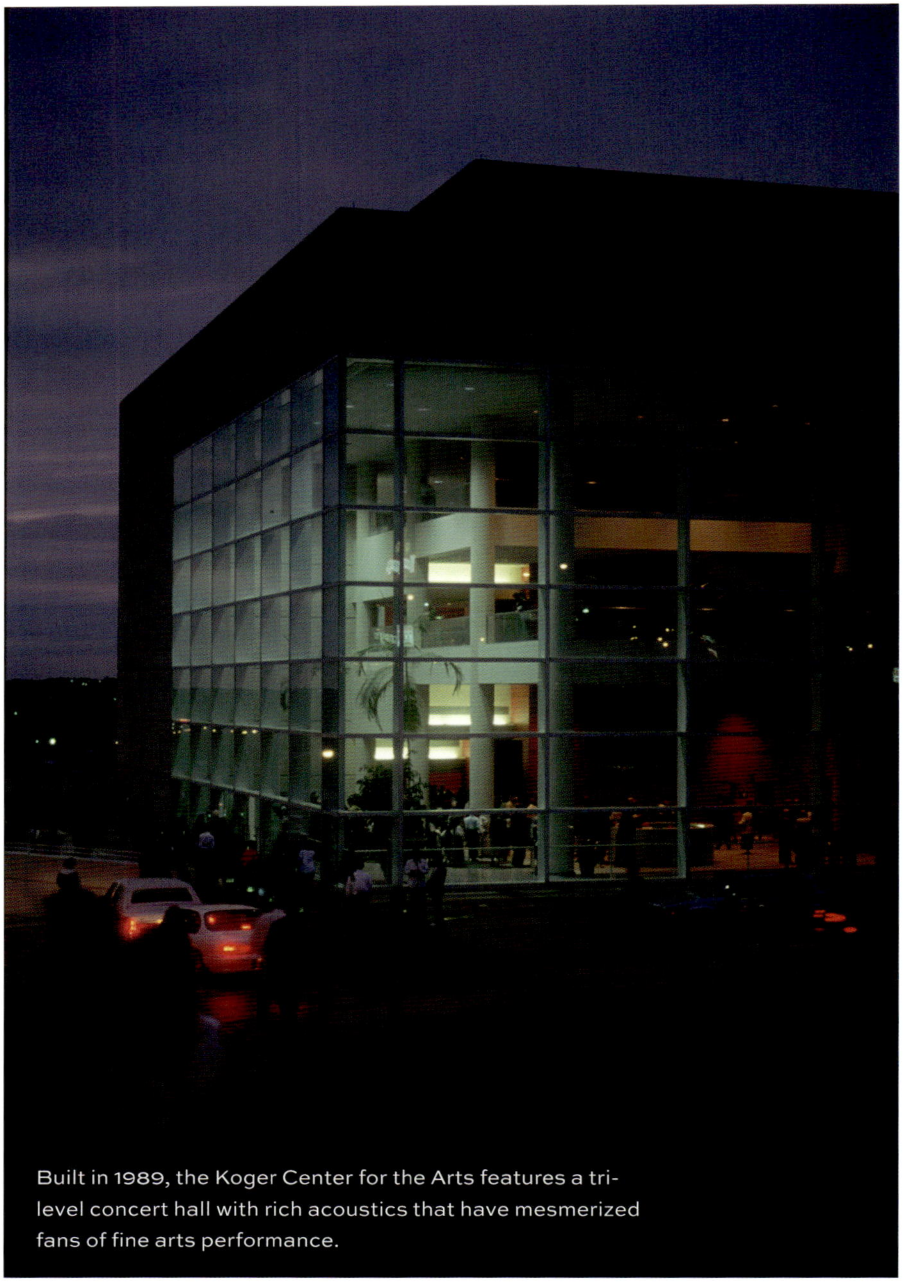

Built in 1989, the Koger Center for the Arts features a tri-level concert hall with rich acoustics that have mesmerized fans of fine arts performance.

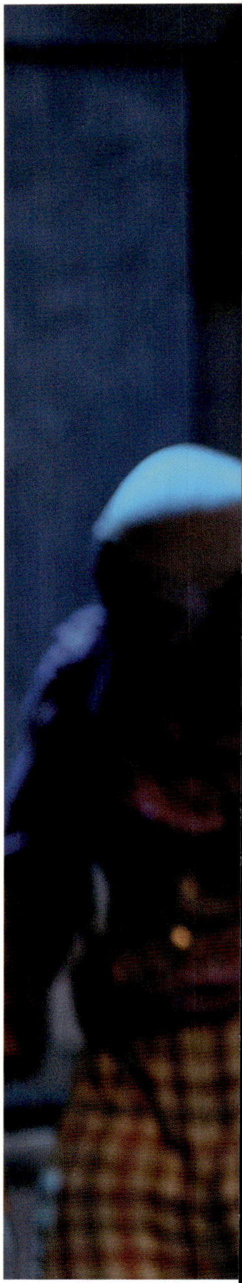

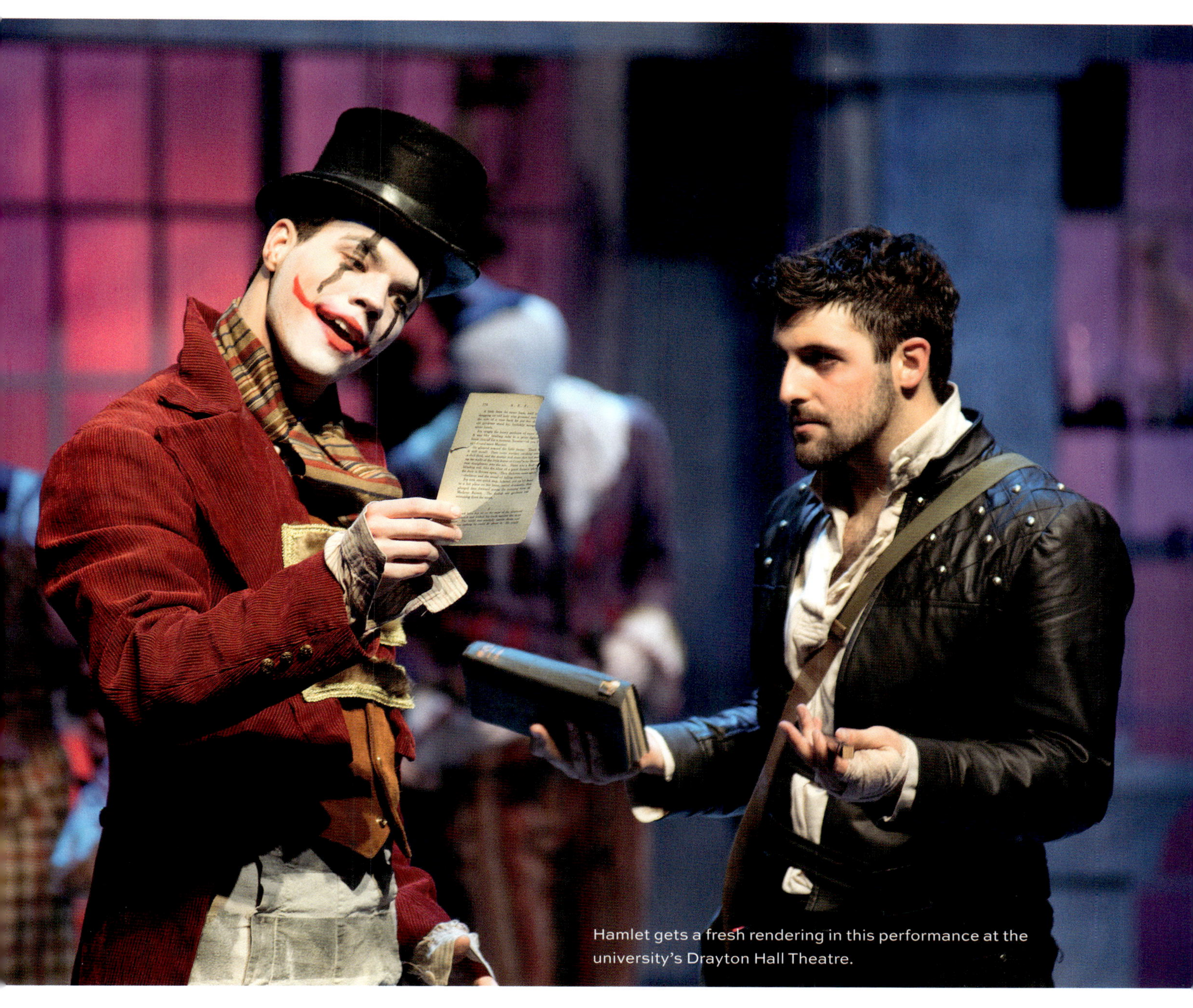

Hamlet gets a fresh rendering in this performance at the university's Drayton Hall Theatre.

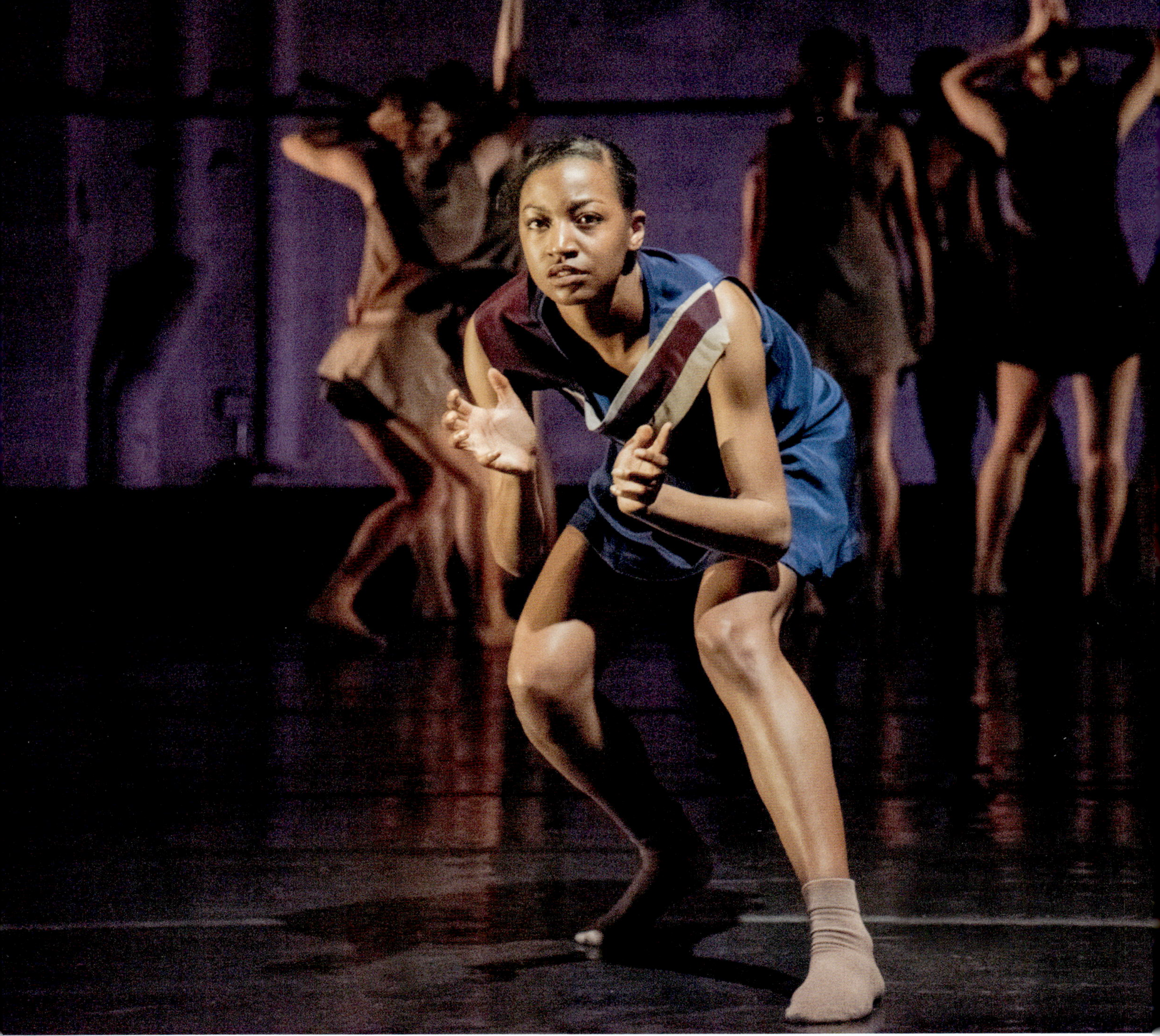

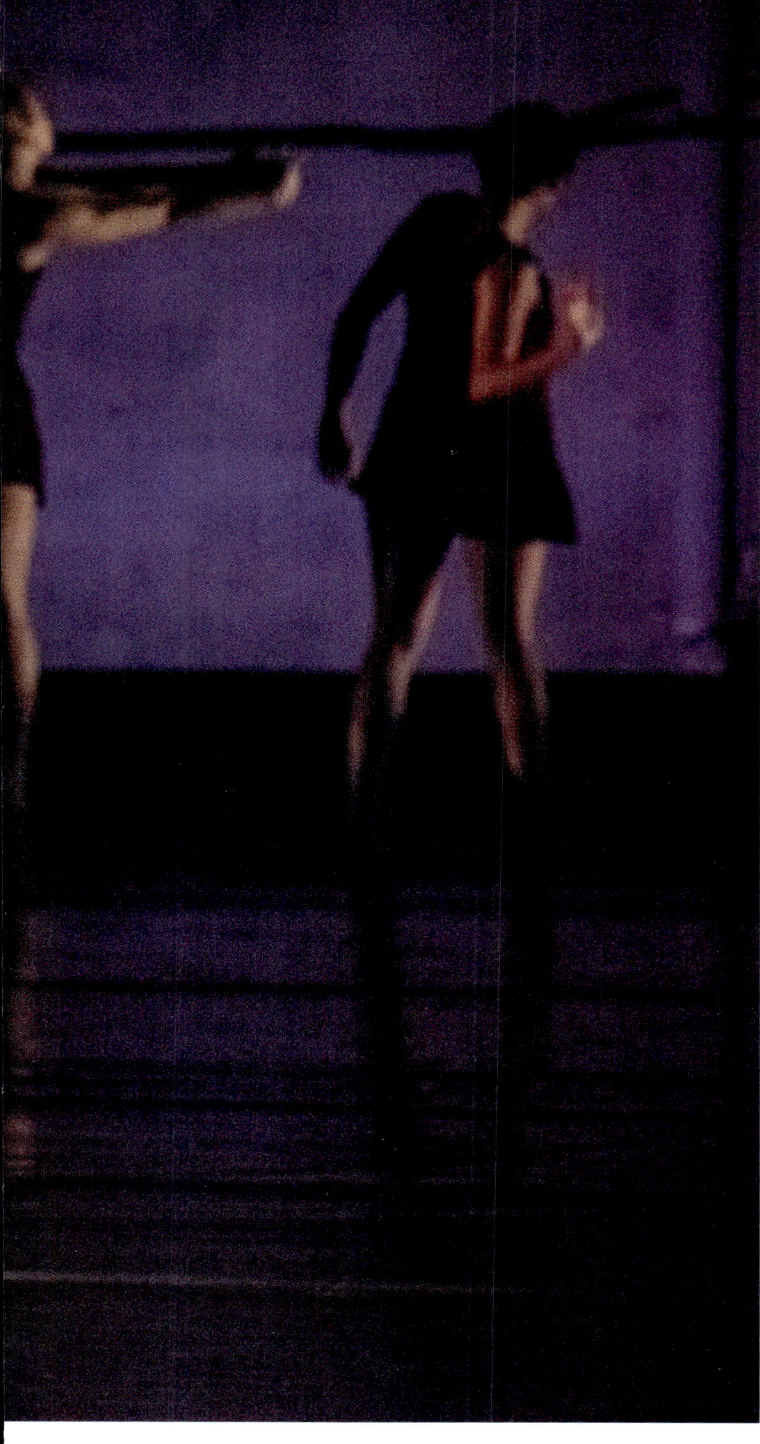

Students in the Dance Company perform "Honor and Ash," choreographed by Shaun Boyle, which they later brought to the Kennedy Center stage in Washington, DC.

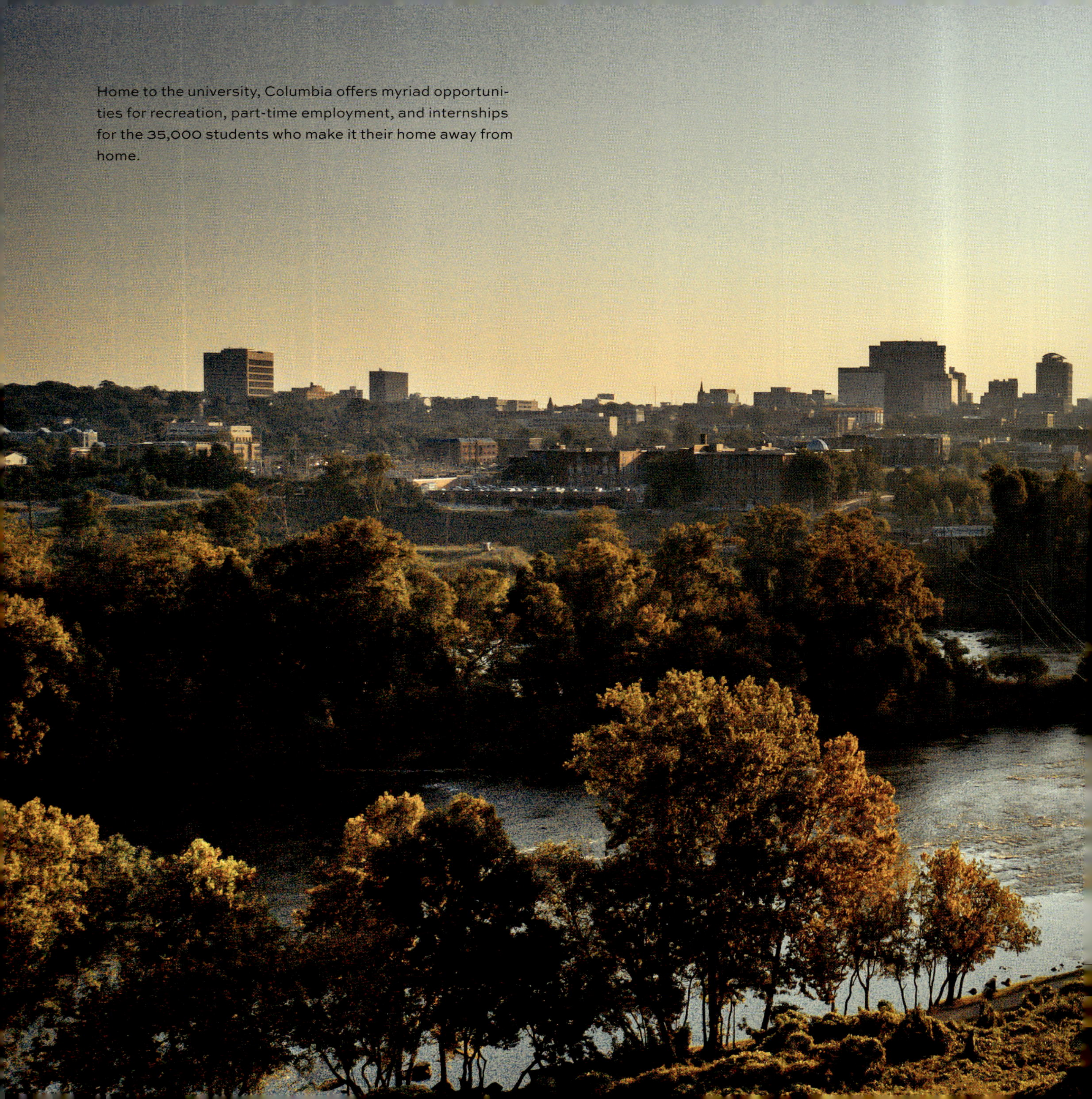

Home to the university, Columbia offers myriad opportuni-
ties for recreation, part-time employment, and internships
for the 35,000 students who make it their home away from
home.

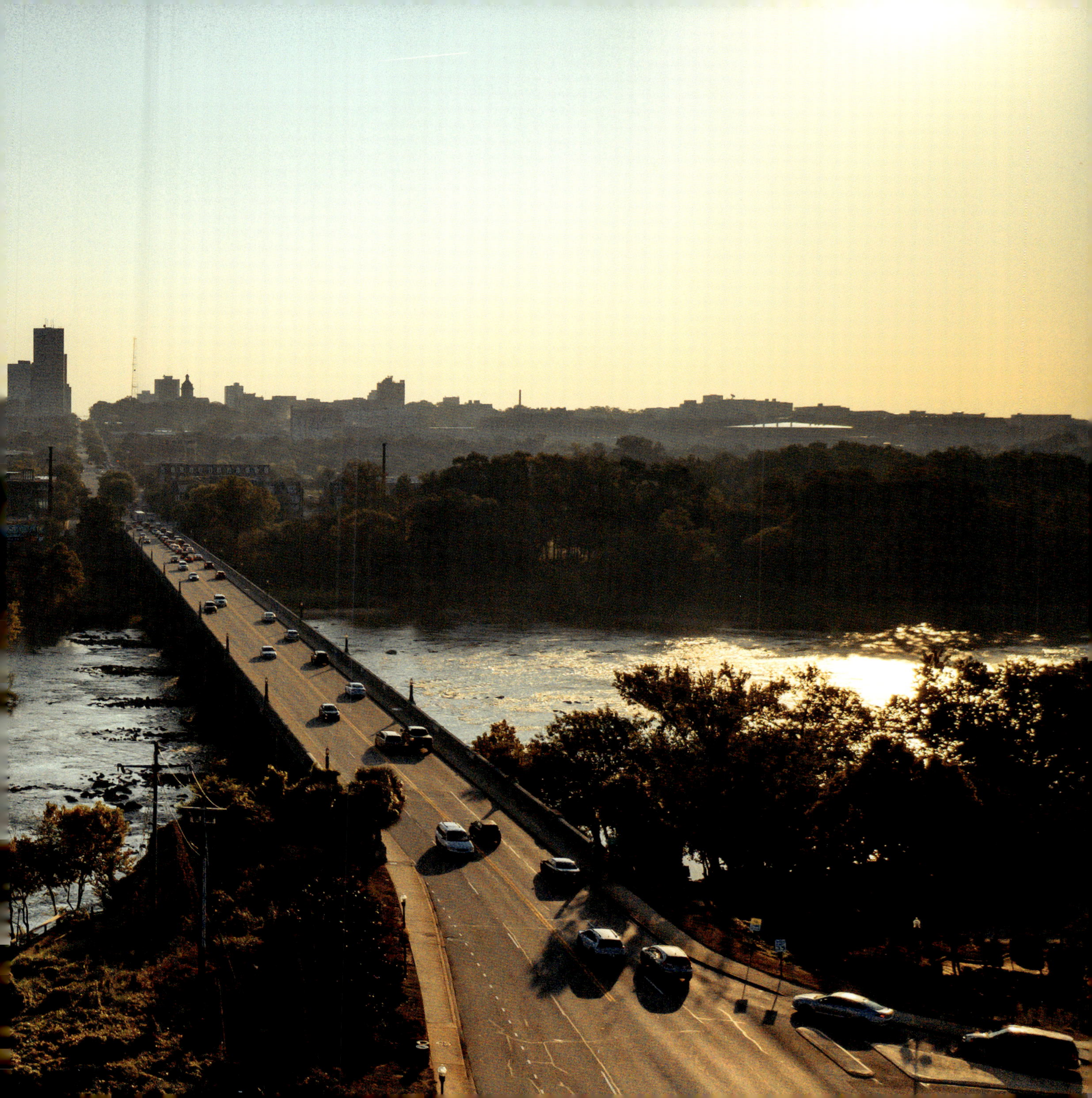

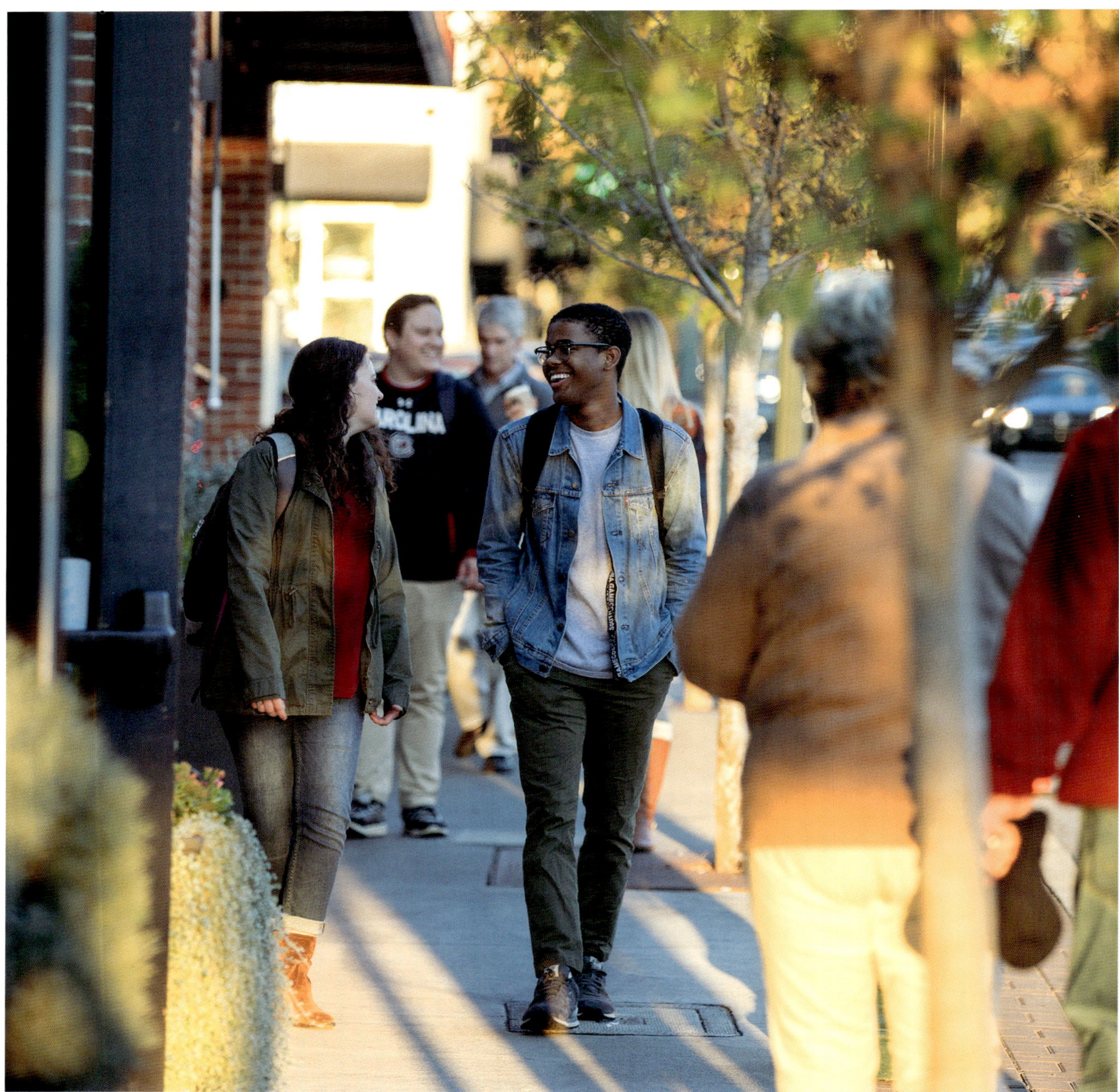

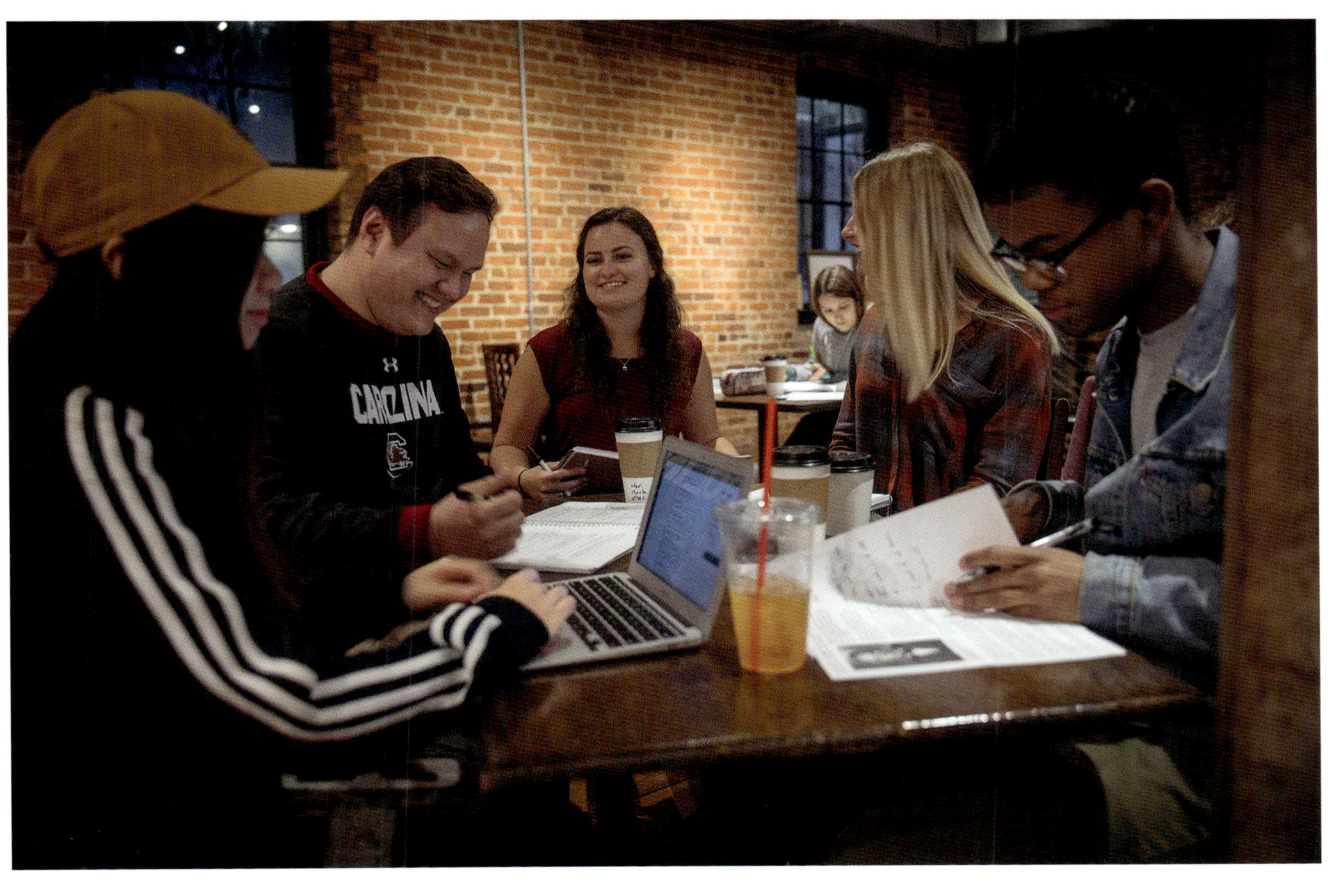

Just a few blocks from campus, Columbia's Vista neighborhood offers dining and shopping venues that attract visitors from across the Midlands and university students alike.

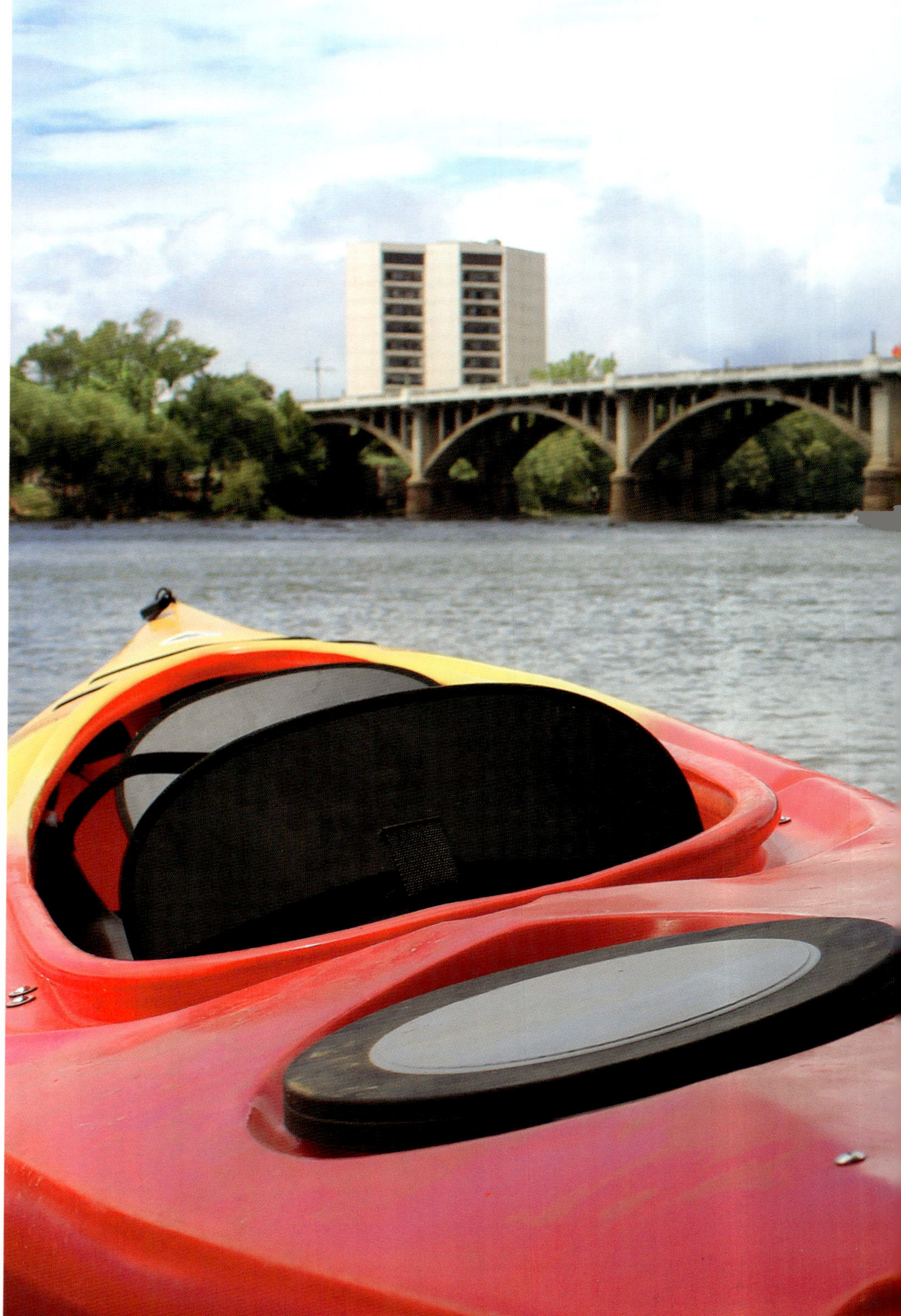

The Gervais Street bridge connects Columbia to Cayce and West Columbia and is a scenic backdrop for kayaking and other recreation along the Congaree River, which winds through the cities just blocks from campus.

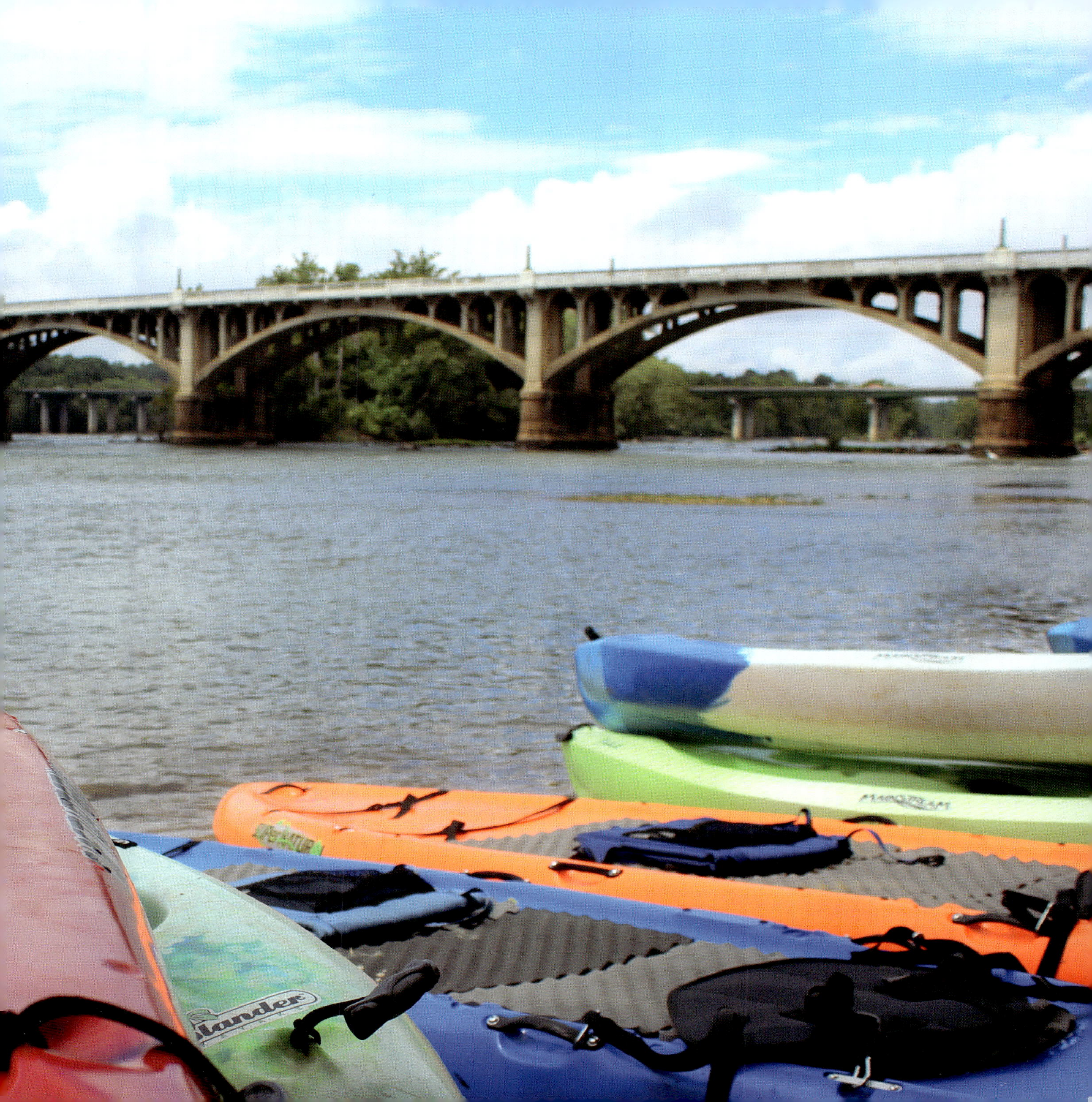

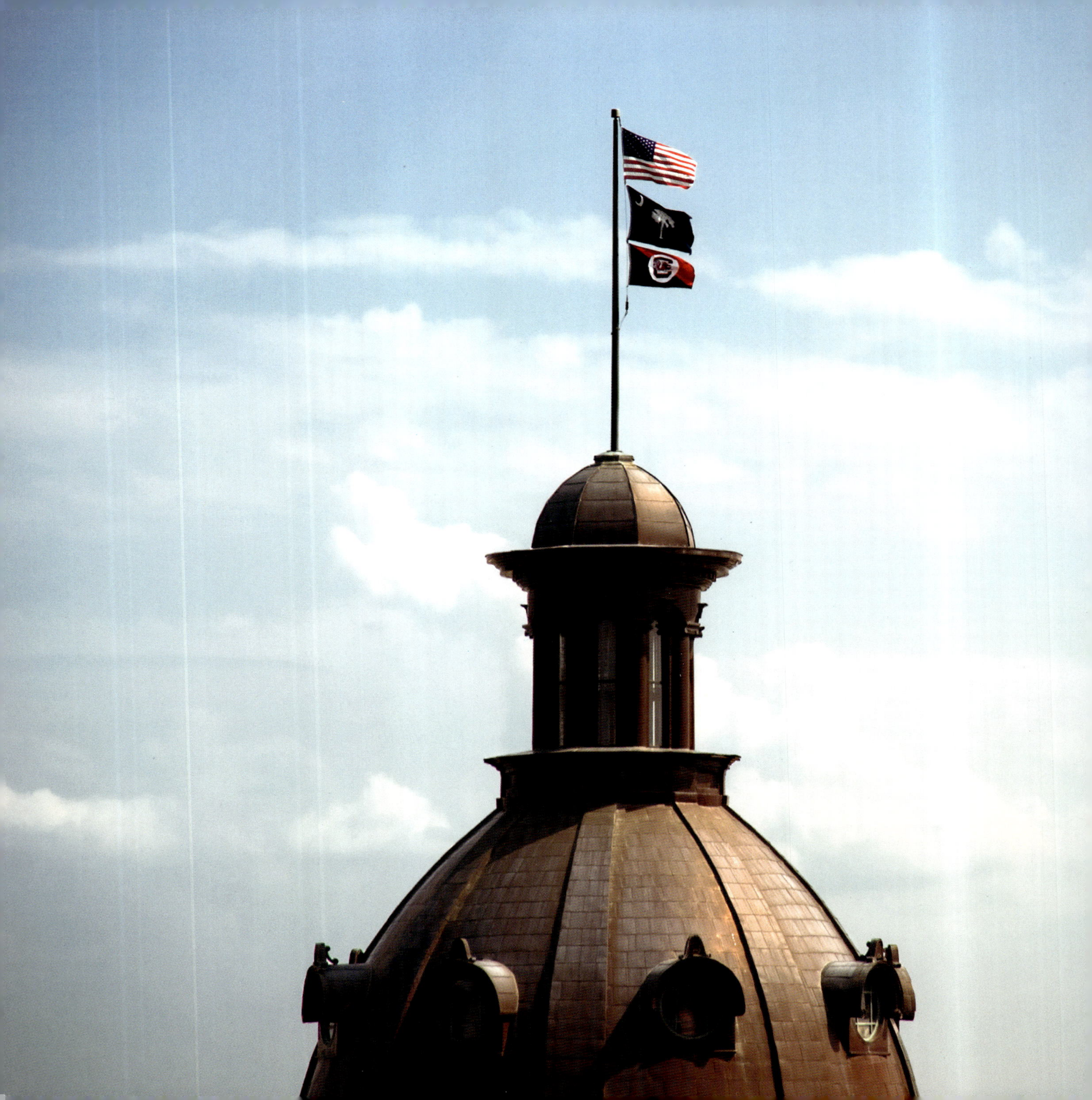

A Gamecock flag with the traditional Block C athletics logo occasionally flies in a place of honor atop the 180-foot-tall State House dome. Major athletics victories, including the baseball team's back-to-back College World Series wins in 2010–11, have earned the prestigious posting.

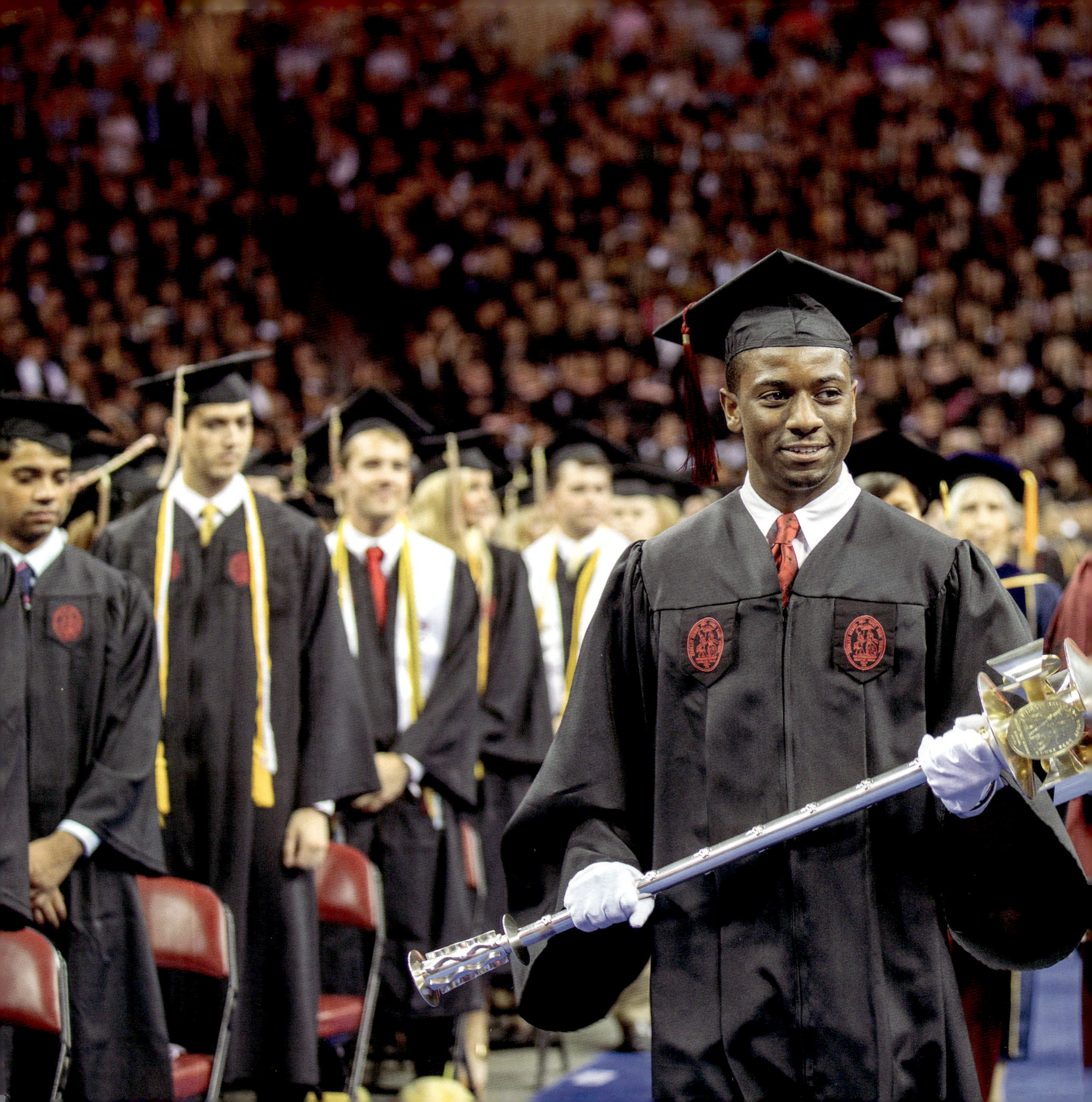

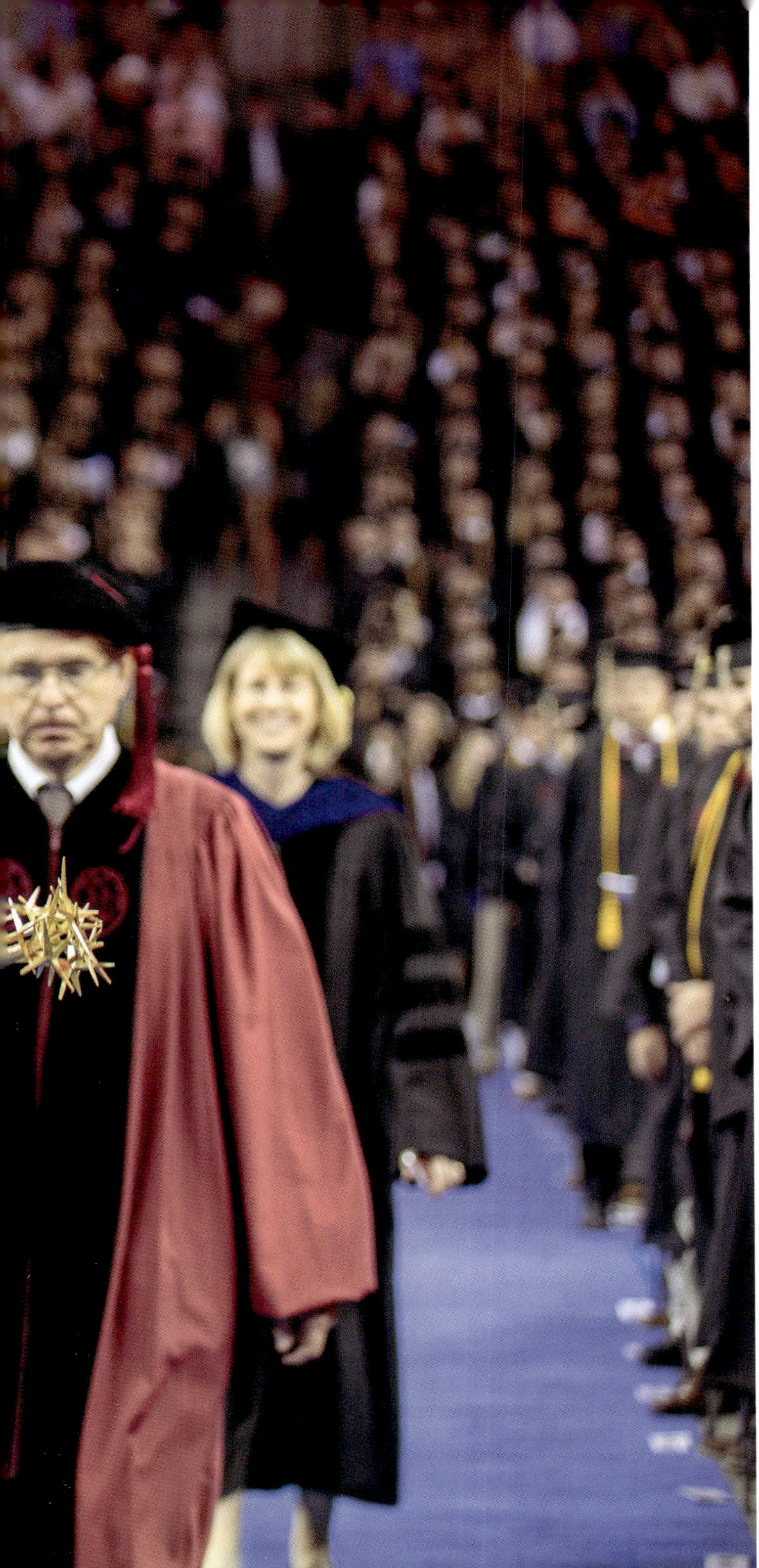

Traditionally carried at commencement ceremonies, convocations, and formal dedications, the silver-and-gilt University Mace includes the seals of the university and state of South Carolina and the Great Seal of the United States.

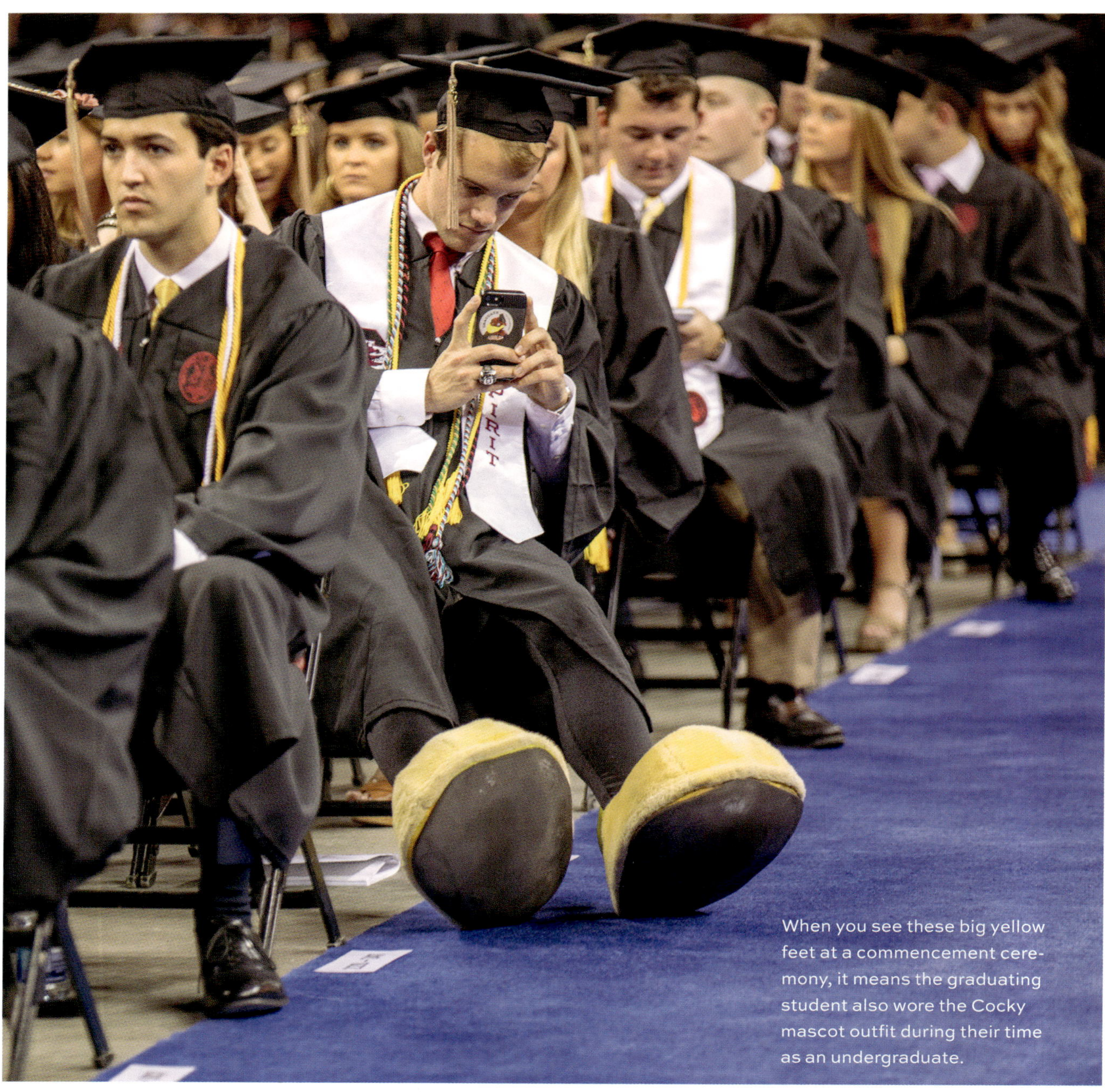

When you see these big yellow feet at a commencement ceremony, it means the graduating student also wore the Cocky mascot outfit during their time as an undergraduate.

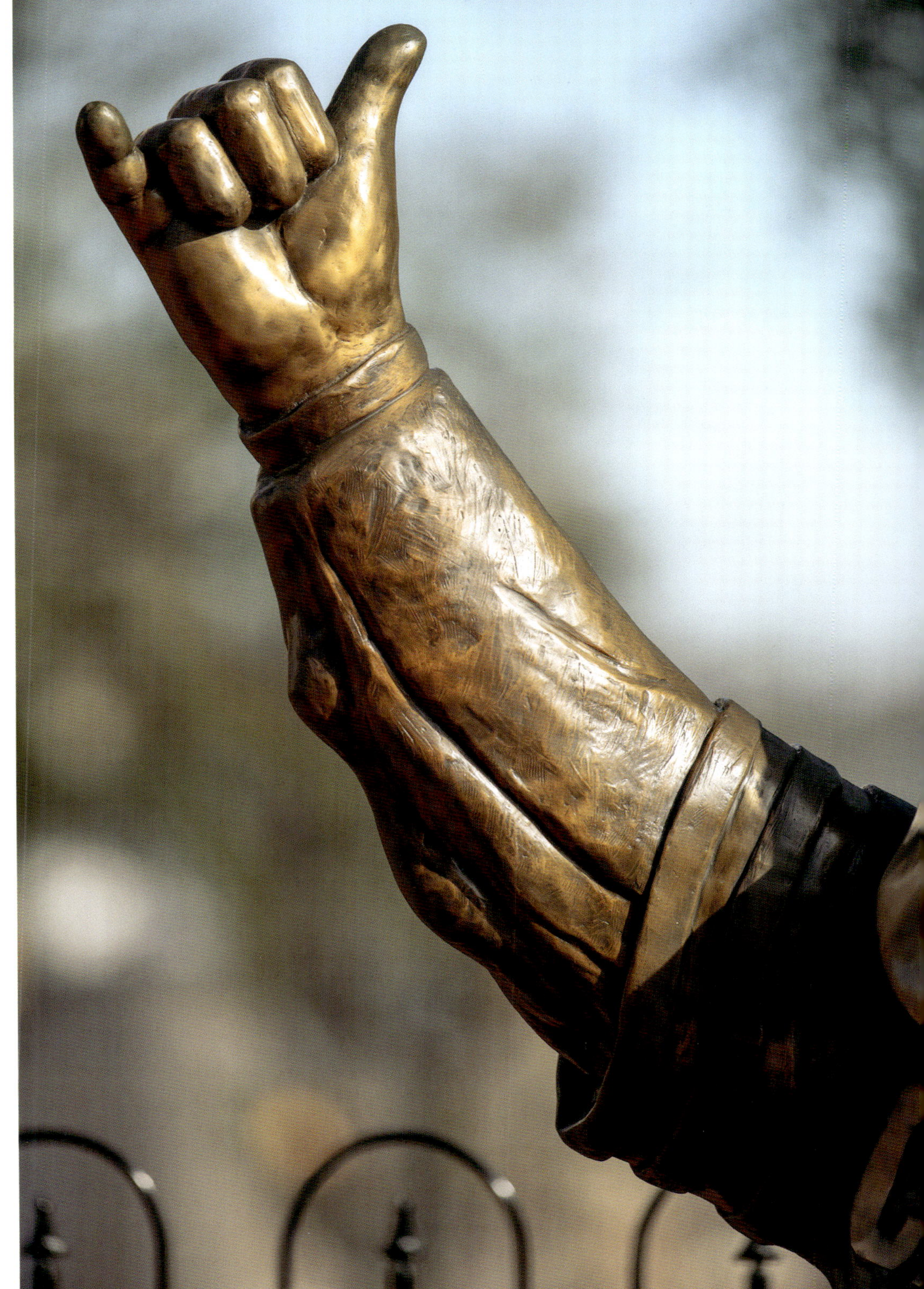

Cocky's bronzed hand—part of the 773-pound, life-size statue of the university mascot—flashes a "spurs up" to visitors from his post near Davis College. The piece, created by sculptor and university alumnus Robert Allison, is a go-to spot for campus visitors taking selfies.

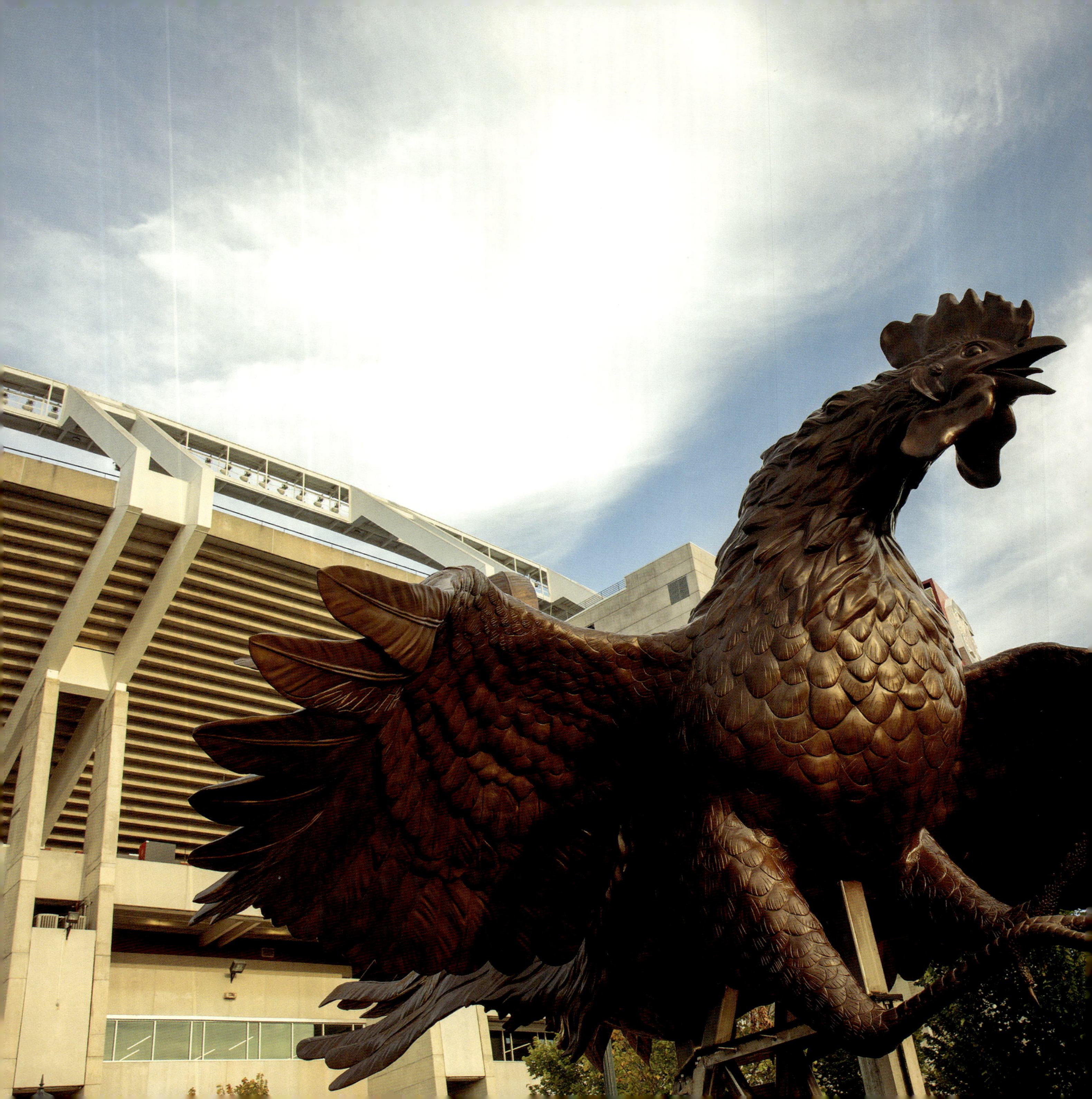

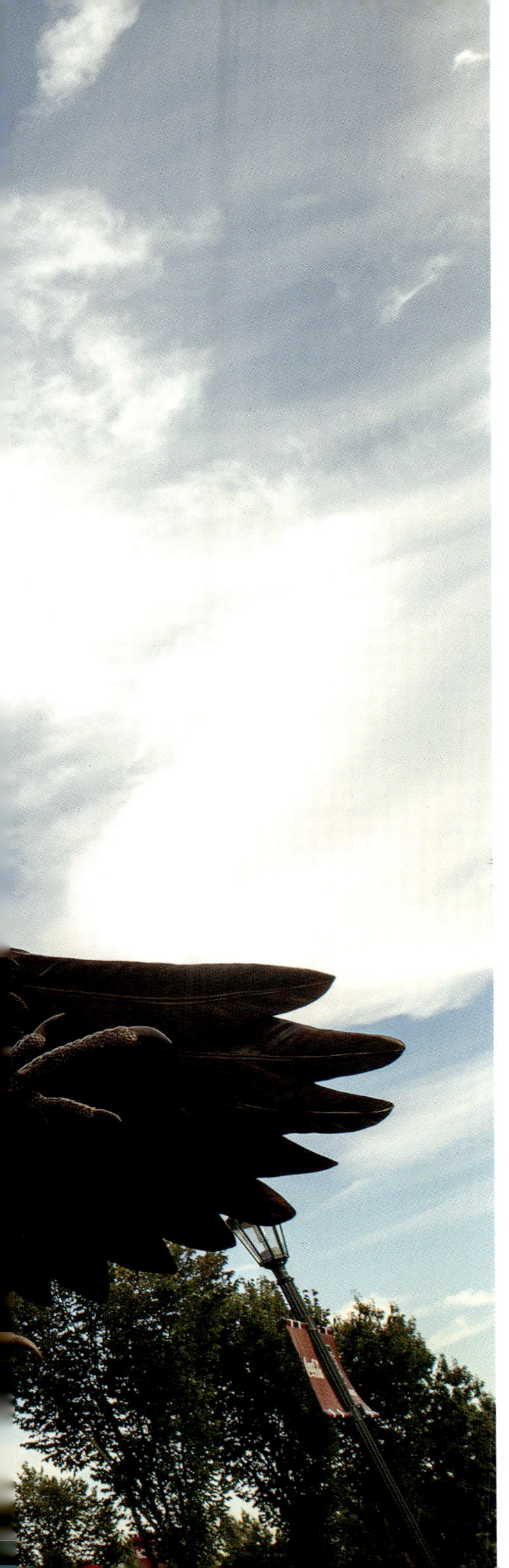

Funded by private gifts from alumni, the twenty-foot-by-twenty-foot bronze gamecock sculpture, created by Jon Hair, came to roost beside Williams-Brice Stadium in 2020. The university's more than 300,000 alumni support the institution through private giving and advocacy efforts coordinated by the UofSC Alumni Association.

Photo Credits

All photographs by Kim Truett, except for the following:

Jason Ayer: pages iv–ix, 26, 28, 41, 48, 87, 89–91, 98
Michael Brown: pages 80–81
Ambyr Goff: pages 96–97
Keith McGraw: pages 84–85
Bryan Vacchio: pages 32–33, 78–79, 92–93
South Carolina Athletics: pages 53–55, 72–75
University of South Carolina: page 88